Handbook of Multimedia and Animation

A. S. Shukla

RAJAT PUBLICATIONS
NEW DELHI - 110002 (INDIA)

RAJAT PUBLICATIONS
4675/21, Ansari Road, Daryaganj
New Delhi - 110 002 (India)
Phones : 23267924, 22507277

Handbook of Multimedia and Animation

Edition 2026

ISBN 978- 81-7880-326-5

[The responsibility for facts stated opinion expressed or conclusions reached and plagiarism, if any, in this volume is entirely that of the Editor. The publisher bears no responsibility for them whatsoever.]

PRINTED IN INDIA

Published by Mrs. Seema Wasan for Rajat Publications, New Delhi and Printed at H.S. Offset Press, Delhi.

Preface

Multimedia is media that uses multiple forms of information content and information processing (e.g. text, audio, graphics, animation, video, interactivity) to inform or entertain the (user) audience. Multimedia also refers to the use of electronic media to store and experience multimedia content. Multimedia is similar to traditional mixed media in fine art, but with a broader scope. The term "rich media" is synonymous for interactive multimedia. Multimedia means that computer info can be represented through audio, graphics, image, video and animation in addition to traditional media (text and graphics). Hypermedia can be considered one particular multimedia application.

Multimedia may be broadly divided into linear and non-linear categories. Linear active content progresses without any navigation control for the viewer such as a cinema presentation. Non-linear content offers user interactivity to control progress as used with a computer game or used in self-paced computer based training. Non-linear content is also known as hypermedia content.

Multimedia presentations can be live or recorded. A recorded presentation may allow interactivity via a navigation system. A live multimedia presentation may allow interactivity via interaction with the presenter or performer whereas Animation is the art of creating moving images via the use of computers. It is a subfield of computer graphics and animation. Increasingly it is created by means of 3D computer graphics, though 2D computer graphics are still widely used for low bandwidth and faster real-time rendering needs. Sometimes the target of the animation is the computer itself, but it sometimes the target is another medium, such as film. It is also referred to as CGI (Computer-generated imagery or computer-generated imaging), especially when used in films.

Animation is essentially a digital successor to the art of stop motion animation of 3D models and frame-by-frame animation of 2D illustrations. For 3D animations, models are built on the computer monitor (modeled) and 3D figures are rigged with a virtual skeleton. For 2D figure animations, separate objects and separate transparent layers are used, with or without a virtual skeleton. Then the limbs, eyes, mouth, clothes, etc. of the figure are moved by the animator on key frames. The differences in appearance between key frames are automatically calculated by the computer in a process known as tweening or morphing. Finally, the animation is rendered.

All frames must be rendered after modeling is complete. For 2D vector animations, the rendering process is the key frame illustration process, while tweened frames are rendered as needed. For pre-recorded presentations, the rendered frames are transferred to a different format or medium such as film or digital video. The frames may also be rendered in real time as they are presented to the end-user audience. Low bandwidth animations transmitted via the internet often use software on the end-users computer to render in real time as an alternative to streaming or pre-loaded high bandwidth animations. A variety of communication media are discussed, from plain text to pictures, audio, sound, and their presentation on both CD-ROM and the World Wide Web.

A comprehensive, step-by-step guide to creating effective multimediaand animation, this book explains all about the components and processes, then helps you complete projects from simple boardroom presentations to dynamic corporate CD-ROMs to Web sites that come alive.

A. S. Shukla

Contents

Preface — *v*

1. Multimedia: Nature And Scope — 1
2. Multimedia Databases — 24
3. Multimedia Networks and Strategies of Innovation — 40
4. Multimedia: Profiling And Regional Restructuring — 72
5. Multimedia Clusters: Formulation and Sustainability — 101
6. Models of Interaction and Designing — 131
7. Multimedia and Industrial Restructuring — 163
8. Designing of Multimedia User Interface — 186
9. Animation: Design and Effects — 226
10. Multimedia Products and Copyright Works — 240
11. Applications and Architectures of Multimedia — 262

Bibliography — 290

Index — 292

1

Multimedia: Nature And Scope

Introduction

Multimedia means many different things to different people. For example, it can mean enterprises, types of communication, products or services. It is rather an amorphous term. People understand it as encompassing interactive television, interactive guides in museums, product catalogues in electronic malls, schedules in train stations, on-line databases which can be retrieved worldwide from networks such as the Internet in the form of virtual reality, simple video, computer games, and so on.

All these products share characteristics that come within the definition of multimedia products and therefore belong to the same generation. However, they are also somewhat different from one another by reason of the particularities they present and the different purposes and functions they serve. The large and vague variety of products that exists in the market constitutes the reason why multimedia is more of a phenomenon than a product which can be pinned down to certain particular functions and characteristics, remaining stable over several years.

Because multimedia is a comparatively new term, inextricably linked with technology and its progress, it is also a fast-evolving term, which inevitably brings with it the characteristics of every new term: broadness and ambiguity. Broadness has a positive connotation in so far as it signifies the capacity multimedia has to accommodate a vast range of things. Ambiguity has a negative connotation in so far as it signifies a reservation as to what it finally accommodates. Thus, multimedia is a notion both rich in content and at the same time vague. In the light of this, this book will deal with multimedia in a broad sense so as to encompass legal solutions which will not soon be outdated by reason of the development of technology in this area.

Multimedia cannot be categorised in one of the existing categories of media. It is rather a descriptive word for computer-based works (in which many technologies are combined) and media which were formerly used separately. In this sense multimedia is a category in itself. In broad terms it is used today as a generic concept, which encompasses new services of communication linked to digital techniques. New services are not, however, 'new' in the literal meaning of the word. In fact, multimedia is a hybrid of heterogeneous technologies, which were formerly used separately and which now permit the exploitation of existing or newly created works in different formats and media. It is a convergence of video, audio and telephony technologies. This convergence signifies new co-existing types of communication, which separate the known material supports from the information they carry and store it in a digitised manner in PCs or create new information, irrespective of any material support.

However, whatever may be the different definitions we give to multimedia, by natural assimilation between the object and its material support, multimedia is essentially used today solely to mean the marketed product, the commercial carrier of the work (often a material support), i.e. the CD-ROM (compact disc read only memory), CD-I (compact disc – interactive), DCC (digital compact cassette), Data Discman, mini-disc, DVD (digital video disc), interactive database on-line, and whatever other form its commercialisation might take.

Definition

The main distinctive characteristic of multimedia is that its technology is meant to combine, in a single medium, diverse types of works or information. In order for this combination to become possible a digital environment is required. The information has to be digitally processed, stored and accessed by a computer. Computers are the only media capable of performing such tasks in a digital environment. In addition to the conversion of the data to a digital format, this format also has to offer, again with the aid of a computer, the option of interactivity, in other words the possibility of a dialogue between the user and the system.

Even though, as mentioned above, a single medium can technically be the combination of many different types of technology, the fact that an essential feature of a multimedia product is the convergence of multiple elements (works) on a single medium has led many commentators to think that the term itself is a misnomer. 'Multi-media' literally signifies the existence of many (multi-) means of communication (media) rather than the multiplicity or mixture of many types or categories of works.

From this point of view a term which has been suggested by Koumantos as being more appropriate is the 'unimedium multiwork' (multioeuvre unimédia), or, perhaps, a simpler abbreviation of it, 'unimedium'. The latter term puts the emphasis on the single medium with which consumers are confronted. Yet it does not exclude the significance of the contents that are included. In the final analysis it is the contents that make a multimedia product sell. The technology only makes it easily and readily available and perhaps commercially more attractive.

However, the term 'multimedia' is by now a well-established term in the area of information technology and, as is often the case with law, it is the trend (or technology) that comes first and the law that follows. Since technology has imposed its terminology in practice, it is the 'multimedia' term that will be used for the purposes of this book as well. As we described earlier, multimedia is an ill-defined notion by reason of its polymorphism. The vast number of products (on-line and off-line) it comprises makes it difficult to limit this notion to a specific and rigid definition. However, there are certain elements that characterise multimedia and that can therefore be found in any product coming within this category. Multimedia is a product or service which combines and integrates in a single medium, in a digitised form, at least two of the following elements: text, audio, still or moving images, computer programs and other data. It requires a software tool that allows for a substantial degree of interactivity and which allows for the retrieval and presentation of the above information. It is clear that the concept of interactivity (or even full integration) is a key one in this debate and one to which we will have to return at a later stage.

Text, audio and images form, in fact, what we call the contents of a multimedia product. By text we mean any material in written form, such as literary works, magazines, newspapers, databases, data, or even entries, instructions or guidelines, as these appear on the screen to assist navigation through the multimedia work. The last three, of course, are regarded more as multimedia product operating materials and less as contents. By audio we mean sounds (natural, instrumental or electronically generated), songs, speech and music. By images we mean any kind of still images, such as photographs, graphics and artwork, or animated works and moving images, such as films and videos, plus any kind of computergenerated pictures.

So far there are three key features which distinguish multimedia products from traditional or conventional works. These are digitisation, combination (or rather integration) of different kinds of works or expressions and interactivity, and they have to exist cumulatively.

It should be noted that the degree of interactivity is capable of introducing differences in quality between the various multimedia products found on the market. Multimedia works with a primitive form of interactivity (such as electronic encyclopaedias or interactive databases) can still be adequately protected by the existing copyright legislation. This is the first generation of multimedia products. However, multimedia works with an advanced level of interactivity (and a sufficient degree of integration of their various elements) constitute the second generation of multimedia products. In this book we will primarily focus on the second generation of multimedia products.

Digitisation

The importance of multimedia derives from the underlying technology of digitisation, which is the necessary prerequisite for any seamless combination of materials. Digitisation is not a new technological development. It appeared more or less when computers appeared and its function, though using many media to circulate its signals, has been inextricably linked with computers. Without the intervention of a computer at some stage, digitisation would not have been possible.

Digital technology should be distinguished from its traditional counterpart, analogue technology. Analogue technology is the technology which has dominated the market up to now. Almost all audiovisual media, such as radio, broadcast television, audio and video cassettes, are paradigms of analogue technology. Analogue technology stores information in the form of a continuous signal, which recognises changes in the information by modulating the amplitude (AM) or the frequency of the signal. Digital technology stores any kind of information in a computer memory, after having translated it into binary code (a sequence of zeros and ones) with the help of a computer program. Because the digitised information is stored in a single format, with only two possible means of expression (0s or 1s), the quality of the information is less prone to errors or deterioration in comparison to its analogue counterpart. Distribution of digitised material can take place in two ways: through physical storage media or independently of any physical storage media. The first category, also known as off-line or non-linear media, includes CD-ROMs, CD-Is, DVDs, Data Discman, floppy disks, and so on. The second category, also known as on-line services, encompasses all kinds of multimedia services which are independent of any material support and which are transmitted by fibre-optic cables, telephone lines and wireless personal communication systems, such as (broadcast) television and integrated digital networks. The Internet is an example of the latter. In on-line services the information itself becomes independent of any material support or carrier on which it was previously stored or kept. The material support is separated from the data it carries; the data is 'repurposed' in a digitised format and is put on-line. We have, in fact, a dematerialisation of information. In this context, information is important as such, irrespective of its presentation on any hard copy, and it also becomes the object of regulation. This is indicative of the fact that fixation, and even more permanent fixation, of works is a notion that is losing ground very quickly as it stands and is in need of being redefined.

Special features of digitisation

In relation to digitisation the following points are worth stressing at this stage:

1. Digital technology, which is indispensable for the creation of a multimedia product, is inextricably linked with computers. The digital language is a uniform language which can be comprehended only by computers. Its transmission, distribution or presentation is, of course, due to the other mediums' compatibility with the particular primary computer that has stored this information in its memory. In this context, multimedia products are in essence computer-based products.
2. Digital technology offers information which can be accessed worldwide (borderlessly) easily, quickly, accurately and with stability. This is also so regarding reproduction, transmission and distribution of this information. Copies can be produced with great ease in infinite numbers, all possessing the same quality as the original.
3. Digital compression techniques abolish the existing constraints regarding the manipulation and circulation of information: data compression techniques abolish (a) any physical constraints regarding the storage and content of the information, and (b) any physical constraints relating to space and time. In this way vast amounts of data can be stored on physical or non-physical distribution systems which are available worldwide. Data is no longer territorially based and it is portable.
4. The convergence of all kinds of works and data into the contents of a multimedia product in a digital format that is seamless renders obsolete any traditional distinctions between literary and audiovisual works. Once digitised, all works form part of a single format (which is the same for all kinds of works) and they are essentially regarded and referred to as information or contents rather than works.
5. Digitisation offers more opportunities than analogue technology for on-line communication of information. Thus, dematerialisation of information is a concept which has started gaining particular ground. The traditional notions of fixation and permanent fixation on some

kind of stable carrier seem no longer tenable as necessary prerequisites for the qualification of a work as an intellectual property work.

6. Digitisation and storage of information do not present any structure and specific arrangement in the sense in which the average person would understand the notion of structure and arrangement. The records containing the information, which are found in the computer memory, are standard normalising entries (data put in the right boxes) which do not represent any special selection or arrangement. The result, however, which is produced on screen under the command of a user, may eventually be an original one. This is important to note with regard to the authorship and originality problems that multimedia poses.

Combination and integration of various forms of expression

The convergence of these kinds of expressions requires a digital environment and PC-processed technologies. All data is transformed into one format: the digital format. This enables it to be seamlessly integrated in a single medium, in such a way as to construct a single information resource.

Interactivity

Interactivity is an equally important feature of multimedia. Although digitisation constitutes the enabling technology for the creation of a multimedia product and for the combination and convergence of different kinds of works (content), this being the main reason for its purchase, it is interactivity (a technique for 'reading' such a product) which makes multimedia different from conventional media and existing intellectual property works. It is the particular feature that makes it appealing and answers the various needs of the users. Interactivity cannot be seen in isolation. It can only be seen in conjunction with the two previous prerequisites: digitisation and combination of different kinds of works. A work cannot qualify as a multimedia work unless all three features are met. Digitisation and interactivity are inextricably linked. There is no interactivity without digitisation, although digitisation can exist in a non-interactive form. Computer technology allows the user to interact with the information contained in a multimedia work by selecting the pathways that will eventually lead him to the bits of information that will serve his particular needs. He is also offered the freedom to organise this information as he wishes by manipulating its arrangement, re-arrangement, selection, combination, inputs or outputs on his screen. Interactivity, however, is subject to two inherent limitations. First, the user's choice regarding the selection, arrangement and presentation of the information is necessarily limited by the choices already made by the producer and the developer of the product. In other words, the user has to limit his choice to the data available in the multimedia product or service, which, however vast, might not be comprehensive or exhaustive. In all cases the work represents the advance selection made by the initiator of the multimedia product. The user has to make his choices from the pathways and commands available in the system and, though they might be great in number, the user is still limited by the capacity and design of the computer system which runs the particular product. It should be noted though that these limits are not narrow and may eventually allow the user to produce a result in which the original material can hardly be recognised. Secondly, the constructive and operating computer software of the multimedia product may also limit the degree of interactivity available, even though it is only over a certain degree of interactivity that a product qualifies as a multimedia product. Five standard levels of interactivity are said to exist:

1. No interactivity, e.g. in the case of a film, where one watches it from the beginning to the end without the ability to intervene in the sequence of the images
2. Manual interactivity, e.g. commands such as those usually found on a video cassette player: slow or quick motion, freeze frame, scan, etc.
3. Limited interactivity, e.g. pre-programming or downloading instructions through an onboard microprocessor in a video player
4. True and versatile interactivity, e.g. interfacing a video player with an external computer, or allowing a user to control graphics, animation and video images
5. Full interactivity, e.g. authoring and delivering with a complete hardware and software package

Multimedia products are thought necessarily to be able to provide the fourth or fifth level of interactivity in order to be considered as such. The user must be provided with the ability to morph (digitally blur and alter images beyond recognition) and sample (sample and blur any kind of works to an unlimited degree). In other words he must be able to initiate newly created works using existing material. The fourth and fifth levels of interactivity are those that offer to the user a real dialogue with the contents of the product. Anything less than that would come close to, if not totally qualify for, one of the conventional existing categories of intellectual property products, but would not be considered as a multimedia product. In this sense, multimedia products are different from the traditional categories of works.

Yet interactivity, as such, is not new. Only its latest and more developed forms are. Interactivity is undoubtedly the evolution, or else an advanced form, of the first search and retrieval software of the early electronic databases. What, however, is the novel (or better, innovative) aspect of it is that it offers to users the possibility of a full direct dialogue, a multifarious interference with the vast amounts of data provided. This it does quickly and efficiently with literally all kinds of expression in a single medium. In view of this, the search and retrieval facilities have to possess two essential characteristics: (1) they have to be complex enough to deal with all the encompassed elements in an efficient and competent way, and (2) they have to look simple, user-friendly, powerful and compelling in order to be marketed successfully and thereby to secure the continuity of their existence in the future.

Layers of Protection

A multimedia product is a complex product in so far as it incorporates many traditional works in a single medium that can only be manipulated by a computer. This alone indicates that many different elements are involved in the creation of a multimedia product and they cannot all come under the same category of protection. Thus, inevitably, different layers of protection exist.

The three essential layers of protection with regard to a multimedia product are: (1) the protection of the contents of a multimedia product, (2) the protection of the multimedia product itself (as a compilation of the works it includes, but not necessarily protection as such from the point of view of intellectual property), and (3) the protection of its technical base. Although this distinction of parts in a multimedia product is theoretically possible, in practice it is not always clear. For example, there is often an overlap between the multimedia product and its technical basis, especially if we consider that whilst a multimedia product might not be a computer program itself, it cannot be accessed unless a computer is used. With such rapid technical progress in the area of information technology leading to computers performing more and more tasks, any distinction might be even more difficult to make in the future. Solutions will eventually need to be somewhat different from the ones that are reached now. This is undoubtedly an area which stresses the need for flexibility as far as legal regulation of information technology is concerned. Moreover, any problems regarding the protection of any one of these three layers will inevitably have repercussions on the other two. All three layers have to co-exist in regulative harmony in order for the creation and proper functioning of the product not to be impeded.

The first layer of protection, that of the contents of a multimedia product, consists either of contents of pre-existing works or of works commissioned for the creation of a particular product. Since the works that are included in the multimedia compilation are independent, they are also the object of a separate and distinguishable protection. This protection is afforded to them by means of copyright, patents, trade marks or any other kind of intellectual property rights. This, of course, does not exclude the possibility that the works included are also protected by other areas of law, i.e. by contract, tort, confidentiality, etc.

If composite works, such as films, videos, live performances, sound recordings, etc., are included, the whole bundle of rights (both economic and moral) of the rightholders have to be taken into account. The inclusion of these works in a multimedia product does not affect the existence of any of these rights, nor does it alter in any respect the regime of their protection. These rights accompany the works in each inclusion in new products. Inevitably the creation of a new multimedia product will take place in a 'multilegia' environment, i.e. one where the laws and the rights corresponding to the particular elements constituting the parts of the multimedia product have to be respected and taken into account by any person dealing with them, from the producer to the end user. The newly evolved rights of the producer, developer or maker of the multimedia product, or any other person involved, are additional to the original rights. Thus, the chain of rightholders becomes ever longer. The rights existing in the works that form the content of a multimedia product are important in so far as they have to be cleared in order for the emergence of such a product to take place. If these rights are not cleared, or are not cleared properly, or are not cleared in relation to all the works needed for inclusion, then the creation of the multimedia product is impossible or, in the last case, its success will be dubious and conditional on possible litigation. Contents are always considered to be the essential marketing features of multimedia. The second layer is the protection of the multimedia product itself. Putting together a number of works in a digitised format with potential interactivity does not assimilate existing rights in the works, but creates new rights in the compilation itself, which now serves a separate and distinctive function. The emerging multimedia product or service produced in the course of an independent idea and plan has an autonomous value. This value is in most cases greater than the value each of the works has on its own. Yet this value should not be confused with the value of a genuine literary work by reason of originality or artistic input in the continental sense. The value of a multimedia product is judged more on market and economic terms than on any other terms.The third layer of protection is that afforded to the technical base of a multimedia product:

1. The platform is divided into two parts: (a) the hardware on which the multimedia application runs, e.g. IBM/PC, Macintosh, etc., and (b) the operating software which is used for the running of a multimedia application on a particular piece of hardware, e.g. Windows 2000, etc. The operating software has to be compatible with the hardware, otherwise no application is possible. In any case, the platform is something clearly distinguishable from a multimedia product. The platform is the compatible environment in which a multimedia work runs in the same way any other application runs.

2. The operating or making program technically creates the multimedia application. This program, which is the authoring program of the newly constructed work, is a separate program and does not accompany the work itself onto the market.
3. The software tool, known as the driver, runtime or engine, allows the user to access, display and manipulate the information available on the multimedia product created. It is the same tool which technically permits the user to interact with the product, by selecting, arranging or transforming the data available. The driver is a component of the multimedia application itself and is embedded in it in object code form. The driver has to be compatible with the platform in order for the multimedia application to be able to run.
4. The operation materials for the multimedia product, also known as the command procedure, are the commands, pathways, entries, indexation systems, thesaurus, crossroads and other means of tracing, arranging and selecting information in the multimedia product. These are the commands which the operating program obeys, in order to perform its function.
5. The distribution media carry the multimedia product. They have the form of either a physical or a non-physical (on-line) medium. The most popular distribution media in the first category are CD-ROMs, floppy disks, CD-Is, DVDs, etc. On-line distribution (or better, transmission) can take place on practically any network which possesses the technology for transmitting vast amounts of data. However, although distribution media incorporate the multimedia work and represent, in the eyes of consumers, the product itself, they are something separate which is protected on its own merits. The technology of the manufacturing of these media is distinct from the technology of the multimedia work. From the point of view of a multimedia product, they can only be regarded as its carriers, which in practice add nothing to its value apart from the fact that they make it easily available to the public.

From the foregoing it can be seen that it is not easy to distinguish between the different parts of a multimedia product in all situations, and this is going to be even more difficult in the future given that computer programs perform more and more tasks every day. The command procedure is an obvious example of a case where distinction is not always possible. The command procedure and the data contained in a multimedia product are linked. Any structure, selection or arrangement of the data is subject to the command that is chosen or inserted by the user. The functions it performs may be functions which are computer related, but the commands themselves as they appear on the screen can still be viewed as data. In this sense the command procedure can be regarded as 'contents' and can therefore come under the same regime of protection as the one applied to contents.

However, there will be cases where the command procedure is particularly sophisticated, especially where the multimedia product is sophisticated as well. In such a case it is very likely that the formal language of the command procedure in terms of syntax, structure and range of expressions will closely resemble a conventional high-level computer language, if not a computer program itself. Thus, the command procedure might also come within the scope of the EC software Directive and qualify for separate protection.

This will also be the case, but from another point of view, when the command procedure itself is embedded in the computer program that designed and constructed the multimedia product. This might happen in cases where the making program has to perform 'classic' or nonsophisticated tasks in relation to the multimedia product. Then, of course, the solution of theoretically including the command procedure in the contents is no longer appropriate. Neither is the solution of considering it as a separate computer program. In this case the one protection afforded to the making program will also apply to the operation of the materials. This will also be so in the more likely case of the command procedure being part of the driver, when the protection afforded to the driver will be the same as the protection of the command procedure. This protection will obviously be a protection of computer programs.

It is clear from the above that only a case-by-case decision is possible on this point. As long as operation materials form part of, or constitute by themselves, a computer program there will be no problem, since an autonomous protection for computer programs is available, irrespective of the legal status of the work these programs operate. Yet problems will arise when such a protection is not possible due to the lack of such a qualification.

A possible solution is found in the sole legal instrument which partly regulates such issues: the database Directive. Recital 20 to the database Directive states that 'protection under this Directive may also apply to the materials necessary for the operation or consultation of certain databases such as thesaurus and indexation systems'. It follows from this that if a database does not qualify for protection under article 1(2) of the Directive, the command procedure is not protected either. The problems which such regulation presents are not discussed here as they fall outside the scope of this book. The problems they present in relation to multimedia products, however, are relevant.

First, in the database Directive the command procedure does not qualify for any kind of protection unless the database itself is protected. The individual merits of the operation materials therefore remain insignificant, in so far, of course, as they do not qualify individually as literary works or computer programs. If this line of thought is followed, the operation materials in a multimedia product, if anything, qualify for the same kind of protection as the one afforded to the compilation. They do not follow the fate of the 'contents'. However, they do follow the fate of the driver, if they form part of it. Although this issue appears to be an important one, not too much practical significance should be given to it, because in most cases the driver itself is bound to contain the command procedure as well. In addition, reproduction of the command procedure is less important if the contents of the particular multimedia product cannot also be reproduced at the same time. If the command procedure is to be used for a similar multimedia application to the one from which it was originally taken, if no originality is attached to it, it will not be worthy of protection as such and thus its copying by a competitor can cause little damage to the original owner. The problems presented by the contents or the technical base will be taken into account in so far as they have direct repercussions on the multimedia compilation itself and on its independent regime of protection. Relevant issues are, for example, the clearing of rights in the contents, the ability to distinguish between the technical base and the multimedia work in new technological developments, and so on.

Project Participants in the Multimedia Product

The most important questions are who the author or authors of a multimedia product are and who qualify as rightholders in relation to which rights. The persons usually involved in the creation of a multimedia product are:

1. The authors of the works which form the 'content' of the multimedia product. These persons are either authors of pre-existing works who have agreed for their works to be included in the multimedia product or commissioned authors who have created works, either independently or in the course of an employment contract, which are to be included in the multimedia compilation. At this point we should note, of course, that other rights, apart from the classical ones an author possesses, exist in many cases in the works that form the contents of a multimedia product. For example, rights in performances or other neighbouring rights are involved, as well as sui generis rights. These rights accompany the intellectual property work in any use and, if clearing proceedings are to take place, clearance will be required in relation to all these rights.

   There might not only be copyright works forming the contents of a multimedia product. Patent, design and trade mark rights may also be involved. The laws relevant to their protection will apply in these cases.
2. The rightholders of the works of the authors mentioned in the first category. Rightholders of the works which form the contents of a multimedia product can be any natural or legal persons. Usually rightholders are publishers, producers of phonograms and audiovisual works (generally employers), collecting societies, and so on. If holders of the rights to a certain work are not the authors themselves but other parties, these other parties do not possess all the rights to a work. They possess the economic rights to the work or a part of it. Any moral rights are non-assignable and they remain with the author until (and in certain jurisdictions even after) the expiry of the copyright in the work. A further layer of rights is the 'secondary copyrights' in the fixation of a work, i.e. the right in the typeface and in the recording. Usually this layer

of rights is possessed by the rightholders of the second category, since in order to publish or record a work they also need some if not most of the economic rights in the work at issue. The producer of the multimedia product (or a provider if it is a multimedia service) can be either a publishing company or an individual (publisher). The producer is the architect of the project. He is the one to select, acquire, bring together and combine the works of all the contributors. He conceives the idea and from him originates the concept for the product. He designs the project and develops the plan of the compilation. When this part of the job is done by a separate person, he or she can be called the editor. The producer also produces or supervises its realisation in terms of production and sinks into it the necessary investments. For example, a CD-ROM is published in the same way as a book, apart from requiring larger investments. The producer usually undertakes the distribution of the product either under his trade mark, if it is considered to be commercially effective, or under the trade mark of the maker of the multimedia work.

The producer should also be the rightholder of those rights that are required for the digital use of the authors' works that will be included in the product. These rights are acquired either through the authors or through other rightholders such as collecting societies. In cases of commissioned works the economic rights of the authors will automatically be transferred to the producer by means of some kind of contract. In the case of employees, that will be done by means of the employment contract, if the particular employee's job is the creation of works that will form part of the contents of a multimedia product.

An issue which is problematic is the moral rights issue. Moral rights are non-assignable. However, in common law jurisdictions, as for example in the UK, they are waivable. Where they have not been waived or where they cannot be waived, they form a separate layer of rights that have to be respected in any use of the copyright work. The producer cannot possess any moral rights in the works he is to use digitally and the same moral rights will apply whether the work is digitally disclosed or not. Therefore the producer has to be very careful not to supersede the limits of normal use of the product and the limits of the use he has been assigned. The users' conduct forms a separate issue.

3. The producer has important creative and production roles. This notion of creation does not have anything to do with producing highly original material. It is creative in so far as he brings various works together, after having selected them and after having put them in a particular structure and arrangement. The more commercialised and commodified the works are, the less original and the more functional they are. His important production role lies not only in the development of the project as such but also in the fact that he adds economic value to the compilation by turning it into a multimedia product: 'The product has distribution and exploitation rights which are worth considerably more than that of the individual elements going to make up the program.'

   The combining elements of a multimedia product are included in a way which enables them to be used in more than one traditional format, e.g. alphabetically. Usually many pathways (or crossroads) are designed, which permit the user to browse the contents in several different ways according to his own needs. The user is given the opportunity to include or exclude information on his screen at any time, as he wishes. This is also the reason why the whole is greater than the sum of its parts.

4. The maker or developer of a multimedia product. The developer of a multimedia product has to be distinguished from the producer in so far as he is not involved in the planning and structuring of the product as a work. The maker is responsible only for the physical development and technical organisation of the product. He designs the operating computer program (driver), the screen displays (the functionality displayed on the screen elements and the positioning of the individual screen elements) and he digitises and stores the information. He may also design the look of the multimedia work as a product, i.e. its form and packaging, etc. The multimedia product is usually produced under the

trade mark of the developer if it is decided that his trade mark is capable of contributing to its market success. However, apart from the very technical issues for which the maker is responsible, in most cases the maker and the editor share responsibility for the creative aspects of the product. Depending on their respective roles, they can be considered as co-authors.

5. Lastly, there are the users. The users do not have any creative role in the multimedia work. The only control they have over the product is that, because of its interactivity, they can manipulate the display of information on the screen of their computer. They can change the outcome of their searches as they wish by selecting or re-arranging the information that is already available in the product but only through the pathways that are available.

Although users of multimedia products are not just passive spectators like film and TV viewers, and although they are given rich forms of interactivity, as for example hypermedia (or hypertext), they are still not deemed to be creators. They are turned from spectators into users and from passive into active users only by the multimedia products which enable them to edit the information provided. Whether they have copyright in the edition of their work is a matter judged on its own merits. The creation of a new visual, artistic or literary work that is original and attracts copyright protection in its own right is probably an extreme and rare case, but it may take place if there is enough creativity involved and if the work is independently created and fixed in some kind of permanent form from which it can be retrieved.

Differences between Multimedia Products

Multimedia works are said to have some unique and distinctive features in relation to conventional copyright works. These features are not new. They are in most cases the combination and evolution of pre-existing, but less developed, characteristics, as was also demonstrated with regard to interactivity. However, their evolution in certain cases has become so significant that it is no longer a change in quantity but one in quality. In this respect some multimedia characteristics can be regarded as new.

Whether or not the particularity and individuality of the multimedia products' characteristics merit a different regime of protection adjusted to their needs is highly disputed and is under investigation. Even if the existing intellectual property laws have to be adjusted to the reality of the new technologies, how far this adjustment has to go, what alterations have to take place and how far these alterations are capable of transforming the original established notion of intellectual property rights, remains uncertain.

Combination of different forms of communication

Various works which are traditionally classified in different categories are combined in a single medium. Such works existed for centuries in the form of a combination of text and images, for example, an illustrated book or newspaper. Audiovisual works are also a good example of combinations of sound and images. The term 'multimedia' has recently become popular as a description of computer-based products or applications. However, some particular features have developed which make it unique.

1. All the works included, irrespective of their nature, are integrated in a single format: a digitised one.
2. There are no physical limits as to the quantity of the works included, because new technologies, such as digital compression techniques, can store almost infinite amounts of data. As Koumantos argues, the quantity of the various elements involved in a multimedia product is such that any quantitative modification becomes necessarily a qualitative one as well. Here, quantity and quality are closely interrelated. Thus, any physical constraints on the storage, the kind of work, the space or time have been abolished and, as a result, information gains value. It becomes portable, quick and easy to access, and capable of been carried by both off-line and on-line media.
3. In relation to on-line transmission of data, no territorial limits exist. Information can be picked up in any place in the world at any time as long as one possesses the necessary technical equipment.
4. The digitised format of the work allows the work to be copied

quickly, easily and cheaply. On top of that an infinite number of copies can be made without any loss of quality.

A Single Material Support

The past combinations of different kinds of works existed, such as text and images, these combinations were based on the combination of the different supports that carried the works, i.e. recordings, pictures, etc. In the case of multimedia products we are no longer tied to any kind of emballage which regroups the different material expressions of the various works under one name, for example a film. Multimedia is a single product which incorporates different kinds of works which have been integrated in this single medium in a single format. The 'Livre blanc du Groupe Audiovisuel et Multimédia de l'Édition' states that: 'on ne devrait pas appeler multimédia un produit regroupant sous un même emballage, mais sur des supports différents, des éléments textuels, sonors ou visuels'. The practical significance of such a differentiation in storing information with regard to copyright will be considered later.

Originality

The value of multimedia products does not necessarily lie in the originality of the works included. If any originality is to be found, it usually consists of the appearance of the product and its userfriendliness rather than the works it incorporates. In these cases multimedia products are valuable because they are comprehensive in terms of information and because their contents are primarily functional and utilitarian in nature. In other cases though, multimedia products can be very creative works. Their creativity is found in the combination and integration of the various components.

Computer-based product or service

A multimedia work's function is computer-based. Although a multimedia product is a work, it cannot as such perform any task unless it is computer aided. That renders it dependent on a computer program but does not necessarily render it a computer program itself.

Combination of Information Technology and Communications Technology

The main technologies that a multimedia application combines are digital video, electronics, informatics and digital communications.

Fixation

One of the most important aspects of a multimedia product, and perhaps the one that determines its market success, is its content. Although content is found at the heart of a multimedia product or service, it is alleged it is not fixed, at least not according to what fixation is considered to mean traditionally, and in relation to conventional intellectual property works. The basis on which lack of fixation in relation to multimedia products is advocated is twofold. Principally, it is based on the fact that information which can be retrieved interactively can circulate and will probably circulate even more in the future as on-line services (lack of fixation in the broad sense). The information will be accessed irrespective of any material carrier. It becomes a valuable commodity on its own without needing to be fixed on some kind of medium. Here the notion of dematerialisation of information is relevant again. In cases where some kind of fixation exists, there is a factual assimilation between the carrier and the data it carries.

Claims which are based on the fact that storing information in the RAM memory of the computer is a form of fixation, though not permanent, add little value to the arguments against dematerialisation. It is the information which counts and its placing in the RAM memory is rather less significant. Interesting in this respect is the draft EU Directive on the harmonisation of certain aspects of copyright and related rights in the information society. This more or less solves the problem regarding the status of temporary reproduction. According to article 2 of the Directive, the reproduction right also covers temporary copies (e.g. RAM). Article 5 provides for an automatic exemption for temporary acts of reproduction 'which are transient or incidental, which are an integral part of a technological process whose sole purpose is to enable: (a) a transmission in a network between third parties by an intermediary or (b) a lawful use of the work or other subject-matter to be made, and which have no independent economic significance'.

The second aspect that is contradictory to the notion of fixation is interactivity (lack of fixation narrowly defined). Interactivity offers the facility to users to revise, re-order and re-organise their data according to their specific needs. They can skip information, reform it and use different pathways to retrieve the data they need. This aspect can be found in both multimedia products and services, whilst the first one is inherent only in the provision of services. Although information is contained on a material support, there is no specific and stable order to which this data is subject. Rather we find information in a 'loose' form as elements and a box of tools, which can be combined when necessary. Up to now fixation has been synonymous with a permanent and stable form; not just the tools and elements needed to be fixed, but also the work itself. New technologies have rendered this notion obsolete. Fixation has become broader in a sense. No order is required, no stability, no permanence. Perhaps the fact that data can be carried in whatever form suffices. If that were not the case, interactivity would not have been possible. Users are the only persons responsible for any potential structure. Of course, as we made clear earlier, users do not create. They select and arrange from what is already available. Their true creative role can be very limited. Often no originality or even effort and labour are invested.

Ease of manipulation and copying

Up to now, apart from intellectual property laws, there have also been physical barriers which prevented large-scale copying of copyright works. As technology has advanced, the problems of volume and time, which constituted the essential barriers against copying, have disappeared. More than ever before digital technology provides users with the ability to manipulate and transform, sometimes to an unrecognisable degree, the data available in the multimedia product. It also allows users to make as many copies as desired or possible, easily, quickly and without any loss of quality. This undoubtedly poses new risks of unauthorised exploitation especially if it is coupled with the fact that copying equipment is now readily available privately (e.g. PCs, etc.). Moreover, it poses risks of infringement of moral rights (as well as economic rights if the copies are to be put on the market and take the place of originals) without any opportunity of tracking down trespassers. More than ever before a more effective and consistent regulation is called for. Copying, which has been the plunder of the last decades, has taken on new dimensions due to the new technological ease with which it can take place. Technological devices to safeguard rights are becoming increasingly necessary. The new draft Directive outlaws the manufacture of any devices that facilitate circumvention of copyright protection technologies. It is a battle which will definitely not be played solely on the field of law. The view that technological devices are to prevent technology inefficiencies in the area is gaining ground. Law can only play a post-factum regulative role. Classical theories of educative and pre-regulative function of the law have been left behind by the new reality.

2

Multimedia Databases

Introduction

Multimedia products at that stage seemed to be blocked in many countries from coming under the protection of compilations on the basis that, although they were considered to form some sort of compilation, they did not contain only works (as originally required in the Berne Convention and consequently in the laws of many of its Member States), but other materials as well. In fact most of their contents were data, information which would not qualify under any regime as material capable of attracting copyright protection. The second problem multimedia products were presenting was the fact that they were not coming anywhere near to the conventional book-format of manually accessible compilations. Multimedia products, if held to be compilations, could only be digital ones. It was not clear in the Berne Convention and the laws of many countries, which did not expressly provide for the protection of databases, that traditional compilations could be legitimately extended to cover digital or electronic compilations. Since, by the enactment of legislation concerning the protection of databases at Community level, these two hurdles disappeared, there were many commentators who stood by the opinion that any distinction between databases and multimedia products would be both unwise and impractical. This would be so especially in a period where the protection for both was seen to be at the heart of developments in the worldwide new technologies market.

The EU legislation was not the first legislation to provide copyright protection for databases. The WIPO Copyright Treaty at a later stage provided for the same kind of protection: 'Compilations of data or other material, in any form, which by reason of the selection or arrangement of their contents constitute intellectual creations, are protected as such.'

Both the WCT and the TRIPs Agreement provide copyright protection for databases by reason of the selection and arrangement of their contents. However, no precise definition of databases is given. The first complete definition found in a legal instrument is contained in the EU Directive. According to its article 1.2, a database is held to be 'a collection of independent works, data or other materials arranged in a systematic or methodical way and individually accessible by electronic or other means'.

A first issue which is clarified right from the start is that the computer programs used in the making or operation of databases are not to be included in the scope of protection of the databases. Any computer programs qualifying for copyright protection are to be dealt with under the software Directive. According to the EU Directive's wording, both manual and electronic compilations are covered. Electronic or digital compilations are those which are arranged, stored and accessed by electronic, electromagnetic, electro-optical or analogous processes. Not all stages of constructing a database have to undergo the aforementioned processes, though. It is submitted that it is the final one which is decisive. Thus, even if a database is manually arranged, stored electronically with the aid of a scanner and accessed electronically by means of a computer program, it is still considered to be an electronic database.

The contents of a database can be wide-ranging. Any literary work or text of any kind, any artistic or dramatic work as well as any kind of image, diagram, figure or number, any kind of musical work or equally any sound can qualify as contents of a database. There is no limit to the number of works or materials included but there are some limits as to the type of content. There is no requirement about the function these materials are meant to serve in the context of a database and no specific type of combination of the materials required. In toto the scope of the contents of a database is very wide. It is perhaps obvious to say that the materials included in a database do not have to be capable of being put in a written format, as was previously required in the UK's Copyright Act in relation to compilations; firstly, because the Directive expressly provides for artistic works as well, and secondly, because the digitisation of the materials inevitably transforms any kind of information into one and the same digital format. Yet, three limitations exist. First of all the materials, which form the contents of a database, have to be independent. The two other requirements are that these materials have to be individually accessible and that the contents of the database have to be arranged in a systematic or methodical way. We will now turn to the detailed examination of each of these requirements.

'Independent' contents

That the contents of a database have to be independent seems to be a simple statement. What is meant by this requirement is not defined, though. If we combine this requirement with what we usually consider as being the classic example of a database, we could surmise that by 'independent' the drafters of the Directive meant materials which can stand on their own, whether they are extracts or whole works. It is reasonable to assume that by 'database' the average person understands a telephone or street directory, or some other kind of catalogue containing various related entries, each with a similar value in relation to the area covered. Independent materials from such projects as these can only be materials which are valuable on their own, because of the information they carry; information which is considered in some sense to be 'complete' information. For example, the information an address gives to its reader can be considered to be a complete and independent piece of information. Its value is enhanced in the context of a database because it brings various pieces of information together and combines them so as to give a global and comprehensive image in relation to a particular area or in relation to a particular subject.

'Individually accessible' contents

The requirement that the materials included in a database be independent forms only the first test for a project to qualify as a database. The second test, which seems to be linked to the first one, is that the materials have to be 'individually accessible'. The fact that these two tests are linked or closely related to each other derives from the fact that an element that is independent in a database can also perform a useful and complete function when it is retrieved on its own. In order for it to be capable of being retrieved on its own, it has to be individually accessible.

The requirement that the materials that are included in a database have to be capable of being accessed individually was put there to exclude any works which serve a different purpose and therefore do not present this option. For that reason any collective works which do not aim at the collection of data, but at a unified literary, artistic or dramatic result, clearly cannot qualify as databases. Films are a characteristic example of this. Although a film consists of separate frames carried on pellicle, these frames are meaningful only when seen as a series of moving images and not separate from one another. In the same sense any recording, or any other audiovisual or cinematographic work, would fall foul of the requirements of the database Directive. Computer programs and video games are further examples. The elements incorporated in them make sense and perform their actual intellectual and commercial functions only when seen in a sequence. They are clearly works which are not capable of being accessed individually. However, a collection of computer programs, of video games or of films is always possible and would fall within the definition of a database.

If the requirement for the elements of a database to be individually accessible did not exist, the wide-ranging definition with regard to the contents of a database would bring within its scope almost every possible kind of work. The result would be the creation of overlapping protection for certain works. Consequently, a second layer of copyright protection would exist, affording more exclusive rights to more people. Apart from the fact that the general copyright system would become confusing, there would no longer be a reason for particular definitions of any specific types of intellectual property products. If, for example, a work could qualify for database protection, there would be no reason to check whether the same work came within the definition of a film as well. The provisions on databases could serve the database author well enough on their own without the need for recourse to any other intellectual property legislation.

This would destabilise the whole copyright system, especially in common law countries where every intellectual property product has to be put neatly into its correct category if it is to qualify for copyright protection. Any interchangeability between the various regimes of protection would lead to abuse of rights, circumvention of obligations and paralysis of certain provisions. What would be the purpose, for example, of offering a database seventy-year copyright protection, if the same database could also qualify for protection as a film, and extend its seventy-year term of protection by starting to calculate it from the death of the last co-author of the film?

One possible solution could be to abandon the different categories of works altogether in the light of their transformation into a single digitised format and provide for one kind of copyright protection only, applicable to all kinds of works. That could theoretically facilitate the use of copyright and prevent possible abuses in the area. However, it would call for a radical reconstruction of the whole copyright system, which would at best disregard the differences in nature between the various intellectual property works. A level of detail would thus be lost in such a system, because these differences in nature lead to differences in the precise format of protection.

Instead of banning the various categories of works altogether, another idea, perhaps, would be to avoid attempts at defining the exact scope of these categories. The EU software Directive, for example, avoided any definition with regard to computer programs, out of fear that any definition was bound to be outdated sooner or later by reason of the rapid technological developments. Another example is the recent Belgian Copyright Act, which does not define the various categories of works, but nevertheless provides for different regimes of protection in relation to different categories of works by referring to them by their generic terms, e.g. literary works, databases, films, computer programs, etc. Such a regime of protection carries with it the danger in the future of losing track of the precise scope of the works it puts into the different categories. Although it is not difficult now to define with a great degree of certainty what a film is, and even easier to recognise one when you see it, this will not necessarily be the case in the future. Different products will be capable of falling into different categories, and there will be no precise definition to prevent them from doing so. That will result in undesirable overlaps between the different regimes of protection. In conclusion, two feasible options remain. However, whether one opts for various categories of works, each linked to a specific bundle of rights and exceptions, or whether one opts for a single category of works, with a single bundle of rights and exceptions, problems remain. Neither system produces an ideal solution.

Systematic and Methodical Arrangement of Contents

The third and final test for a work to qualify as a database is whether its contents are arranged in a systematic or methodical way. The mere storage of quantities of works or materials in electronic form will fall foul of such a requirement. Yet, it will only be rare or remote cases where the contents of a database will not be subject to some kind of method or arrangement. In most cases this method or arrangement is also the one that enables the contents to be individually accessible with the help of a software tool. Yet, the kind of method or arrangement required is not specified in the text of the Directive. What is likely is that any arrangement of the contents of a database in most cases will not be the result of the individual judgment of its author. More and more databases are the result of planning on the part of their developers, who, in order to realise them, have to make them subject to certain technical rules, dictated by their making and operating software. Thus, part of the planning of a database is initiated or semi-initiated and realised by computers. Any arrangement would look even more absurd, if one applied it in relation to the storage of the contents in the memory of some computer in binary code. This requirement, of course, is banned by Recital 21 to the Directive. What is not specified, however, is whether any method of arranging the materials will be judged before or after the materials have been inserted into the memory of the computer. If it is the latter, what is the role, if any, of the user of the database who initiates the various selections and arrangements of this material on his screen? Are these selections and arrangements to be taken into account? Is the user of such a product to be afforded any rights, at least to works that give him a wider scope of discretion and creativity, as is the case with interactive multimedia products?

Once these three requirements are met (independent materials methodically or systematically selected or arranged and capable of being accessed individually), a work can qualify as a database. No express, or even indicative, examples of such cases are given in the Directive. Yet, a number of works which do not meet the above tests are excluded. Amongst these works one work, which does not immediately seem to fall foul of the aforementioned requirements, but which is however excluded from the scope of the Directive, is an ordinary audio CD. According to Recital 19 to the Directive, 'the compilation of several recordings of musical performances on a CD does not come within the scope of this Directive, both because as a compilation, it does not meet the conditions for copyright protection and because it does not present a substantial enough investment to be eligible under the sui generis right'.

These requirements can refer to two points only: either to the originality requirement regarding the selection and arrangement of the contents of a database, or to the elements of the definition of a database. The former point has to be examined on a case-by-case basis and no theoretical conclusion is to be drawn in advance. In relation to the latter there is nothing to indicate that an ordinary CD does not include independent works, which have been arranged subject to a particular method or system, and which can be retrieved independently. However, the inclusion of CDs in the scope of the Directive would unnecessarily extend a protection already afforded to sound recordings in the national copyright laws as neighbouring, related rights or copyright. Yet, it is not clear whether the exclusion of CDs implies the exclusion of phonograms in general. This might eventually cause problems in case of databases seeking to provide information in the area of music. CD-ROMs and CD-Is, however, remain expressly within the Directive's scope of protection.

Beyond Copyright

The information which constitutes the contents of a database, whilst independent, is not separately or additionally protected by the copyright which is afforded to the database itself. This is so irrespective of whether the contents themselves are within copyright protection or not, or within any other kind of protection, e.g. trade marks, trade secrets, know-how, confidentiality, etc. Since databases are considered to be, in fact, an extension of traditional compilations, and since their value consists of the assemblage of the various materials, copyright protection can be afforded to them only in relation to the selection and arrangement of their materials. This selection and arrangement has to be the author's own intellectual creation, according to the wording of the database Directive, which is the same in all EU Directives. This is the yardstick against which databases are measured in order to pass the hurdle of originality.

The originality criterion for a database to constitute its author's own intellectual creation, though lower than the continental one (which requires creativity and personal involvement to a greater degree), is still higher than the common law one (which requires skill and labour only). That means that many databases, which previously qualified for copyright protection under the common law system, will no longer be able to do so. There are, however, databases which remain outside the scope of copyright, even though a substantial amount of skill and labour has been invested in them, not to mention a substantial financial investment in most cases. These databases are in need of protection, albeit to a lesser degree, and that need for protection has been addressed.

It was essentially the aforementioned need which dictated the introduction of a sui generis regime of protection in relation to the contents of a database. That need is created irrespective of the fact that the contents of a database are themselves already protected by copyright or by some other right. The role of their initial copyright is to stop them from being copied without the authorisation of their rightholder. The role of the person who has incorporated those contents into a database, after having acquired the authorisation of their rightholder, is insignificant or nonexistent in relation to their potential inclusion in a new database. That results in all the investment in time, money, effort and energy put into the construction of the database remaining unprotected, or partially protected through unfair competition law in those countries which provide such a law.

It is exactly the solution to this problem that the sui generis right, which was introduced by the database Directive, offers. The sui generis right is granted to the maker of the database, so as to allow him to prevent third parties from extracting and/or re-utilising the whole or substantial parts of his work without his authorisation. Yet, this right is subject to one prerequisite. The making of a database has to involve a qualitatively and/or quantitatively substantial investment in the obtaining, verification or presentation of its contents. This requirement constitutes the raison d'être of the sui generis right, which in fact is an unfair competition rule conceptualised and transformed into a positive intellectual property right.

It is essential to note three things so far. First, the sui generis right is a right afforded to the contents of a database and not to the database itself (meaning the selection, arrangement or other structure of its materials). Second, granting of a sui generis right instead of copyright to the maker of the database removes the potential danger of having two copyrights in the same material owned by different parties; one owned by the author of the original work or his successors in title, and the other owned by the maker of the database, in which the work is included. It could even be argued that the sui generis right itself has the potential to create ownership conflicts with the owner of the copyright in the database. Lastly, we have to bear in mind that the sui generis right is a passe-par-tout right, which is afforded to the contents of a database, irrespective of the fact that they themselves are protected by copyright or some other right, or irrespective of the fact that they form part of a database which is protected by copyright. The sui generis right is an additional layer of protection for any kind of independent materials of a database, which form the contents of a copyrightable or non-copyrightable database.

Multimedia Products as Databases

Many of the elements contained in the definition of a database are not easily transposed to a multimedia context. We will consider these points in more detail in the next pages. Suffice it to say here that the requirement of systematic and methodical arrangement of materials does not create problems in relation to multimedia products. In the same way as a database, a multimedia product contains many materials and these materials are always arranged, one way or the other, in a systematic or methodical manner.

Interactivity versus 'individually accessible' contents

One could argue at this point that Recital 22 to the Directive, which expressly provides for the protection of CD-ROMs and CD-Is in relation to electronic databases, may actually refer to multimedia products as well, or at least refers to them in so far as interactive databases are held to be multimedia products. With regard to the definition that we gave of multimedia products in the first chapter of this book, we could argue that it is broad enough to include interactive databases as well. Still, more than one expression is combined on a single medium, either non-linear or linear, in a digitised form. Even if the database at issue contains only text accessed through hypertext links, the presence of a computer program, which allows for the retrieval of those texts and for the interactive dialogue between the user and the information included in the database, allows the database at issue to meet the requirement of combining more than one element of expression.

If we now look at the definition of a database, we will arrive at similar conclusions, though from the other end of the spectrum. The database definition allows for the simultaneous existence of more than one expression, and dictates the use of a computer program. However, there is no mention of interactivity. That does not seem to create any problems since it is not true of databases that by not expressly mentioning something, we imply that it must be excluded. Interactivity sits perfectly well with databases. It does not add to or transform any of their essential characteristics. On the contrary, it makes the requirement of 'individual accession' of their contents easier and more commercial. On top of that, some could also argue that interactivity is a feature attached to the computer program that runs the database, and that it is not to be judged under the definition of a database in the first place. Since interactivity substantially affects the image, nature and function of the whole multimedia product, we have to admit that, on this point at least, distinguishing databases from their operating software tool might make sense.

Yet, not all multimedia products are databases in this sense. The modern multimedia applications do not aim to collect pieces of information, which the user can simply track down and access individually. Nowadays multimedia products are more than that. If we look into the components of a modern multimedia product and those of a database, we will probably see that both databases and multimedia products include a computer program to operate them. They both contain a large number of different kinds of works and expressions in some kind of systematic or methodical arrangement. In the case of a database, however, some things remain out of the scope of qualifying contents. For example, three-dimensional objects are not included. Some, of course, would regard this exception as insignificant compared to the bulk of works qualifying, but in the case of multimedia this is not so. If we admit that multimedia products will very soon move into the virtual reality world, where three-dimensional objects are more common, even if as will be seen later there is at least an issue as to whether all virtual works are really three-dimensional, excluding them is in fact putting a substantial obstacle in the way of their evolution. Of course, the exclusion of three-dimensional objects is not incorporated as such into the actual provisions of the database Directive. It is found only in the guidelines offered in its Explanatory Memorandum. This Memorandum has by no means the same value as an express provision. It can only be interpreted with regard to the historical and social environment present at the stage of drafting the legislation to which it refers. That implies, of course, that it would not be illegal in the future if three-dimensional objects were found by a national judge to qualify as contents in a database. In reality, of course, most of the three-dimensional works that will be included in a multimedia work will be represented in a two-dimensional format that creates a three-dimensional impression. For these works the problem does not arise.

Apart from the computer program operating the work (both for databases and multimedia products), and the arrangement of almost the same scope of contents in a systematic or methodical way (as the law for databases requires), multimedia products seem to distinguish themselves when it comes to the requirement for their contents to be 'individually accessible'. Two options are possible in relation to a multimedia product. The first is where the contents are both individually accessible and accessible in conjunction with one another, depending on the command the user of a database enters into the system. The second option is where the contents have been integrated into one another to such an extent that no individual access to them is possible. The question arising here is whether these multimedia products can still come under the protective umbrella of databases.

Multimedia Products containing 'individually accessible' contents

We have to look separately at each of these two possible cases. In the case where the contents of a multimedia product are both individually accessible and accessible in conjunction with each other, part of it, relating to the entries which are individually accessible, can qualify as a database. The problem is, however, that it is not in practice feasible or advisable to protect only a part of a work, as would be the case here with the multimedia product. One of the possible protections has to take precedence. The question is which one? In a case where all (or most of) the contents of a multimedia product are individually accessible, undoubtedly that product qualifies as a database. The fact that the same contents can also be viewed in conjunction with each other should not normally create a problem. In this sense the multimedia product could qualify as a database.

In addition, the protection of a multimedia product as a database also presents the advantage that the contents of the former, by analogy with the latter, will also be protected when they are not selected or arranged in an original way. This protection will be afforded to them by reason of the sui generis right, if substantial investment in their collection, verification or presentation is made by the developer of the multimedia product. The mere storage, of course, of quantities of works or materials in electronic form will not qualify for copyright protection nor for sui generis protection. Since the cases where such an investment will not exist will be rare, and since multimedia products do not necessarily always involve an original structure (selection and/or arrangement) in relation to their contents, the sui generis protection in relation to the latter is both desirable and commercially advantageous.

Moreover, sui generis protection seems at first sight capable of closing gaps in the protection of multimedia products, analogous to those faced by databases some time ago. Although the existence of a sui generis protection for the contents of a multimedia product is good, it does not go far enough. This is because a multimedia product is more than the collection of its contents. The protection of the original structure of its contents by copyright and the protection of the assemblage of those contents by the sui generis right fails to encompass the whole of a multimedia product.

It encompasses only two-thirds of it, which in fact constitutes only the database that a multimedia product includes as part of its functions, together with the computer program. Yet, as we mentioned earlier, the multimedia product is more than just a database. It is a new creation, the functions of which share few of the functions of a database. The protection of only parts of it disregards the nature of the multimedia product and disregards its arguably different needs as a totally new product.

In order to represent a multimedia product graphically, we could present it as a circle. One-third of the circle will be occupied by the computer program and the operating materials of the product. The second third will be occupied by the database contained in the multimedia product. The final third will be occupied by the new creation, which allows for the contents to be viewed in conjunction with each other. It is this final third which outstrips the concept of a database. Here we can refer only to a new creation which, though it encompasses a database, is the multimedia product.

Exceptionally, very simple, or should one say simplistic, multimedia products may present a different picture. If there is no real added value in terms of original work, and if the interactivity element is contained solely in the software, it might be argued that one is really confronted with a combination of a database and a computer program. In this exceptional scenario, where there is no full integration of the contents and where, in combination with the interactivity, this does not lead to the addition of another layer of added value, the resulting multimedia product could be protected as a database if one keeps in mind that the database model also includes separate protection for the computer software.

Conjunctively retrieved contents in multimedia products

The second case is where a multimedia product does not contain a database at all, because its contents can only be accessed in conjunction with each other. The application of the protection of databases in a multimedia product is not possible, since the database Directive specifically requires works to be individually accessible.

In such cases we have to look for a regime of protection, the purpose of which is not the mere collection of materials, their systematic editing and their individual access. What is required is protection which covers the collection of materials and their systematic editing, so as to produce a literary, artistic or other outcome, which shows its value only when accessed as a whole, or at least as a sequence of some of its contents. This is where the emphasis is shifting: away from the collection of existing materials and towards the creation of a new integrated work. The new work has a substantial added value superseding that of the sum of its parts and deserving protection for that reason, rather than simply for the structured collection of materials. This is something which is rather different from the normal concept of a database.

Alternatively 'individually accessible' could in relation to multimedia products also mean that the work or component as such appears or can be made to appear independently on screen. That requirement can be met even if at the same time some other item appears too. Examples could be background pictures that go with text, or sound that is combined with images. In this sense a vast number of multimedia works could be taken to meet the database criteria. This interpretation bends the rules on databases to a great extent, and is clearly motivated by an overriding desire to find an adequate regime of protection for multimedia. Those who advocate it see the investment in a multimedia work (that uses other original works as components) as the essential point. The database model has that kind of protection as its essential feature and is therefore a suitable model. In reality this is not what 'individually accessible' is supposed to mean. The user should be able to lift a single item out of a compilation of data in isolation, otherwise almost anything could potentially be seen as a database. A multimedia work does not make that possible. Rather it offers combinations and integrated versions of bits and pieces of elements that are contained in it. It tries to offer added value on top of that of the single components.

The compilation alternative

If databases are to be abandoned (wholly or partly) as a possible or as the only possible regime of protection for multimedia products, the first obvious alternative which comes to mind is compilations. A compilation may in certain cases, where this is provided by the law of a state, contain materials other than works. These materials are not necessarily capable of being put into a written format and do not have to be individually accessible. This addresses the difficulty raised in the previous paragraph in respect of databases. In that sense at least, certain multimedia products might have more in common with the concept of a compilation. However, as we explained in the chapter on compilations, this is not entirely true since a compilation puts the emphasis of the protection it offers on the stable selection and arrangement of existing materials, whilst the multimedia work is in need of protection for the new work that is created and that corresponds better to the content rather than the structure. A study by the Max-Planck-Institut demonstrated that both compilations and databases suffer from the same defect when they are drafted in to protect multimedia products. They focus on the selection and juxtaposition of individual elements. A multimedia product focuses on the integration of these individual elements into something 'extra' that gives added value to the product. This means that the compilation model is as little suited to multimedia products as the database model. In addition, compilations present all the problems that are associated with the requirement of a written format and with the exclusion of certain types of works from their scope, at least in certain jurisdictions. This means that compilations cannot be a universally accepted alternative. A last important point is the fact that multimedia products are associated with the concept of interactivity. This means that they take the integration of the materials contained in them one step further than traditional compilations. In compilations the integration of works is given a fixed format. Such a fixed format will in most cases still allow individual access to each of the materials. Interactivity is the antithesis of any fixed format and allows for the full integration of the contents in a flexible way.

The second obvious candidate for protection with regard to multimedia products is films. In a film, different pre-existing works are put together in a systematic and methodical combination, so as to produce the artistic and/or informative result that the film is aiming at. In relation to films, the requirement of 'individual access' to their contents is also missing as it is in the case of some multimedia products. In the chapter that follows, we will discuss whether films are obvious or realistic candidates for the type of works that will offer effective protection to multimedia products.

3

Multimedia Networks and Strategies of Innovation

Introduction

The concepts of new media or multimedia refer to products and services combining the video, audio and print/graphic dimensions of computer technology, telecommunications and content that can be used interactively by consumers and business users. The products and services of multimedia firms include content design and development; consulting in such areas as marketing, design, and technology; content packaging and marketing, including CD-ROM publishing and online/Internet services; content distribution, such as online/Internet; electronic commerce such as financial services; software development and 'generic' applications, including information retrieval and management; and content creating tools such as audio recording, design and illustration.

The organizational dynamics of this new segment of advanced producer and business services are unusual, to say the least. About two-thirds of the firms have been in business for three years or less, and about 30 per cent have been newly established over a period of eighteen months from March 1996 to September 1997. During this last period, about one-sixth (17 per cent) of the firms have dropped out as independent entities either by merger, relocation or bankruptcy.

Besides providing a description of the structure and dynamics of this new segment of the post-industrial services sector, my purpose is to concentrate on the special affinity between innovative corporate strategies and certain structural characteristics of the new inter-firm networks that are central to this dynamic process. I focus on the expansion of the new media industry in Manhattan since 1992, its economic effects on the tri-state region (New York, New Jersey and Connecticut), its internal structure, the typical organizational profile of its new innovative firms, and the emerging competitive effects of the new media on the old media.

Growth of 'Silicon Alley' before and after 1992

From the perspective of urban sociology in general, and the theory of regional economic development and innovation in particular, the case of New York City is rather atypical, if not unique. New York has been an economically thriving metropolis for a long time. It is a central site for a region already leading in the development of post-industrial and especially business services as well as communications and entertainment. It has a highly concentrated clustering of multimedia firms whose development, while contributing to the regional economy, can be said to feed mainly on their own success, thus creating a highly dynamic and self-sustaining, almost autonomous, development.

The New York City multimedia industry participates actively in the process of globalization. It continues to attract investment from domestic and transnational financial centres, is an exporter of multimedia services, and thus benefits from a highly competitive-cooperative-integrative environment without as yet showing signs of being overly fragmented, over-integrated, or destroyed by these processes. During the 1990s, it has been a case of growth feeding on growth. The central causal assumptions of the theory of industrial districts, that production and service networks will generate innovative regional economic growth, are therefore supported from the start. In the case of New York, indeed, they are somewhat tautological since the process already occurs at a high level of 'institutional thickness' and sustained development rather than starting out from ground zero. The special features of multimedia firms and networks, and discuss some of the likely consequences of new media growth for the older media.

New York's pre-1992 economic development in thecontext of a 'global city'

Like most major world cities, New York has experienced a disproportionate growth of the service sector (relative to manufacturing) since the early 1970s. Within that sector, business, commercial or producer services have been the fastest growing and transnationally most relevant component. The leading producer services are the FIRE services, i.e. financial (banking), insurance and real estate, as well as accounting and consulting, advertising and legal services. To these must be added communications and a host of other business services such as administration and management, research and development, personnel and security, not to mention maintenance, cleaning, and related 'personal' services.

Nationally, total employment in the United States grew from 77 million in 1970 to 117 million in 1991 (52 per cent), whereas producer services jumped from almost 6.3 million in 1970 to 16.35 million in 1991 (160 per cent). Within the category of producer services, the two fastest growing items during this twenty-year period were legal services (211 per cent) and miscellaneous business services (314 per cent). A persuasive case can be made that a significant part of this dramatic expansion of producer services is due to the concentration of transnational corporate headquarters in global cities like New York.

As mentioned, the growth of the post-industrial urban service economy has not been one of unbroken monotonic increases. In the mid-1970s, the New York City government experienced an unprecedented fiscal crisis which was 'solved' only by subordinating the 'sovereignty' of financial decisions on credits and expenditures to the Municipal Assistance Corporation. This was a financial control board constituted and heavily influenced by banks, investment houses and other financial institutions. From 1977 to 1987, New York City's share in the national employment level in producer services declined slightly from 8.3 per cent to 7.6 per cent, due in part to the municipal fiscal crisis and in part to an increasing dispersion of such services regionally and nationwide. The ten-year decline varied slightly among services, from insurance (6.5 to 4.8 per cent), real estate (10.1 to 7.5 per cent) and business services (8.4 to 6.2

per cent) to legal services (9.4 to 8.2 per cent). Only banking and finance remained stable at 11.7 per cent during this period. It should be noted that, in all of these figures, Manhattan always shows a higher concentration of services than New York City as a whole.

After the October 1987 stock market crisis, there was a sharp decline in employment as well as considerable restructuring in the securities and banking industry, including mergers among large domestic banks. Employment in banking fell from 169,000 in 1989 to 157,000 in 1991, a drop of 7.6 per cent. Nevertheless, the growth of foreign investment and banking continued to ensure New York's role as a leading world financial centre. The city retained six of the world's top ten securities firms as of 1990; not to mention the continued importance of Wall Street, the New York and American Stock Exchanges, the Dow Jones Company (ranking as the world's fortieth largest media corporation which includes the Wall Street Journal) and numerous other business and financial service enterprises.

New York City was and is, of course, also the media capital of the United States, where some of the nation's largest publishing firms, television networks and advertising agencies are located. 'These corporations', as Moss and Ludwig put it, 'produce the information and images that are communicated across the country and the world, in the form of newspapers, magazines, books, and radio and television programmes. The presence of information-intensive firms in New York City contributes to the economic well-being of the city' and serves 'the larger metropolitan region surrounding the city itself.

As of 1988, the four major daily newspapers had a total circulation of about 4.6 million. City residents can receive at least fifteen television stations without subscribing to cable TV and there are fifteen AM and twenty-three FM radio stations. Moss and Ludwig identified eighty foreign language newspapers serving the city's vast and growing immigrant population. Cable television has grown from two cable TV franchises for Manhattan in 1971 to four franchises serving all the boroughs since 1986.

Yet Moss and Ludwig point out that the riches of media coverage in the city are double-edged: 'a small number of firms control the major television channels, radio syndicates, and major daily newspapers. On the other hand, a multiplicity of grassroots media outlets have emerged to counter the inadequate coverage and appeal of the mainstream, and often national, media'. There is a growing disparity between the traditional television and print media that serve the area and the highly diverse ethnic and minority groups that make up the majority of the city's population. 'Moreover, there is growing bifurcation of the media, with the city-wide print and television increasingly serving the affluent middle class within the city and surrounding region, while radio and community newspapers serve specific ethnic and minority groups'. It stands to reason that this social division will continue to be reflected in the bifurcation of old and new media consumers since educational differences, as well as the costs of equipment and access, are likely to restrict the new media market to those with adequate economic resources and cultural capital. Unfortunately, continued global economic expansion is likely to exacerbate the existing socio-economic inequality within cities as well as among them. There are also growing disparities in the stratification among sub-national, national, and transnational regions.

The growth of Silicon Alley since 1992

The traditional media have always been concentrated in urban areas and have played an important role in the economic and cultural life of cities like New York for many decades. The last few years, however, have witnessed the explosive growth of a qualitatively different symbiosis of information technologies, structural innovations and cultural creativity which has come to be known as the 'new media', multimedia, or cyber-industry. To be sure, personal interaction and participation remain distant ideals in these new media, but they provide a new technical infrastructure in which interactive and response capacity is a central, built-in feature. One could view the electronic bulletin board and interpersonal e-mail as transitions to these new computer-integrated forms. Local area networks and, finally, 'The Internet' and its subsets, such as the World Wide Web with its websites, home pages and voice-audio-video-graph-print combinations have become emblematic of a new interactive virtual reality and the notion of 'virtual communities'. Multimedia products and services represent a new symbolic environment, a 'culture of real virtuality'. While there is plenty of myth-making that surrounds the secrets of the Internet and the new media, there is a tangible and highly profitable infrastructure of producers and providers that constitute the core of this cyber-industry.

Multimedia firms, as described in the following account, include companies specializing in entertainment software, those providing online/Internet services, CD-ROM title developers, website designers and an assortment of related production and service networks connecting suppliers, producers, distributors and consumers. Advertising, marketing, entertainment, education, publishing and video-film production are the new media providers with core businesses outside the new media. It is useful to distinguish at least three layers of the New York cyber-industry: the corporate giants, the new media industry as a whole, and its most creative and volatile subset, Silicon Alley. In reality, these layers are, of course, interrelated.

The Corporate Giants

New York is home to seven of the world's largest multimedia firms including Time Warner (ranked number 1), Viacom (4), Advance Publications (15), National Broadcasting Co. (NBC) (19), the Columbia Broadcasting System (CBS) (24), The Hearst Corporation (37), and Dow Jones and Co. (40). Each of these giant corporations consists of several subsidiaries: they are the result of multiple mergers and acquisitions and are continuously involved in processes of reorganization and restructuring. The world's largest media firm Time Warner, for example, includes Turner Broadcasting (and the popular CNN) since 1995 and holds the Manhattan Cable TV franchise. Time Warner had a total of 72,500 employees in 1995. In the same year it had a total media transaction volume of $25.37 billion but, significantly, due to a large volume of corporate debt, in fact made a net loss of $124 million.

Viacom Inc., the fourth largest media corporation with a $17 billion transaction volume and 81,700 employees, had a net profit of $163 million for 1995. It controls a variety of subsidiaries, including Paramount Pictures, the Blockbuster Video chain and a host of cable-TV networks (MTV, Showtime, Nickelodeon, Nick at Nite and ten other channels, some of them joint ventures), film, multimedia, publishers and entertainment park groups. In 1996 Viacom entered into a joint venture with the Kirch-Group in Germany. Should the Internet ever become accessible via home television, a corporation like Viacom would be well situated to reap enormous profits from its wide-ranging corporate network.

Still another well-known example is Dow Jones and Co., the fortieth largest media firm world-wide. It includes The Wall Street Journal (WSJ), Business Information Services, the WSJ Television Group, the Dow Jones Investor Network and the business journals Barron's and Smart Money. In 1995, it had 11,200 employees in over 100 countries and a transaction volume of $2.284 billion, with a net profit of $190 million.

It goes without saying that each of these corporate giants constitutes the core of a series of partly hierarchical, partly lateral inter-firm production, service and supplier networks. The New York Times, for example, is represented among Silicon Alley firms by its subsidiary The New York Times Electronic Media Company which is headed by a content development specialist and has sixty employees. Sony, the sixth largest media concern world-wide, has had an 'entertainment' subsidiary Sony Online Ventures Inc. since 1995.

Finally, Microsoft maintains three subsidiaries in Silicon Alley with an undisclosed number of employees (Microsoft Multimedia Productions, Microsoft Sidewalk.com and Microsoft Developer Relations Group).

It is likely that the new media industry will increasingly be dominated by an ever-smaller number of large, transnational enterprises. Despite a large number of new entries into the industry, many of the small multimedia firms to be described below will ultimately become integrated into the larger firms by joint ventures and strategic partnerships or will develop into sizeable corporations themselves through mergers and acquisitions.

The New York area new media industry

The new media industry as a whole provided 105,771 full-time equivalent jobs in 1997, including 55,973 (53 per cent) in New York City proper. The eighteen-month increase from the end of 1995 to mid-1997 alone amounted to 48 per cent for the whole area and 105 per cent for the city proper.

The breakdown for the type of employment in 1997 was as follows: of the total of 105,771 employees, 56 per cent were full-time, 21 per cent part-time and 23 per cent freelancers. While the category of freelancers has remained stable, the proportion of part-time employees jumped from 12 to 21 per cent in eighteen months, whereas the proportion of full-time employees shrank from 64 per cent to 56 per cent.

In April 1996, the big accounting and consultancy firm Coopers and Lybrand had estimated that new media area employment as a whole would increase by at least 100 per cent by the end of 1998. So far, the increase has been 50 per cent for about half of that three-year period and about 200 per cent since 1992. Thus, despite criticisms of the firm's methods and projections as inflated and advocacy oriented (it was criticised as an 'industry booster'), it is worth noting that most of the figures reported for 1997 have been remarkably close to the earlier projections and that the firm cannot be faulted for lack of accuracy.

The economic picture points to a success story as well. A total of 4,259 area firms generated $3.8 billion in gross revenues in 1995 (these totals for the new media industry include related firms in New Jersey and Connecticut). The corresponding figure for 1997 is 4,881 firms generating $5.7 billion, a 50 per cent increase. Manhattan alone, with 2,128 or 44 per cent of all the new media enterprises, generates $2.8 billion or almost half of the area's gross revenues derived from new media products and services. This represents a 56 per cent increase in revenues over 1995 for the Manhattan enterprises, which tend to be larger than those located outside Manhattan and New York City.

However, there has been a significant structural change in the New York area industry in the eighteen months from April 1996 to October 1997 that signals a rapid increase in economic concentration. Significantly, '1996 was the year of the shakeout in Silicon Alley'; '1997 was...the year of continued consolidation'. For example, in 1995-96, the ratio of large multimedia firms with annual revenues of over $5 million to those under $5 million was .235 or 235 per thousand. By 1997, in contrast, this ratio had shrunk to .0526 or 53 per thousand. This amounts to a four-and-a-half-fold increase in corporate concentration in a year and a half.

This means that while the 250 largest multimedia firms or business units make up only about 5 per cent of all New York area firms, they account for 72 per cent of the total revenues. Moreover, since the percentage of revenues spent outside the local economy increases with firm size, a growing portion of the $4.1 billion generated by the 250 largest multimedia corporations in 1997 was spent outside the New York economy. To be sure, the total number of firms increased during the period in question, but the size distribution has become more skewed.

Another type of concentration, this one related to the Internet itself, can be ascribed to the 'normally' high corporate density of metropolitan areas. Not surprisingly, Manhattan is also 'the hub for the Internet with almost 150,000 Internet hosts in New York County'. More importantly, in 1997 New York City had the largest Internet presence with 17,579 registered domains or 4.2 per cent of the national total. A domain represents a single organizational entity or naming authority such as 'nyu.edu' which is used by thousands of computer work stations and e-mail addresses at New York University alone. According to Moss and Townsend (1997:5), 85 per cent of the domain registrations are commercial domains that use the abbreviation '.com'. The remaining 15 per cent are domains like '.org', '.gov', and '.edu'.

Manhattan alone had 15,139 or 86 per cent of the area's registered domains. With a population of over one and a half million, Manhattan had a 'domain density' of 9.9. Only San Francisco had a higher domain density (10.2), although it has only half of the actual number of registered domains (7,518 to Manhattan's 15,139). Thus, the five American cities with the largest number of domains and the highest domain density are Manhattan, San Francisco, Seattle (4,080), Dallas (3,988) and Boston (3,981).

Silicon Alley

The district that is most interesting and relevant for purposes of this chapter is 'Silicon Alley', which comprises the southern third of Manhattan. It represents the area south of 41st Street which is constituted by the 30s and 20s, the Flatiron District, Chelsea, Greenwich Village and the East Village, the Lower East Side, Soho and Downtown. The latter includes Wall Street, the New York and

American Stock Exchanges, the World Trade Centre, and the famous 55 Broad Street building with its broad bandwidth, high-speed wiring which is home to many firms.

The 'institutional thickness' of this geographical area is proverbial and illustrates the embeddedness of Silicon Alley firms in a rich economic, social and cultural environment. For example, many of Silicon Alley's multimedia service and training networks involve institutions of higher education such as New York University and its Tisch School of the Arts Centre for Digital Multimedia, now the Centre for Advanced Technology with its famous Interactive Telecommunications Program (ITP). Directed by Professor Red Burns of NYU, the ITP has produced a number of top executives in Silicon Alley, including Jaime Levy (Electronic Hollywood), Howard Greenstein (now director of the Microsoft Developer Relations Group), Rebecca Odes and Esther Drill of gURL, and Stacey Horn of Echo, a virtual community firm. Burns began her career in 1971 when she founded the Alternate Media Centre at the Tisch School which is also nationally known for its outstanding film and video training programmes.

Other examples of New York's rich array of training networks are the NYU Taub Urban Research Centre, the NYU Stern School of Business and the Courant Institute of Mathematics with its computer facilities. In addition, there are various research institutes, colleges, business and law schools (some of them part of the City University system) as well as smaller educational establishments such as the Parsons School of Design (New School of Social Research), the Fashion Institute of Technology and Pace University, to name just a few. Some of these institutions are themselves connected by network ties among teaching and research faculty, the supply of new student cohorts and the placement of graduates.

As mentioned before, publishing houses, advertising agencies, and a host of older media conglomerates complement this densely structured service environment. Many of these institutions pre-date the multimedia revolution, but there is no doubt that the new media industry and the highly saturated educational environment benefit from each other.

Silicon Alley comprises 1,106 new media establishments, which represent 52 per cent of all new media businesses in Manhattan and generate $2.8 billion in gross revenues. An increasing number of these firms provide specialized products and services. Thus, the average number of products and services provided in 1995-96 was 3.6, but dropped to 2.4 in 1997. 84 per cent of the firms provide content design and development as a core product/service. The other top six products and services provided by firms in descending order are consultancy (37 per cent), content packaging and marketing (34 per cent), content distribution and transport (22 per cent), software development (20 per cent), content creation tools (17 per cent), and electronic commerce (16 per cent).

In terms of their service relationship to various market segments, the firms in this area are most closely associated with advertising and marketing (59 per cent), entertainment (37 per cent), information/reference (43 per cent), education (31 per cent) and financial services (28 per cent). The largest business customer segments besides publishing, advertising, new media and information technology are entertainment, financial services, telecommunications, education, broadcasting, retailing and other business and commercial services.

Publishing, new media, information technology, financial services and telecommunications saw the largest amounts of growth, between 14 per cent and 48 per cent, after 1995-96. The increase in the share of financial services (48 per cent), new media (39 per cent) and information technology (33 per cent) illustrates the tendency for Silicon Alley growth to feed on itself. Smaller customer industry segments such as health care, culture and government also experienced disproportionately large increases; government, for example, almost doubled its share from 8 to 15 per cent.

A close-up view of Silicon Alley firms

Besides the many network ties, alliances, partnerships and joint ventures that are characteristic of firms in the multimedia industry, there are also larger associational entities that reflect the phenomenal growth of the Silicon Alley cluster. For example, the Flatiron Partners venture capital group has more than 120 'associates'; there are over two thousand members of the New York New Media Association (NYNMA) located at 55 Broad Street. The scale of growth is also reflected in the number of subscribers to the Silicon Alley Reporter itself, an industry journal that was established in late 1996 and published its tenth issue in the winter of 1997-98. In the following account, I draw on a number of these indigenous sources of information, given the absence of a comprehensive empirical study of Silicon Alley to date. The latest membership directory of the NYNMA provides perhaps the best illustration of the great diversity of firms located in Silicon Alley. Of the 2,058 members listed for Fall 1997, 1,878 designate their primary business within one of sixty-five product and service categories. If this total of 1,878 corporate members is taken as a base (clearly non-random, but probably fairly representative), one arrives at the following distribution in declining order of frequency.

1 The largest category is constituted by a total of 573 digital media firms which represents 30.5 per cent of the 1,878 firms. Of these 573, almost one-third (10 per cent of the total) are in web services and design. Another third (9.2 per cent) are in online news and information, almost 5 per cent in CD-ROM development, and almost 4 per cent in advertising design.
2 Financial services constitute the second largest group with 202 (10.8 per cent) of the 1,878 firms. Banking, venture capital and investment make up the lion's share of this category with 142 firms (70 per cent). Accounting, financial management and consultancy come in second with fifty-eight firms (29 per cent).
3 A third major category is represented by a variety of professional services. By far the largest group here is legal services (132 firms, or 7 per cent of the total 1,878). This is followed by management consulting (84 firms or 4.5 per cent), and marketing and promotion (83 or 4.4 per cent). 'Recruitment' accounts for 76 firms (4 per cent); this probably includes the important networking activity of talent and head hunting. Finally, there is advertising and sales (66 firms or 3.5 per cent). All other professional service firms account for 3.9 per cent of the total.
4 The print media (newspaper, magazines, and book publishing) are represented by an astonishing 113 firms (6 per cent).
This suggests that old media corporations are likely to have new media subsidiaries and that there is a considerable'

degree of interpenetration of old and new media rather than outright competition. The additional 64 broadcast media firms, especially radio and network and cable TV, could be seen as similarly bridging the old and new media sectors. The same is true of professional services like graphic design, photography and writing.

5 Finally, there are 103 software development firms (5.5 per cent of the total), a category that includes publication and distribution, interactive software and contract consulting.

These groupings reflect the organizational and corporate diversity of Silicon Alley, not necessarily the shares in profits or total value added. The diversity of products and services is obvious and is reflected in the sixty-five separate categories in terms of which the 1,878 firms are listed.

Some industry clusters outside New York have a fairly high degree of area specialization. This is reported, for example, by Allen Scott in his work on the San Francisco Bay Area in Northern California (business applications and information repositories) and the Los Angeles/Hollywood centred area in Southern California ('self-enhancement' products). Silicon Alley markets seem to combine and integrate both of these specialty areas and appear generally to be more highly diversified than either of the two California area clusters. Unfortunately, the product market categories represented by Scott's 431 California firms are not commensurable with the categories used by the Coopers and Lybrand study or the NYNMA directory. Hence, there is no easy way to compare the findings of Scott's meticulous study short of a systematic comparison and replication.

Another way of looking at the 'typical' Silicon Alley firm is provided by a listing of 100 top multimedia executives and their firms published in the tenth issue of the SA Reporter. This is by no means a random sample but it does represent the range of both successful and struggling multimedia firms and provides a behind-the-scenes look at the dynamics of this unusual industry cluster. I have selected forty firms from the 100 entries published and believe they can serve as a basis for constructing a kind of 'ideal type'.

Half of these 'typical' Silicon Alley firms are in the business of producing 'content' and thus represent the more creative aspect of multimedia service production. The other half are in design, advertising and marketing, public relations and accounting, software, virtual communities and chat groups. Among these forty firms, the average number of employees is twenty-two, with a range from two to fifty-five. The average age of the Chief Executive Officer is thirty-two years, with a range from twenty-three to forty-six. Finally, the average length of time the firms have been in business is twenty months with one firm being barely six months old.

Four companies out of the 100 listed and not included in the above ideal- type profile are significantly larger: the average number of employees is 168. They are in accounting and financial services, Internet advertising (DoubleClick), commerce, content and software (N2K), and 'online community' content (iVillage). They have been in business for an average of two and a half years, with the average age of the executive being forty-eight years.

By contrast, the typical Silicon Alley firm is small and entrepreneurial, relatively young, and headed by a relatively young executive/owner. Most of these Silicon Alley firms, however, share the feature of extensive 'networking', be it in the form of mutual client and supplier relationships, subcontracting, joint ventures, partnerships or strategic alliances. Informal cooperation is also of course a common pattern.

It is worth noting that Coopers and Lybrand's demographic profile for 1997, based on all 4,881 multimedia firms in the New York area, is only marginally different from the above ideal type. Their 1997 report shows that 60 per cent of all firms have their primary business in content design and development. These firms generate about 50 per cent of the industry revenues. The average age of the new media top executive is forty years. In addition, the report emphasizes the network structure of the industry, in that new media firms show a 'high degree of reliance on suppliers and subcontractors'. New media firms are also shown to have a relatively young workforce; 36 per cent of the employees are under thirty years old and another 35 per cent are between thirty and forty. Only 38 per cent of the employees, however, are female.

Finally, in the absence of an in-depth empirical study of Silicon Alley, one may draw upon a gradual accumulation of a fund of knowledge and 'wisdom' by knowledgeable participants and observers. One of these is Thomas Hirschfeld, a journalist who provides an informative description of some of these firms. For example, AdOne Classified Network collects classified ads from hundreds of newspapers across the US and publishes them on a single website. Users can search AdOne not only by category and region but much more narrowly by type of house, car, job or other commodity. Atnet provides business-to-business communications. Through Virtual showrooms' and company directories that can be searched by product and price, businesses in the fashion industry can locate suppliers and customers. Data Downlink is a service for business users. It aggregates quantitative information such as economic figures, industry statistics, company financial data and market facts, and makes it available to subscribers who can download the data directly from the web. Index Stock Photography functions as an electronic photo-research centre for advertising agencies, publishers, and others. The 'Riddler' website of Interactive Imaginations entertains visitors with trivia contests, crossword puzzles and other games. Playing is free and real prizes are offered, but the games take players on tours of other websites whose owners pay Interactive Imaginations for the traffic.

According to Hirschfeld, the service is very popular and serves as a marketing tool for consumer-focused businesses. iVillage was originally founded by a partnership of executives from the magazine industry, cable home shopping and other services. It publishes 'magazines' on the Internet for sharply defined consumer groups one of which (Parent Soup), for example, gives parents medical advice, guidance from child-rearing experts, news and other information. It organizes online 'chat groups' where parents can discuss particular issues with one another while being offered child-related merchandise for online sale. Founded in January 1996 with $14 million in venture capital, iVillage got into rough water within a few months and had another capital infusion of $21.5 million in June 1996. In November 1996, all of iVillage's sites were integrated at a separate site called Life Soup devoted to parenting, health and work from a women's perspective. 'A convergence of message boards, chat areas, and "advertorials", the sites are integrated with commerce zones and sold to advertisers on claims of 51 million page views per month'.

Juno provides almost a million consumers with free electronic mail services in return for showing them advertisements while they are writing or reading messages. Medscape, supported by advertising from pharmaceutical manufacturers and others, is an Internet site for doctors. It has some 200,000 members. For a fee, users can get important information, including journal articles and research abstracts.

N2K (Need to Know), founded in 1995 and one of the large Silicon Alley firms mentioned above, operates some of the major music-related websites where browsers can hear excerpts from new releases, learn what their favourite artists listen to, and buy from a vast assortment of CDs. Such new media services are highly competitive vis-à-vis the old media firms, as Hirschfeld points out; for example, traditional stores have begun to offer some of these services but cannot match N2K's selection and convenience as well as the scale and scope of the Internet. Like iVillage and other firms, N2K encountered some rough going in the beginning, but seems to have recovered after 1996. It established sales alliances with America Online, Netscape, MTV, @Home, PointCast, AT&T, and WebTV and added a software component with e-mod (encoded music online delivery), a technology that plays CD-quality music over the Net.

Nature and Importance of Multimedia Networks

The network structure of clusters like Silicon Alley, it is useful to distinguish analytically between the technical information infrastructure or technical networks, on the one hand, and social networks on the other. Technical networks such as computer or telecommunications networks (e.g. local area nets and the Internet as a whole, as the net of nets) are 'technical' in the sense of requiring computers (hardware), the necessary programs (software), protocols (traffic rules) and electronic or optical telecommunications connections for purposes of access and use. One of the quantum differences of these networks from the one-to-one connection between users of a conventional telephone system lies in their one-to-infinitely-many simultaneous, multimedia, interactive capability. For the remainder of my discussion, I will treat these technical networks as given.

Social networks are the specific weblike patterns of informal social relationships among different nodes, as constituted by persons, firms, organizations, and other collective actors (agents, agencies). Among social networks, I want to further distinguish between emergent ('natural', expressive) and instrumental or strategic networks (formed for explicit purposes such as exchanging information, obtaining resources or solving problems) and concentrate mainly on the latter.

Inter-firm production and service networks (such as intercorporate and inter organizational networks among multimedia firms, their suppliers, distributors and corporate customers) are prime examples of consciously enacted strategic alliances and economic networks. While such networks could conceivably develop and function without the technical infrastructure discussed here, the scale and scope of their operations are vastly enhanced by the availability of the Internet.

There are, of course, other important types of strategic networks, such as quasi-governmental and policy networks, and the clandestine networks of organizational, governmental and élite corruption as well as organized crime. In all of these cases, there is likely to be an underlying 'milieu effect' which results from the embeddedness of actors in a common social environment or subculture ranging from simple and homogeneous to highly diverse and multiplex settings.

A third, intermediate category of networks are either strategically produced by, or emerge more or less randomly from, technical networks. As such, they can be said to be the social by-products, as it were, of techno-social linkages. I call such technically based or net-induced social structures socio-technical networks. They are characterized by a great variety of purposes, contents, themes or orientations. Socio-technical networks are 'virtual communities' in the dual sense of representing a community of interacting 'netizens' whose connection to each other is nevertheless based on mere cybernetic links. Thus, in talking about socio-technical networks, it seems important to analyse the origins and nature of the technical infrastructure of networks separately from their generative, productive and innovative effects on organizational and social network formation. One should distinguish the technical aspect from effects such as the creation of specialized electronic markets, target groups, interest associations and value-adding partnerships. Similarly, since the development of markets, hierarchies, groups and associations from any kind of prior social network involves a process of formalization and institutionalization, it too requires a separate logic of analysis.

While technical, social (especially organizational and inter organizational) and socio-technical networks can be analytically distinguished, this is not quite so easy in actual practice. As Hoogvelt and Yuasa point out in a comparison of Japanese and Western conceptions of information technology, technical information networks cannot be easily separated from production and organizational technology. They argue that 'in the West, the absence of a psycho-cultural infrastructure comparable to that which enables Japanese network capitalism to operate, has resulted in the conviction that information technology is not primarily part of production technology, but mainly organizational technology. As organizational technology, it is designed to overcome the "precarious" dependency which the new systems of production entail and which, in the Japanese context, as we have shown, are relatively unproblematic. The function of electronic data processing (EDP) and electronic data interchange (EDI) in particular is organizational: providing procedures, communication and memory patterns and ways of linking, controlling and coordinating personnel and companies with one another and with machines. Emerging patterns of hierarchization of EDI flows are important determinants of future constructs of power and regulation'.

In sum, there are many types of techno-social linkages in the sense that the nature and capacities of computer networks have consequences (or create opportunities) for the formation, structure and operation of social networks. It is in this latter capacity that the Internet and its constituent sub-nets can be seen as factors in the acceleration of competition and innovation. Self-reinforcing processes are set in motion in which competition leads to cooperation and further integrative social network formation. This, in turn, may stimulate innovation and competition at a higher level. Something like this has undoubtedly animated the phenomenal growth of the new media industry in Silicon Alley in the last half decade.

The negotiated work agreements of multimedia networks

In the strategic social and socio-technical networks among the multimedia firms of Silicon Alley, we find all the well-known types of relationships characteristic of production and service networks. They range from relatively open and informal cooperative arrangements among producers, service providers or suppliers to strategic alliances and joint ventures. They also include the more formal and long-term aspects of relational contracting and the bi-lateral agreements of quasi-firms. The mixed and often contradictory nature of some of these relationships in terms of formal informal, contractual non contractual, managerial competitive or cooperative competitive elements is indicated in such terms as managed competition, managed trade and negotiated market relations, mutual advantage and profit sharing, mutual transparency and joint target costing.

Relational business practices, however, have a tendency to marginalize or bypass formal contractual ties, seeking to get a maximum of cooperation, effort and response out of interactive episodes or partnerships with a minimum of formal commitments, institutional obligations or legal consequences. Yet interactive and relational practices in service settings in general, and in knowledge-intensive services in particular, have a much broader significance for social network formation involving co-producers, service providers, clients, consultants and related expert services. Insofar as the participants and members of such interactive network-based practices develop and share a common definition of the situation (the terms and conditions, expectations and rules, definitions and standards, rights and obligations which make these practices possible), they can be said to have a negotiated work agreement that tacitly governs their interactions and relations.

It is these more or less implicit work agreements that are the core of multimedia networks. In contrast to the analytical separation between process and product in manufacturing, the product of human services inheres in the process of providing the service itself. The quality of the customized performance is constituted in part by the nature and quality of a human relationship. This process typically involves a kind of co-production based on intensive symbolic interaction and negotiation between two or more people, for example between the service provider and the client.

Human professional services, from medicine and law to teaching and consulting have always been based on this model of more or less cooperative interpersonal negotiation in a somewhat ambiguous, indeterminate, non-routine situation. In such settings, it is understood that experts, due to their technical know-how (or one might say, 'professionals, due to their technical autonomy and their monopoly over skill and knowledge'), exercise a certain degree of influence over clients which hovers between persuasion, charisma and the substantive rationality of professional authority.

As the vast literature on the professions and professional practice shows, however, social expectations, negotiated agreements and implicit contracts can also be disrupted or negated by asymmetrical power relationships or, more precisely, by the conversion of knowledge into power. Misunderstandings and distortions based on unequal power relationships may already be present at the time so-called 'agreements' and 'contracts' are negotiated. They may develop later during the course of the 'consummation' of the negotiated relationship. It goes without saying that asymmetry and inequality of resources and power underlie most problems in the 'fulfillment' of contracts. This is an endemic modern condition that tends to surface also in other fairly institutionalized relationships such as employment and marriage contracts. Formal legal definitions and contractual arrangements were historically designed to stabilize such problems.

In the knowledge-intensive settings of contemporary high-tech production and service systems, the work of 'symbolic analysts' is frequently evaluated in terms of the specific interpersonal skills and performance they exhibit in the process of providing a service. As Powell puts it with respect to network forms of work, 'certain forms of exchange are more social that is, more dependent on relationship, mutual interest and reputation as well as less guided by a formal structure of authority'.

While trust plays an important part in such settings, the partly cooperative, partly competitive situation is often sufficiently ambiguous to warrant a more or less rational recourse to the terms and conditions of the work agreement. In other words, strategic social networks do not, and probably cannot, operate merely on 'blind trust' but are contingent and conditional on some reflexive evaluation of the 'performance' in and of the service relationship. This is likely to be even more true of socio-technical networks and virtual communities, in which the anonymous and liberating nature of the virtual reality produced may also generate a degree of social distance, if not estrangement. Let me illustrate these considerations with some examples of typical service network structures that one is likely to encounter both within and among firms in the multimedia industry.

Project networks in advertising and consulting

In a typical advertising or consulting agency, a given project is organized around both business and management functions. These are centred in a client consultant and his or her account as well as an associated technical and creative organizational unit consisting of a technical or art director, a copy writer and a creative director. Contact with the client is maintained by the consultant who brings the client's viewpoints and wishes into the agency and provides the project team with the appropriate conceptual and technical specifications.

Since teams are sometimes working on different projects and accounts at the same time, there is a good deal of ongoing restructuring and rotation in the division of labour. The agency may resemble a loosely-coupled network of activities or 'adhocracy' rather than a professional bureaucracy with its hierarchy of specialists. Occasionally, in-house teams are asked to compete against each other, especially when customized campaigns are developed to attract a new client.

An ad agency may either provide (make) or outsource (buy) needed support services such as print, film and video, interactive online computer screen design, EDP and direct dialogue marketing. There may be independent management consultants and trend researchers who specialize in certain markets or 'future trends' and who mediate between client firms and ad agencies. Short-term technical services may be provided by freelancers who often develop personal relationships with creative personnel in a multitude of different agencies and who constitute a crucial resource in local multimedia markets.

In many of these cases, the project teams must contact and activate these external service providers and develop social networking skills to use them effectively. Thus, the external relationship between agency and market is constantly pulled into the agency itself; economic principles of competition and the control of transaction costs may assume the function of internal organizational direction and control, especially when agencies are dependent on powerful clients.

The network form of organization also governs the constitution of more external 'core teams' or 'integrated communication networks' among firms. A powerful client, in consultation with an ad agency, may initiate and finance the development of an ad hoc project network pulling together various firms for the production of advertising campaigns involving music, film or other performance media, promotion, and public relations. Different networks may be put together for different purposes. Clearly, it is in the agency's interest to be able to have a number of such multimedia service suppliers available at short notice and to develop long-term relationships with them. However, shifts in market trends, clients, and the constant need to weigh make-or-buy decisions also generate a degree of rotation, turbulence and change. Project networks and core teams, therefore, do not necessarily exist for long periods of time or have a determinate structure and stability. Indeed, the term 'core team' has sometimes been viewed as too static and may give way to terms like 'integrated communication agencies' or 'integrated communication networks'.

In advertising, project networks within and between agencies and clients are usually connected by local area computer networks which parallel or supersede the traditional connections by telephone. An agency may have 'internal' computer networks ('Intranets') both for in-house staff located in its various branches and for its clients, although cross-access may be limited. Usually, of course, both staff and client networks are also connected to the Internet.

Other knowledge-intensive service networks

It should be clear that the kinds of service and project networks described above are not simply an added element of traditional organizational forms in knowledge-intensive and multimedia services. Service and project networks constitute the core structure of a new type of organization of work in which cooperation across institutional boundaries becomes a new force of production, creativity, and innovation. This understanding informs research on a variety of advanced producer and business services and their inter-firm networks. It is relevant to fields such as management consultancy, corporate auditing, and tax, legal, and marketing consultancy; computer and EDP services, software development, communication, and marketing services, as well as advertising in a number of different countries.

The work organization of services in these areas is characterized, according to Strambach, by an intensive process of cooperative interaction and exchange of information between service provider and client which derives from the client's need for explanation, clarification, interpretation and detailed instructions. Clients in this service sector demand a highly particularized and individualized 'product'. Their specification results, in part, from the cognitive nature of the tasks to be processed and the non-routine problems to be 'solved'. It also, in part, comes from the very availability and increased use of new information and communication technologies themselves. Such highly specialized products-as-processes can, in turn, often be provided only by a cooperative arrangement between service provider and one or several suppliers. The service process has to be adapted to the specific needs and circumstances of the corporate client. 'Only then can a qualitatively optimal problem solution be achieved from the perspective of the client. From the perspective of the service provider, on the other hand, a high degree of adaptation and flexibility is required'.

Strambach concludes that knowledge-intensive firms use network structures in order to respond effectively to complex and dynamic work situations and to adapt to rapidly changing external environments. By using combined network strategies (e.g. cooperation and externalization) flexibly, they establish a competitive advantage over those firms that do not use network structures.

These conclusions agree broadly (provided production and service networks are analytically distinguished from marketing networks) with those of other students of inter organizational networks such as Berkowitz, Faulkner and Anderson and Perrow. A particularly interesting formulation of a typology of social networks in marketing comes up with the concept of 'stakeholders' (other than consumers') networks not under the control of the firm'. The authors state that 'companies are adopting the concept of the hollow corporation which suggests that, through strategic alliances and outsourcing, the firm can obtain many of the functions it requires without having to perform all of them internally, and there is increased interest in...the management of a network of organizations'. Obviously, there are analytical parallels between the notions of the 'hollow corporation', the highly networked Type 1 service network, the 'borderless enterprise', the 'Virtual enterprise' and the 'lean supplier system', even though one could quibble over the analytical differences between 'system' and 'network'.

Thus, the process of learning, adaptation and managerial transformation with respect to networking appears to complement the population-ecological process of selection of those organizational forms that opt for network-based innovations. Moreover, in addition to their technical or socio-technical aspects, such networks have a social character that appears to have a particularly innovative potential which renders multimedia networks phenomena of more than technical interest. One aspect of this development is the strategic significance that Peter Drucker and others have ascribed to knowledge-intensive human capital, a type of capital vastly enhanced in the context of social and socio-technical networks.

Another aspect is the blurring of boundaries among firms and between them and their environments, a theme developed by neo-institutionalist organization theory but not yet fully articulated with the theory of social networks except for Powell's seminal contributions. Finally, there is the question of the spatial/global and longitudinal/historical dimensions of interorganizational network formation and development, especially when viewed in terms of the transitions from inter-firm competition to possible later stages of cooperative, exchange and oligopolistic or neo-corporatist networks and, ultimately, hierarchical or transnational integration. Much of this work in tandem with the object it describes finds itself in statu nascendi insofar as the intimate connection between economic globalization and the emergence of strategic alliances and networks is only now evolving. It is as yet barely studied or understood.

Competition between old and new media firms in Silicon Alley

The putative competitive advantage of multimedia firms in Silicon Alley is a particularly fascinating issue when it is viewed through the Schumpeterian lens of 'creative destruction'. There seems to be little doubt among the 'new media partisans not just the militantly non-conformist employees of the start-up companies themselves but their whole support network of venture capitalists, lawyers, landlords, consultants, accountants...that new media are destined to triumph over old media'. Hirschfeld adduces five basic reasons for this scenario.

1 Since Internet users spend forty to forty-five hours per month online, they tend to cut back on the most time-consuming old media activity: television viewing.

2 Television and other ad-supported old media will lose advertising dollars as their mass audiences are reduced by the new media's ability to offer advertisers 'narrowcasting', the capacity to reach carefully targeted audiences through socio-technical networks. Through a kind of 'informating' process, that is, the possibility of collecting background information on Internet users through user-search practices (e.g., while clicking on an advertisement on the web), firms can build up invaluable data sets on specific target groups.

3 New capabilities such as 3-D simulations or cheap, high-quality video-conferencing (already used for pornographic purposes) promise to be expanded for business- and family-oriented mass market applications.

4 Although the old media conglomerates own large sets of valuable content (e.g. the Hollywood film files originally brought to Time Warner Inc. by Warner Bros, and Ted Turner), these assets are not easily turned into a competitive advantage since re-tailoring or translation of old content for new media use appears to be dragging. Hirschfeld observes that Video games based on movies usually fail, and websites created by old magazines [cannot compete against new] start-ups'

New media, in turn, can create 'brave new worlds of content' and can 'customize content for individual users in a way that no old-media company can'. Hirschfeld continues:

Above all, the new media allow subscribers to create their own content, to build the sense of 'electronic community' that many customers want. In thousands of so-called 'chat rooms', the content consists of never-ending conversations about everything from car repair to knitting to politics, offering far more variety and personal contact than a conglomerate's polished product. These 'rooms' make money by charging chatters per minute or by displaying print ads. The king of such communal, subscriber-created content is America Online (AOL) which is like a digital bartender, bringing like-minded people together and collecting more money the longer they schmooze.

It is estimated that by the end of 1997, AOL had more subscribers in Manhattan than Manhattan Cable and more New York subscribers than the New York Times. Clearly, newspapers and other local media are beginning to see the writing on the wall.

5 The old media conglomerates, finally, may find it difficult to change their corporate cultures and transform their corporate structures. They have large operating units and multi-level hierarchies that obstruct the flow of information, resist the processes of constant reorganization and restructuring so typical of the new networked corporate entities, and are ill-adapted to start new programmes and projects on short notice.

Hirschfeld points out, however, that the sheer money and power invested in the old media conglomerates may prove to be a formidable source of resistance for some time to come. Old-media revenues have still been growing even as some giants like Time Warner, which is participating simultaneously in both old and new media markets, operate in the red (due largely to a huge debt service). The traditional entertainment industry is 'an export powerhouse, second only to aerospace'. Advertising itself is a potent factor in the relatively low cost of using television and radio as compared to start-up costs of the (ever-changing) computers and the new media subscription fees, and established big media firms may still have the advantage of name recognition, large mass audiences and huge advertising budgets.

Some difficulties may also face the new media in terms of the undue cost and amount of time spent individually on the Internet as well as some degree of cultural resistance to becoming a 'netizen' in a virtual community, factors that appear to be even stronger in Europe than America. Old media corporations may, however, seek to conquer the new rivals by integration, as has already been suggested by the extent to which large corporations like the New York Times, Sony, Time Warner and the big national TV networks have managed to put their foot in the door and begun to operate simultaneously in old and new media markets.

Nevertheless, the 'war between old media and new will be fought in every segment of the industry', according to Hirschfeld, and estimates as to the likely outcome require a differentiated analysis. All print media are most vulnerable to competition from the new media because computerized texts offer new possibilities as compared to paper. Searchability by subject, author, date or specific publication, and capabilities like alphabetization, archiving, filtering and electronic cutting and pasting are powerful alternatives to traditional modes of using print media. Newspaper advertising and, hence, newspaper circulation stand to lose the most in comparison to the ad-listings-cum-pictures and other information offered by the World Wide Web.

Magazines, however, may be better prepared for the threat from the interactive periodicals called 'zines' because they have their own websites and can meet the competition on its own turf, for the time being. For example, Time Warner's Pathfinder 'allows visitors to chat on topics related to Time Inc.'s various magazines, to communicate directly with reporters and photographers on key stories, and even to play games related to the subject matter'. Here the new versus old media competition takes place within the belly of the beast itself.

In the case of the book market, the verdict is mixed. The book industry, currently growing at 5 per cent annually, also partakes of both old and new media advantages. Books are still easier to read the old-fashioned way as compared to consuming them on the computer, but they can be marketed and bought more easily via the new media, for example through the one million title 'Virtual inventory' of Amazon.com in Seattle. As a result, large publishers and distributors profit more from the Internet than do ordinary bookstores.

In contrast to newspapers, magazines and books, business information services are among the most profitable segments of the new media industry and generate $31 billion in annual revenues for companies in the New York metropolitan area. 'Business information naturally lends itself to on-line delivery' which, due to lower costs, benefits the owners of content such as McGraw Hill, Dun and Bradstreet, Dow Jones and Thompson Business Services.

As to the film, music, TV and radio industries, Hirschfeld believes that they 'will feel the new media's effects later than the print industries, but they will feel them even more profoundly, for reasons that Thomas Edison would find very familiar'. Clearly, the new technologies need a while to be perfected and to catch on but, once they do, technological 'breakthroughs such as high-speed connections over cable TV lines, TV sets with built-in web software, and "hybrid" CD-ROM's that combine copious data with online updates' will sweep the field, mainly because of lower costs. This is particularly significant in the area of film, where 'Hollywood studios (most owned by New York-based conglomerates) now routinely use supercomputers to generate special effects' , making previous techniques and practices of the film industry obsolete. In the recorded-music industry, the new media effects derive from distribution and marketing, not production. Since 'music is already in digital form thanks to compact disk technology, customers will soon be able to download entire albums directly onto their hard drives over the Internet (something they will eventually be able to do with movies too)'.

Broadcast television and cable TV will be affected by the new media, but in opposite ways. Hirschfeld reports that 'in 1995, Americans spent slightly more buying PCs than TVs, and TV usage fell 40 per cent on average after the purchase of a household's first PC', a fact likely to hit the country's four major New York-based TV networks. Cable TV networks, on the other hand, will benefit from the broadband data lines into homes, ultimately capable of delivering data a thousand times faster than a fast telephone modem. 'Speed matters', argues Hirschfeld, 'not only because consumers get responses more quickly but also because multimedia content containing too much information to download effectively over phone lines will soon be available'.

Radio is the only old medium likely to continue to serve the same audiences that have always been listening: the millions who drive to work and those in low-income and minority groups who, as Moss and Ludwig point out, have little or no access to other media, especially in expensive new forms.

In sum, the competition between old and new media may enhance rather than destroy the field, partly because it may occur more and more within rather than between media conglomerates such as Time Warner Inc. As Hirschfeld's informative analysis suggests, the Internet provides for cheaper and more effective marketing and distribution at the expense of newspapers and broadcast television. At the same time, however, the Internet will increase the value of ideas and thus enhance the cultural significance and economic scope of the multimedia industry as a whole.

Interim conclusion on multimedia networks

The multimedia networks of Silicon Alley are, to some extent, spin-offs from the producer-services sector and the information technologies that have developed since the 1970s and contributed to spectacular global expansion since 1992. Multimedia networks are, of course, not the only factor in the process of economic and financial globalization, but they are a significant and indicative part of it and have grown at the same dramatic pace in the last few years. Yet this is not all. Multimedia networks in global nodes such as New York City are themselves centres of self-activity, organizational learning and high-density interaction with other units. It would, therefore, be too simple to describe them as merely a link in a one-dimensional, mono-causal, or unidirectional chain of 'value creation' in which they are seen to influence the creation, diffusion and adoption of technical and social innovations, or to determine regional economic development.

Multimedia networks are, rather, part of a process of mutual causation. In other words, they are self-organizing core structures in a series of relationships of partly competitive, partly cooperative interactivity with other production and service networks. As members of networks in a transitional phase between competition and integration, actors in multimedia networks may indeed perceive greater benefit from temporary cooperation rather than single-minded competition and conflict. This is reflected in slogans like 'everybody benefits', 'rising water lifts all boats', 'increasing the size of the pie as a collective strategy is more important than competition for the pieces'. In a period of global block formation, such arguments are particularly persuasive. Given the central location of Silicon Alley in one of the world's major cities, the various multiplier effects and synergies of such a combination of cultural and economic density tend to translate into the kind of positive feedback loop I mentioned before.

The multimedia industry, by its very nature, tends to contribute to a new culture industry which is in the business of providing new images, interpretations and meanings of what is happening globally at the same time that it offers redefinitions of changing cultural traditions and practices at the national, regional and local level. Thus, the new multimedia-based culture industry benefits from the very social and economic reality it helps to describe and define in the virtual reality of cyberspace.

Discussion and conclusion

The short historical trajectory of New York's Silicon Alley shows the tremendous potential for sustained economic development of production and service networks in general, and of multimedia networks in particular. The new production and service networks, whether in Europe, Japan or the United States, exemplify the dual role of being part of economic globalization and at the same time constituting the backbone of reactive regional development strategies in the face of global competition. In this dual role, they are supported and their effects augmented by the new media industry.

The special nature of interactive virtual communication makes multimedia networks into something more than a sub-category of service networks. Because of their technical capabilities and socio-technical convertibility as well as their strategic significance in the new culture industry, multimedia networks provide an additional level of communicative capacity and cultural sophistication. They are networks of networks. As such, their effect seems to reach beyond the conventional advantages of agglomeration because they are in the business of self-enhancement and creative self-representation. Moreover, they may harbour the key not only to self-transformation, but to local/institutional and regional/socio-economic transformation. Network formation normally benefits from cultural homogeneity and other categorical similarities among actors as well as homophily in their choices.

Multimedia networks, however, appear to thrive on diversity and difference, thus encouraging collective learning and experimentation as well as creativity and innovation under conditions of freedom of speech and self-expression. If their accessibility were not so frequently limited by virtue of unequal resources, education and other restrictions of cultural capital, they could become the medium of a liberal-democratic culture par excellence.

The case of Silicon Alley, however, is difficult to separate from other aspects of the unique context in which it is embedded. New York's conditions of organizational density are hard to duplicate in regional clusters that find themselves in the incipient stages of economic development. The experience of Silicon Alley points to the kinds of potential synergies that emanate from a diversified economic and cultural context. Even a limited constellation, such as a mid-sized urban environment with two or three institutions of higher education, research and development, and creative-technical training (art, computers, design, film, music), one or two major employers sponsoring a series of production, supplier, and service networks, and a few networks of multimedia firms self-sufficient enough to constitute a relatively autonomous, but attractive basis for further development, would be a viable baseline for any regional cluster. Examples from the American heartland are the 'Research Triangle' of North Carolina or the urban-regional high-tech clusters around Ann Arbor, Atlanta, Austin, Baltimore, Bloomington, Boston, Houston, Ithaca, Madison, New Haven, Princeton, San Francisco, Seattle and Washington. None of these cities are particularly large or even comparable to New York, but they all have either a major research university, or a state government or major employer large enough to anchor some other knowledge-intensive service network or multimedia venture. The crucial factor seems to be the avoidance of a highly specialized or homogeneous, single-industry base which might be internally networked, but not sufficiently diversified.

All of these cases also benefit from the active participation and encouragement of local, state, and sometimes interstate or regional economic development agencies and policies. For the State of New

York, these roles are performed by the Office of Economic Development in the State Office of Management and Budget, Albany, N.Y.; the New York City Mayor's Office of Economic Development which is highly pro-active in attracting out-of-state and foreign venture capital and arranging for tax credits and tax abatements; and the Port Authority traditionally active in planning tri-state infrastructure and advanced economic development.

In addition, a multicultural and multi-ethnic urban environment always seems to have an edge over culturally and ethnically homogeneous settings if only because the latter tend to be boring, offer a limited quality of life in terms of choices of entertainment and life-styles, and are often artistically, culturally and intellectually impoverished. Multicultural university towns, by contrast, have often proved sufficiently attractive for young urban professionals to provide the right kind of dynamic, liberal, youthful, future-oriented milieu.

If this sounds like an advertisement from a local chamber of commerce or from a regional economic development corporation, it is perhaps not so far from the mark because these characteristics also figure in the 'quality-of-life' ratings of cities, their demographic composition and their economic growth rate. All told, the new multi-layered types of social and socio-technical networks discussed here seem to fit well with this larger socio-cultural diversity. Multimedia networks tend to spring up and develop in a relation of mutual causation and transformation with the rich, image-laden and meaning-producing texture of cities, and thus also help to create and reflect the current dynamics of global change.

4

Multimedia: Profiling And Regional Restructuring

Introduction

Since the achievement of full employment in the early 1960s, the number of employees in the city and environs of Munich has continuously risen to approximately 1.3 million. The increase has primarily been in the Munich periphery during the past twenty years, although more than two-thirds of the jobs, approximately 850,000, are still situated in the core of the city itself.

The sectoral structure has changed with this general growth in employment. The manufacturing and service sectors once employed almost equal numbers, but the proportion of persons employed in the manufacturing sector has decreased to a quarter while the service sector now accounts for three out of four employees. This remarkable increase is Munich-specific to the extent that it is not only production-oriented but primarily technology-oriented. It has resulted in a remarkable rise in the level of qualified labour in the region ('academization'). There has also been a considerable externalization of technical activities: an indication of flexibilization strategies and a corresponding cooperation intensity.

This structural change towards 'post-fordistic' industrial structures has been supported by numerous public and private training and research institutions, by the communication and transport infrastructure, and by highly developed 'soft location factors'. In comparison to other agglomeration areas in Germany, the Munich location has the additional advantage of offering an attractive leisure-time and recreational area in its immediate and outer environs, as well as in the proximity of the Alps.

The Munich area in comparison to other locations of the media and communication industry

Apart from these production/service complexes, an important media industry has developed in Munich. Alongside Cologne, Hamburg, Düsseldorf and Berlin, the Munich area is considered one of the most important media centres in Germany. Each of these four conurbations has a stronger specialization than Munich in specific sectors of the media industry (e.g. the newspaper sector in Berlin, the magazine sector in Hamburg, the radio and TV sector in Cologne, and the advertising sector in Düsseldorf). The Munich area, in contrast, has achieved prominence across a wide range of media and communication sectors. Among the four agglomerations, Munich boasts the broadest media range and the greatest functional diversity.

In comparison to Berlin, Hamburg and Cologne, Munich has an extremely strong competitive position as a telecommunication and media location. The location advantages of the Munich area are especially evident in the telecommunication and information technologies, software production, electronic media hardware and television. 'Munich is represented in the various sub-sectors of the telematics and media sectors in a balanced manner, which in a great number of sub-segments has resulted in a leading role and in an adequate presence in virtually all of them'.

Media industry in the Munich area and the trend towards 'multimedia'

Among the important media locations in the Federal Republic, Munich is certainly the 'Number one'. This was already ascertained in the first study 'Media City Munich' dated 1983 and confirmed in the two subsequent studies conducted in 1988 and 1995. Approximately every tenth employee in the Munich area is currently employed in the media sector. The study entitled 'MedienStadt

München III' (Media City Munich III) was jointly commissioned by the City of Munich and the Chamber of Industry and Commerce (IHK) for Munich and Upper Bavaria and published in 1996. It shows that in the City of Munich and its environs there were 101,000 persons in full and freelance employment in 6,700 enterprises in the printing, film/radio/TV and advertising sectors. Their turnover amounts to 25.1 billion DM. Since the first study in 1983 the figures have doubled, not only as regards employment but also as regards the number of enterprises and turnover.

Between 1988 and 1995, a total of 28,440 new jobs were created in the media industry. In 1995, 72,060 persons were employed in this sector as full-time staff and 28,700 as freelances. Compared to 1988 and 1983, the share of freelances among all employees has continually grown to approximately 30 per cent at present.

Since 1988 the number of enterprises has increased by 60 per cent; between 1993 and 1995 1,200 new media enterprises were established. Since 1988 the turnover of the industry has risen to 25.1 billion DM, an increase of 8 billion or a 47 per cent increase. This does not take into account the turnover generated by non-Bavarian and foreign subsidiaries.

In the same period, capital expenditure has risen from 893 million to 4.2 billion DM, representing an almost five-fold increase. About half of the approximately 6,700 media enterprises in the Munich area are active in the advertising industry (3,078), a further 2,074 are associated in some way or other with the printing media. Approximately 1,500 (every fourth enterprise) are associated with film/TV/radio etc. The printing sector is the largest industry in the media sector, not only in terms of the number of employees (38,000 or 53 per cent) but also as regards turnover (11.3 billion DM or 45 per cent). It is primarily the publishing sector that contributes to growth (more than 8,000 employees), while the printing sector itself, above all the pre-print stage, is declining. Approximately one-fifth of employees (13,800) work in the advertising sector and the industry's turnover is in proportion to this (4.9 billion). In contrast to the previous years analysed, printing and the film/radio/TV sectors managed to increase their percentage for 1995 while the advertising industry had to face a loss of approximately 5 per cent.

The media industry is characterized by small and medium-sized companies interspersed with some large-scale enterprises. Only about thirty enterprises can be referred to as large media-industry enterprises although even these, in comparison to other industrial enterprises, are of a rather modest size. About 90 per cent of the Munich-based media enterprises generate a turnover of under 10 million DM, half have a turnover of under 1 million DM, and a third produce an annual turnover of 250,000 DM or less.

More than half of the media enterprises consist of independent contractors and are therefore not listed in the commercial register. These include two-thirds of all enterprises in the advertising industry, but only a third of those in the printing sector. Approximately half of the radio/film/TV/video sector is made up of small enterprises.

Due to the digitization of the information, communication and transmission technologies, the various media sectors have started a process of integration and mergers. Innovative multimedia products and services are emerging at the interface between the traditional media sectors of audio media (sound), visual media (picture, movies) and printing media (text). The producers needed only a few years to create a multimedia industry (in the narrow sense). Although there is neither a generally valid classification and distinction of the economic multimedia segment nor a clear definition of its contents, it is largely agreed that the terms integration, interaction and networking may be used to describe three multimedia directions or qualities.

Integration is promoted by digitization from a technological point of view and by the liberalization of the media and telecommunication markets from the point of view of economic policy. It is an ongoing process which involves an increasing number of sectors of the economy. The media industry is currently merging with the information and telecommunication industries, which has led to the coinage of the term 'TIME industry' (telecommunication, information technologies, media industry and entertainment). In view of this tendency the approximately 14,000 employees in the enterprises and companies of the computer and telecommunication technologies must be included, so that in 1995 approximately 115,000 persons were employed in the TIME sector. The total number of employees in the city and environs of Munich is 940,000.

Figures based on the number of employees paying social insurance (taking into consideration the statistical error margin) show a steady development, with a slight regression in some manufacturing technologies but an overall increase.

Historical preconditions

The media and communication industry in Munich has various technological, economic and political origins. These include the precision mechanical/optical and the printing industries. Inventions and developments made in Munich in the late eighteenth and early nineteenth centuries promoted the establishment of enterprises concerned with the manufacturing of cameras, lenses and photographic material. Munich's political role as state capital and the central function of the city for its environs and indeed all of Bavaria have always enhanced the theatre and other cultural institutions such as museums as well as a broad range of training facilities. Before the Second World War, the electrical engineering industry was already represented by numerous enterprises in Munich. It received a decisive impetus immediately after the end of the war with the move of the headquarters of Siemens AG from Berlin to Munich and the resulting expansion of the Munich plant. The enterprise currently employs approximately 35,000 people in the Munich area. The growth of the defence industry in the Munich area in the 1960s and 1970s also attracted a large number of foreign companies, in particular American electronics enterprises (Texas Instruments, Digital Equipment, Motorola and others), who have established subsidiaries (responsible for marketing, customer service and training) and some production facilities in the Munich area. A broad range of software companies has settled and developed around them (including Microsoft Deutschland in Unterschleißheim and CompuServe in Unterhaching, an Internet provider that has recently been taken over by AOL). The fact that Munich is one of the most important training and research locations in Germany is a decisive condition of development and an important location factor. More than 100,000 students are enrolled at ten universities and colleges. Particularly close links have been established between Technische Universität München and industrial enterprises. Munich also holds a predominant position as regards extra-university research. Those groups whose headquarters are situated in Munich have concentrated their research and development facilities there. This concentrated research and development competence provides an employment and labour market climate for high-tech development in Munich which thus directly or indirectly benefits from the communication and media sectors. This enhances flexibility, especially among more highly-qualified personnel and increases their opportunities for transferring to other enterprises. This, in turn, contributes to the diffusion of knowledge and experience.

Location requirements and location factors of the communication industry

The attractiveness of Munich for the media and communication industries is based on a number of special, primarily 'soft' location factors, which are either general location advantages' or the concentrated presence of elements which are important to the industry. These include:

- Proximity to a great variety of media providers and users.
- A comprehensive range of qualified staff and a creative labour pool ('good people').
- A broad range of training facilities and sites for media and communication professions.
- A well-established media and communication infrastructure.
- An urban ambience (regarded as a fertile ground for creativity and diversity).
- The image as an area boasting concentrated media and communication competence, thus attracting other professionals.
- Support by state and local governments for the media and communication industry.
- An attractive residential and leisure environment; the Munich conurbation is the 'sunbelt' of the Federal Republic.

A survey showed that 85 to 90 per cent of the media enterprises were satisfied or extremely satisfied with the location. The agglomeration Munich per se with its (media) diversity is emphasized as being the most important location factor. 'The prime aspect is Urbanity with a capital U'. The fact that other media producers and providers are also located in situ is regarded by enterprises as the main asset. It enhances close customer relations and offers numerous opportunities for contact with customers and sub-contractors. The pool of qualified labour, an efficient transportation network, the size of the local community and the unbureaucratic attitude of the local authorities are also of great importance to them. Location disadvantages are also mentioned (expensive location, high rents both for residential and business premises considerable competition, high taxes) but none of these aspects outweighs the advantages of the location.

In a current study by the IMU Institute and the Catholic University of Eichstätt, experts constantly refer to the positive aspect of agglomeration size, geographic proximity, media diversity and urban environment. These factors all contribute to a creative environment for which the sectoral media diversity in the Munich location prepares the ground. A thriving urban culture is the expression, prerequisite for and result of this creative process. Proximity offers interaction advantages, facilitates many immediate face-to-face contacts and thus enhances and secures the availability of information.

Media producers require an urban environment which enables their largely freelance employees freely to organize the working-time during which the task at hand is to be fulfilled. Many of them are not unwilling to work at night in order to be able to spend their days elsewhere. The separation of day and night work becomes blurred, and the same applies to the separation between work and non-work. This mode of working and living is possible in a city region offering creativity and stimulating diversity but not in residential and commercial deserts situated on the fringe of the agglomeration.

Core areas of the media industry and multimedia activities

The media and communication sector in the Munich area consists primarily of small and medium-sized companies. It is grouped around a very few production service cores that represent a considerable percentage of the media employees and is, moreover, important for the orientation of the media and communication policies in Munich. It will be useful to detail the most important protagonists of the communication and media industry.

Newspaper publishers

Five daily newspapers with a total circulation of 1.2 million copies are published in Munich. The national Süddeutsche Zeitung is published by Süddeutscher Verlag, owned by five publisher families. One of them, the Friedmann family, also publishes the tabloid Abendzeitung. Münchner Pressehaus is the second largest newspaper publisher. It publishes the Münchner Merkur, which is primarily distributed in southern Bavaria, and the tabloid tz. The south German editorial office of BILD-Zeitung is also situated in Munich.

There are various interrelations between the publishing companies, particularly in the form of printing cooperation but also through interlocking capital arrangements. For the print publishing companies, expansion towards the new media is an attempt to open up further exploitation channels in addition to the traditional media such as newspapers, magazines or books. As is the case with other newspapers and magazines, the articles of the Süddeutsche Zeitung are also available online. The Süddeutsche Verlag issues a TV magazine SZett (which is fed into the programme of the privately-owned TV broadcasting company VOX situated in Cologne). It also holds a share (26.4 per cent) in the Munich radio station Radio Gong 2000 and in the regional programme slots of RTL and SAT.1. Münchner Pressehaus has acquired the local radio station Charivari and the local TV station M1.

Magazine publishers

Judged by the number of editorial offices, titles and publishing companies, Munich ranks second after Hamburg in the magazine publishing sector. In 1983 the Burda Verlag moved the editorial head office of the Bunte magazine from Offenburg in Baden-Württemberg to Munich. The editorial offices of other magazines already located in Munich but spread throughout the city area were merged with the Bunte editorial office at the same time. Other editorial offices were moved from Stuttgart to Munich. The news magazine

Focus, published by Burda Verlag, has been the most successful new venture in the German weekly magazine market in the last few years.

According to media analysis '96, the Burda group ranks third among the ten major German publishing ventures. Approximately 800 out of a total of 5,000 full-time employees are on the Burda payroll in Munich compared to a mere 380 employees in 1983. The Burda group has concentrated a substantial share of its radio, TV and multimedia activities in its subsidiaries Burda New Media and Burda Broadcast Media, both housed in Munich. The Burda Verlag for example also produces the TV magazine focus TV (in the 'virtual' studio of Bavaria Film GmbH in Geiselgasteig) which is broadcast by the privately-owned TV station Pro Sieben.

Important magazines are produced in the Munich location for the Hamburg publishing companies Grunerand Jahr, a Bertelsmann subsidiary, as well as for the Heinrich-Bauer Verlag. Some of these magazines have also acquired offshoots in the electronic media sector. Besides general public magazines, numerous specialized publishing companies are located in the Munich area. Their publications focus on telecommunication issues and high-tech products. Most of the computer and PC magazines available in Germany are produced and published in Munich.

Book publishers

Munich is second only to New York in global book publishing. 12,000 new titles are issued annually by 319 book publishers. A quarter of all the books produced in Germany are published in Munich. Although not all of the books published in Munich are also printed there, its position is strengthened by the printing industry located in Munich. The same applies to the wide range of agencies and other service providers in sectors ranging from photography and graphic arts to distribution. Publishers view 'new media' or 'multimedia' as an opportunity for opening up additional channels of exploiting traditional contents by means of technologically novel information media. The question for publishing companies is to what extent they themselves can make use of and control the new technologies and the associated new distribution channels, or whether these have to be opened up by third parties.

With its book and music production, the Bertelsmann group, situated in Gütersloh, constitutes an essential node in the media industry complex of the Munich area. Bertelsmann is one of the biggest media groups in the world with a turnover totalling more than 22 billion DM in the business year of 1995-96. In Munich, Bertelsmann Buch AG, together with its publishing subsidiaries, has approximately 1,500 employees. Bertelsmann AG achieves the bulk of its turnover with music, entertainment and multimedia. Its product line is integrated in the BMG Entertainment AG, which also has its headquarters in Munich.

BMG Entertainment International holds a 14 per cent share in the global music market and continuously expands into non-music oriented entertainment sectors, such as video and interactive entertainment. The subsidiaries of BMG Entertainment in the Munich area include BMG Ariola Media, Ufa Musikverlage, Ufa Video and BMG Entertainment TV. It has interests in the radio firms RTL2 (8.5 per cent) and Antenne Bayern (16 per cent) and in the Arbor TV film production in Tutzing (74 per cent).

Further important publishing companies in the Munich area include R. Oldenbourg Verlag (with publishing company, graphic industries and data systems divisions) with approximately 1,700 employees; Bruckmann Verlag, with F. Bruckmann Medien GmbH as a media subsidiary; Langenscheidt-Verlag, which currently also distributes a major part of its language tuition programmes on CD-ROM; and publishing companies like Markt und Technik, Magna Media and Franzis', who have focused on electronics, computers and PCs.

Film/radio/television

Munich is the leading centre for film and TV production in Germany. 34 per cent of this industry's turnover in Germany is generated in Bavaria, primarily in the Munich area. Two-thirds of all feature film producers in Germany are located there. The film/radio/TV sector boasts the highest growth rates in personnel among all sub-sectors of the media and communication industry. The granting of licences to privately-owned radio and TV programmes by the authorities has opened up a new sphere for capital investment. This comes primarily from the printing and publishing sectors as well as the licensing of media products and recently also from the trading sector. In addition to the established public stations Bayerischer Rundfunk and Landesstudio Bayern of ZDF and the privately-owned Bavaria Film GmbH, an important electronic media constellation developed in Munich during the 1980s when the Radio and TV sector was liberalized. The availability of a large number of radio and TV channels has opened up new, additional presentation and advertising opportunities. Yet there is also a need for additional programmes and adequately qualified staff.

The activities of the Kirch group (film licence trading, film production, film dubbing) have given rise to the TV station Pro Sieben with its subsidiary Kabel 1 and the sales station H.O.T., a joint venture with Quelle Versand. DF-1, the first German TV channel based on digital transmission technology, and Deutsches Sportfernsehen (DSF) are located in the immediate vicinity of the studios of Bayerischer Rundfunk and ZDF in the northern outskirts of Munich. The two TV stations RTL2 and tm3, the latter generally regarded as catering primarily for women, have also started operation. The local TV station tv-münchen, originating from TV weiß-blau, has opened up a transmission centre east of Munich.

Bayerischer Rundfunk (BR), a public radio and TV station, is integrated into ARD (Arbeitsgemeinschaft der Rundfunkanstalten Deutschlands). In addition to its share in the Erstes Deutsches Fernsehen programme and the 'Third Programme' (Bayerisches Fernsehen), it broadcasts five radio programmes. With regard to a regional multimedia cluster, one has to mention the cooperation with Süddeutsche Zeitung as regards text archives, the merging of the BR studio capacities with the ZDF subsidiary FSM (Fernsehstudio München) and Bavaria Film and a corporate participation in Bavaria Film decided on in summer 1997.

With the acquisition of the transmission rights for films like La Strada and Casablanca in the 1950s, Leo Kirch laid the foundation for one of the largest film and media licensing enterprises in the world. In the 1970s and 1980s Kirch founded numerous subsidiaries and acquired majority shares in film and TV productions as well as dubbing enterprises, film distribution companies, cinemas, licensing agencies and other enterprises. The Kirch group employs 1,400 people, of whom approximately 800 work in the Munich area.

In the late 1980s and early 1990s the Kirch group also expanded into the TV business. Kirch currently holds 43 per cent of the privately owned TV station SAT. 1, 66.5 per cent of Deutsches Sportfernsehen (DSF), 25 per cent of Hamburg pay-TV station Premiere and 100 per cent of the digital TV station DF-1. His son, Thomas Kirch, increased his share in Pro Sieben Media AG to 60 per cent when it went public in July 1997. Moreover, he owns 40 per cent of the local TV station tv-münchen and one-third of the teleshopping station H.O.T. (Home Order Television).

Kirch's television flagship is the TV station Pro Sieben, located in Unterföhring. It was founded in 1988 after the purchase of the Munich news station Eureka TV and started transmission in early 1989. In 1992 Pro Sieben acquired the station Kabel 1 as a subsidiary. Pro Sieben is the only TV provider of the Kirch group that operates in the black; with a turnover of 1.67 billion DM in 1996 the station earned a profit of approximately 170 million DM. In July 1997 the station went public as Pro Sieben Media AG. Thomas Kirch acquired further shares so that the direct Kirch stake in the station now amounts to 60 per cent. The new name is indicative of an entrepreneurial development that commenced in 1993 and expanded the activities and business segments of the station to include almost the entire multimedia sector.

In the radio sector a comparable supplier expansion has taken place in the last ten to twelve years. Parallel to the expansion of the public Bayerische Rundfunk from three to five programme segments, a privately-owned broadcasting network has been established with Antenne Bayern as a second regional broadcasting station located in Unterföhring, as well as a number of local broadcasting stations including Radio Gong 2000, Radio Arabella, Radio Energy, Radio Charivari, Radio Two Day and scene radio stations like Radio Feierwerk and Radio LoRa among others.

The Bavaria Film premises have existed since 1919 in Geiselgasteig, the Grünwald suburb on the southern outskirts of Munich. These premises are among the largest film production sites in Europe. Refounded in 1959 as Bavaria Atelier Gesellschaft, the Bavaria Film area serves as a production and service institution for German and foreign film and TV productions. Bavaria Film GmbH boasts the whole range of state-of-the-art film and video recording facilities, as well as film laboratories, dubbing studios, distribution departments, and other facilities. The Bavaria studio has approximately 2,000 employees and in 1996 achieved an annual turnover of 277 million DM.

Westdeutscher Rundfunk (with Westdeutsches Werbefernsehen) and Südwestdeutscher Rundfunk Stuttgart are the majority shareholders of Bavaria Film GmbH. The remaining shareholders include banks and insurance companies. This association of Bayerischer Rundfunk and Bavaria Film is supposed to give a boost to the media location Bavaria. In spring 1997, Bavaria and ZDF combined their studio capacities to form the Bavaria-Film und Fernsehstudio GmbH, the largest studio association in Germany. As well as ZDF and Bavaria, the Bayerische Landesanstalt für Aufbaufinanzierung also has a share in this. Hitherto the ZDF studios had been subsidiaries of the FSM Fernsehstudios in Unterföhring. The new company has 14 studios and 200 employees. Its services are expected initially to generate a turnover of 30 million DM.

The advertising industry

The advertising industry is represented to a lesser extent in the Munich area than in other locations. Among the fifty advertising agencies with the largest turnover in Germany in 1996, fifteen were located in Frankfurt, eleven in Hamburg, ten in Düsseldorf and only six in Munich. The biggest Munich advertising agency, Heye and Partner GWA, with a turnover of approximately 48 million DM, ranks 16th, up three ranks compared to the previous year. It has approximately 200 employees. The business segments of the advertising industry are changing with the new media and communication technologies. The trend points towards marketing consultation and access to the electronic advertising market. Here a segment is developing in which advertising agencies will increasingly compete against multimedia producers and suppliers in the foreseeable future.

Multimedia

The multimedia sector in its narrow sense can be defined as including production companies and service providers for offline and online applications (such as CD-ROM games, computer-based training (CBT), archiving systems, Internet and Intranet, etc.). It is currently made up of at least 150 enterprises with about 5,000 employees (full-time and freelance staff) in the Munich area.

The Munich area has become the leading centre for multimedia taking the number of multimedia development and production companies and their staff as indicators. The wave of newly-established companies in this sector peaked between 1992 and 1996. About ninety of today's multimedia enterprises were founded during this period. Most of them were originally established as multimedia agencies; others came into existence as a result of the re-orientation of existing producers and service providers or of expansion strategies aimed at including multimedia applications. The third part of the multimedia sector foundation was laid by spin-offs of subsidiaries or hiving-off parts of large media and telecommunication groups, such as Siemens and Burda publishers.

Siemens-Nixdorf Informationssysteme AG (SNI) is a fully owned subsidiary of Siemens AG located in Munich. It was established by Nixdorf AG in Paderborn (subsequently taken over by Siemens) and the information and communication sectors of Siemens AG. Approximately 7,400 people work at the SNI headquarters in Munich. In autumn 1996, SNI opened the new business area of 'Advanced Services & Media' (ASM), in which the enterprise interest in the multimedia market segment was combined with the areas of computer-based training, Internet and Intranet, teleworking and telecooperation. It includes consultancy, design and operation of the corresponding multimedia services and is targeted mainly at multimedia concerns of medium-sized and large-scale industries. In 1996, SNI founded the Computertraining und Services GmbH Munich as well as the Waste and Recycling Information Services GmbH (WARIS) in Grasbrunn near Munich. This is the first global waste and recycling exchange that by using the Worldwide Waste Management Information System (WWI) in the Internet offers both information and a business platform for an optimization and recycling of resources to suppliers, inquirers and service providers of the waste disposal industry as well as the authorities concerned.

.Many multimedia companies see themselves as advertising agencies using specific media technology platforms (CD-ROM, Internet, Intranet). Another part of the enterprises is just like book publishers concerned with the production and distribution of information (modern history, edutainment, language courses, games); a further aspect is drawing up concepts for the communication between enterprises ('business to business').

The majority of the enterprises active in the multimedia sector are small and very small enterprises. Two-thirds of all enterprises employ up to twenty persons (full-time employees and freelances). One-quarter of all enterprises have twenty to fifty employees. This means that over 90 per cent of all multimedia enterprises employ fewer than fifty people. Only 3 per cent (four entries) have between fifty and 100 employees, while only 5 per cent (six entries) have between 100 and 300 employees. The German branch office of the Internet and software company Oracle in Munich distorts this picture: they have approximately 1,300 employees, more than a quarter of all those employed in the multimedia sector in the Munich area. The other large-scale enterprises also include companies with a range of interests in addition to multimedia. They are included among the multimedia sector only because they provide services for the multimedia sector by offering facilities for training or further education.

Although the market currently continues to expand, especially where online multimedia applications are concerned, the multimedia sector as a whole seems to have entered a phase of consolidation, particularly among major enterprises. The number of new business starts has decreased. The same decline is seen in the growth of employment and turnover, which in some cases has been enormous in the last few years. Enterprise structures have sometimes not been able to catch up with the fast-moving development of the industry and need to be adapted. Some multimedia agencies are trying to promote growth and the use of their existing resources by restructuring their enterprises, part of which developed in a rather unsystematic manner during the boom in the early years. They are also trying to stabilize their customer relations. However, even these in-house consolidation efforts are not sufficient for some of the major multimedia agencies. Enterprises try to meet increased financing requirements (a rising share of fixed costs) by gaining support from well-funded external shareholders, by company take-over bids or by going public. At the same time, agreements on the medium and long-term management of key accounts make the enterprises more aware of the need for security.

The initial upswing and the specific profile of the multimedia sector is closely related to the existing manufacturing and service structures prevailing in the high-tech Munich location. During their start-up phase, almost all multimedia agencies worked for one or several large Munich enterprises, drawing up offline or online company and product presentations or training projects for them. Working for enterprises in the automotive and electrical engineering industries, publishing houses and banks, and for the television and film industry in the Munich area has led to an orientation towards specific technologies and programming in the multimedia industry. Coping with these tasks often provided the multimedia agencies with so much thrust that they have been able to go beyond southern Bavaria and do business on a national or even international scale. Nevertheless, most Munich-based multimedia agencies continue to focus on the south of Bavaria.

Although multimedia enterprises in general have to regard most of the other multimedia agencies as competitors, these enterprises maintain an open relationship which is due, among other things, to the continuing expansion of the multimedia market. In principle, every enterprise is able to cooperate with any other enterprise and in fact will do so if a project requires a competent partner for tackling specific tasks. Competence is the decisive factor in cooperation even if the search for potential partners is often limited to a circle of enterprises whom the company already has found to be completely satisfactory. A large number of the multimedia agencies try to specialize in specific areas of know-how, thus identifying a niche for themselves where, although the competitive pressure is remarkable, they enjoy some degree of shelter from it.

Multimedia is a fast-moving industry. The requirements to be met by the enterprises are changing fast. The life-span of multimedia know-how is extremely short, and those responsible for professional training often cannot update courses as quickly as the industry requires. The qualifications required to work in an enterprise are therefore imparted to a large extent by the enterprises themselves. Formal professional education is not an absolute requirement for new employees. Prerequisites include skill, talent, the ability to work in a team and the readiness to meet new challenges. The output-oriented approach pursued by multimedia agencies requires creative, flexible, ambitious, adaptable and in general young employees who will take on the tasks involved in a project as their own and be ready to commit themselves beyond traditional working (time) rules. Some of the employees work as freelances or regular freelances, and some routinely work at home and are connected online to the enterprise.

Until now, enterprises have been able to meet their demand for new creative thinkers when they need to expand their skeleton staff by tapping a broad-based and diversified regional labour market. They are only faced with bottlenecks when recruiting qualified programmers. Staff seldom move from one enterprise to another on account of a generally very positive working atmosphere, though such movement might be desirable to ensure a continuous restoration of the creative potential. Independent freelances are often highly qualified in a specific segment (for example 3D applications) and work for several companies at the same time.

Most multimedia agencies regard all forms of Internet or Intranet presentations as their particular strategic spheres of multimedia activities in the future. They focus on the business-to-business sector, that is the design and handling of commercial relations between the protagonists in the enterprises. A broad range of activities will open up in this area within the next few months and years, while the private household demand for online services will only increase significantly after a sustained improvement in convenient online features: This will incur communication costs.

Although multimedia enterprises must (still) be considered as belonging to a small segment of the labour market and the industry, their innovative potential is expected to promote the restructuring of the location and to provide further positive employment impulses to the Munich labour market.

Telecommunication

As the telecommunication sector was liberalized, this market was subject to substantial changes. New business start-ups, alliances and cooperation between enterprises characterize the sector. The information and communication sector in Europe is expected to overtake the automobile industry by the year 2000.

When the Bavarian utility group Bayernwerk AG was privatized in 1994, the utility company VIAG AG took over the majority share from the Free State of Bavaria in 1994. At the request of the Bavarian Government, it subsequently relocated its headquarters from Düsseldorf to Munich. It founded the VIAG

Interkom GmbH, as a joint venture together with British Telecom in May 1995. In June 1997, VIAG Interkom already had 700 employees and is expected to expand its workforce to approximately 9,000 by 2006.

As a telecommunication provider, VIAG Interkom offers the international language and data services 'Concert' in Germany, a joint venture between British Telecom and the US MCI Communications Inc., which is aimed at providing with global communication services to international enterprises. Technical services through the link-up of fixed networks and mobile phones are also expected to be offered to private clients. In February 1997 the enterprise was granted the fourth German mobile phone licence E2.

Public authorities also wish to participate in the expected telecommunication boom. The restructuring of the postal and telecommunications services in mid-1996 broke the monopoly on the transmission channels in the telecommunication network. It is now possible for owners of efficient data transfer networks other than Telekom above all public and private utility companies to make their networks available. In July 1996 representatives of the City of Munich, Bayernwerk Netkom GmbH, Bayerische Landesbank and Stadtsparkasse München signed a partnership agreement to found a joint city network telecommunication company M'net. Currently based on 50 km. of fibre optic cables and 1,800 km. of copper cable, M'net has developed its own telecommunication service. Apart from basic services such as the link-up of computer centres and local mainframe networks, M'net is also involved in the implementation of value-added services and video conferences. The Bavarian Ministry of Industry and Technology has earmarked 3.3 million DM for the sponsoring of its trial runs.

An indication of the importance of the Munich data processing and telecommunication enterprises is also given by their presence at important computer fairs. At the CeBit 1995 in Hanover, 498 enterprises from the Munich area were represented, making up 12.2 per cent of all German exhibitors. The annual 'Systems' trade fair takes place in Munich and is one of the leading information and communication trade fairs in Europe that links technology and contents. It provides an international forum for producers and suppliers of hard- and software in the EDP and communication sectors.

Production and working conditions

Unlike other industrial production, the product of the media industry or of multimedia constitutes the unique output of a creative, innovative formation process. Let us distinguish the (multi-) media product from its carrier medium—newspaper, magazine, book, film, radio broadcast, CD-ROM, Internet presentation, etc. and focus on the content that is to be conveyed by means of the medium. The content is essentially the individualized output of a constantly new and diversified creative process although the related manufacturing technology reaches an ever increasing in some cases even high level of standardization. Right up to the point where it is reproduced, the media product is the result of a craftsman-like manual design process.

The media formation and production process primarily consists of projects which produce 'interaction goods'. It is frequently achieved not by an individual (as in the case of a novel) but by cooperation and joint action, partly by formally independent creators, in an organized cooperation process such as a film or video production, a music production or a CD-ROM production.

Cooperation is a primary principle in the creation of media products; without it very few would come into existence. The more the media production process resembles an industrial production process (as in the production of a daily newspaper) the more cooperation is required within an enterprise. The more it represents a unique event (as in the production of a feature film) the more likely it will be a cooperative process between numerous different partners led by one management. This cooperation is flexible and temporary; the personnel involved in production differ according to the form and purpose of the product. The team is disbanded after the termination of the project to re-form for a different project in a different constellation. Qualification and flexibility of those involved is an essential factor. Urbanity and a creative environment are the most important conditions for the creation and formation process of an 'interaction product'.

The media sector has always evinced a high proportion of so-called self-employment activities in comparison to other industries (consider the actors, journalists, graphic artists, photographers and other persons employed in the film, radio, publishing and theatre sectors). This is due to the fact that the media product is a cooperative project. Behind the forms of free cooperation, a broad range of diverse employment opportunities is evident. In some cases it is a matter of so-called 'make-do' independence: an employment relationship where in fact there is a high dependency on the individual employer and little or no creative liberty is granted to independent work.

In almost all new working places created in the media industry, vacancies are currently apparent, just as recently vacated posts in which hitherto full-time employees were active are metamorphosing into working places for freelance employees. At the same time the tendency towards multiple employment increases; hence the employment in different, parallel spheres of activity.

Changing qualification and training requirements

There has been a change in qualification requirements with regard to employment in the traditional and 'new' media sectors. While traditional commercial professional knowledge and professional experience decline in importance, the requirement for skills and qualification in EDP-supported working places increase. This is the case not only in the hitherto traditional printing sector but also in the various categories of the new media.

Apart from the expansion of existing professional profiles to include EDP know-how in training and further education, new professional profiles arise by way of the integration of hitherto subdivided activities. Thus it will not be possible in future to carry out activities without formal training ('learning by doing'), as in the initial phase of the 'new' media industry. Here, too, the requirement for specifically designed training courses in the new multimedia sectors in training centres especially established for this purpose will increase.

The diversity of qualification in the Munich area is supported, safeguarded and funded by a broad range of training and further education facilities for media professions. In its scope and diversity this is the equal of any in other media locations in Germany. Apart from the established training facilities, some of which have existed for decades, a number of new training and further education facilities have been created in the last few years to cater to the changing media landscape. No fewer than thirty different (high) school and further education facilities can be listed, not counting the numerous private actors' studios in Munich.

The expansion in the telecommunication sector in the last few years and the boom that will undoubtedly result from the loss of Deutsche Telekom AG's telecommunication monopoly in 1998 threaten to lead to a shortage of specialized labour in the Munich area as far as the telecommunication suppliers are concerned. Siemens AG is a case in point. In July 1997 Siemens had 200 vacancies in the telecommunication sector. By the year 2000 the company will employ an additional 3,000 telecommunication specialists. Multimedia enterprises are complaining about a noticeable lack of qualified programmers. Meanwhile, the number of students in such subjects as information technology, electrical engineering and communication engineering has continuously declined both at the Ludwig Maximilians and the Technische University of Munich as well as at senior technical colleges. The current number of enrolled students is 3,800, which is an indication of a considerable shortfall of newcomers. Hence enterprises like Siemens have increasingly started to boost their recruitment programmes in the form of mobile information fairs at the Technical University and the Fachhochschule München.

Multimedia Infrastructure

Apart from the entrepreneurial protagonists immediately involved in the media and communication industry, a network of supplementary facilities, associations, regular events and other infrastructural conditions has developed for their support. Its density and diversity is a further indication of the importance of the media and telecommunication cluster in the Munich area. This multimedia infrastructure includes interest groups and other associations, including public or semi-public institutions, to support and monitor prize awards and other events.

Associations

In the Munich multimedia cluster, numerous associations come together to represent and try to implement the interests of their respective customers (in general, professional groups or groups of companies) with regard to other social groups, the state and administration or the public.

Table 4.1 Professional training facilities

Institution	Supporting organization
Institut für Kommunikations -wissenschaft (previously: Zeitungswissenschaft)	Munich University (State of Bavaria)
Institut für Theaterwissenschaft	Munich University (State of Bavaria)
Hochschule für Musik	State of Bavaria
Deutsche Journalistenschule	Public and private TV and radio stations, newspaper and magazine publishers, Deutscher Journalisten-Verband (Association of German Journalists), Industriegewerkschaft Medien (media trade union), Evangelische Medienakademie (Protestant media academy)
Hochschule für Fernsehen und Film (HFF)	State of Bavaria
Akademie der Bayerischen Presse	Bayer. Journalistenverband (Association of Bavarian Journalists), Verband Bayer., Zeitungsverleger (Association of Bavarian Newspaper Publishers), Verband der Zeitschriftenverlage in Bayern (Association of Magazine Publishers in Bavaria)
Bayerische Akademie der Werbung	Non-profit institution sponsored by thirty enterprises, associations, chambers, Bayerische Landeszentrale für neue Medien (BLM)
Bayerische Akademie für Fernsehen	Bayer., Staatsministerium für Unterricht, Kultur,

Fernsehen	Wissenschaft und Kunst (Bavarian State Ministry for Education, Culture, Science and Art), privately owned broadcasters, BLM, numerous enterprises
Bayerische Theaterakademie im Prinzregententheater	State of Bavaria
Fachakademie für Fotodesign	State of Bavaria
Otto-Falckenberg-Schule (Fachakademie für Darstellende Kunst)	City of Munich
Mediadesign Akademie	Privately-owned training institution (mediadesign CAD Trainingscentre München GmbH)
Burda Journalistenschule	Privately-owned magazine group (Burda)
BLR Dienstleistungsgesells chaft für Bayerische Lokal-Radio-programme mbH & CoKG	Privately-owned radio broadcasters

Table 4.2 Associations

Sector	Association
Printing and publishing sector	Verband Bayerischer Verlage und Buchhandlungen e.V. Verband Bayerischer Zeitungs-verleger e.V. Verband der Zeitschriftenverlage in Bayern e.V. Landesverband Bayern der Industriegewerkschaft Medien Presse Club München e.V. Club Wirtschaftspresse e.V.München

(Contd.)

Advertising sector	Konferenz der Akademien für Kommunikation, Marketing, Medien
	Arbeitsgemeinschaft der ARD-Werbegesellschaften
	Wirtschaftsverband der Filmtheater e.V. Bayern
Film industry	Verband der Szenenbildner, Filmarchitekten und Kostümbildner in Europa e.V. Grünwald
	Verband Deutscher Schauspieler-Agenturen
	Interessenverband deutscher Schauspieler e.V.
	Verband Deutscher Filmexporteure e.V.
	Export-Union des Deutschen Films e.V. (EXU)
	Verband Neuer Deutscher Spielfilmproduzenten e.V. (55 producers/production firms out of 115 members are based in Munich)
	Verband Privater Bayerischer Fernsehanbieter (VPGBF), Freising
	Verband Bayerischer Lokalrundfunk
	Vereinigung Bayerischer Rundfunkanbieter
TV and radio broadcasting sector	Arbeitsgemeinschaft Privater Rundfunk (APR)
	Lokal-Fernsehen München e.V., Unterföhring
	Kommunikationsverband Bayern e.V.
	Bundesverband Deutscher Fernsehproduzenten e.V. (52 out of 134 German members are based

	in the Munich area)
	Verband Deutscher Schauspieler-Agenturen
Theatre and music business	Landesverband Bayerischer Tonkünstler e.V.
	Interessenverband deutscher Schauspieler e.V.
	Gesellschaft für Musikalische Aufführungs-und mechanische Vervielfältigungsrechte (GEMA)
	Gesellschaft zur Wahrnehmung von Film und Fernsehrechten mbH (GWFF)
Performing rights organizations (ensure adherence to copyright regulations)	Verwertungsgesellschaft (VG) Wort
	Clearingstelle Multimedia Verwertungsgesellschaft mbH (CMMV)
	Verwertungsgesellschaft der Film und Fernsehproduzenten mbH (VFF)
	Verwertungsgesellschaft Bildkunst
Labour unions	Industriegewerkschaft Medien—Landesbezirk Bayern

In August 1995, the Deutscher Multimedia Verband e.V. (dmmv) with headquarters in Munich was established by several multimedia entrepreneurs, including some based in Munich. They realized that there was a need for joint action in the multimedia sector, above all as regards quality control, legal and training issues, quotation and calculation issues. The association has also been designed to maintain contact between industry, politics, the authorities and the press. By early 1997 the dmmv had already expanded to an interest group representing more than 220 members of the German online and offline multimedia industry. A survey dating from October 1996 shows that thirty-one of the 118 associated multimedia enterprises come from the Munich area.

Supervisory and Coordination Institutions

The Bayerische Landesanstalt für neue Medien (BLM), as the second public corporation in the radio and TV sector in Bavaria licences and supervises private radio and TV providers. The Münchner Gesellschaft für Kabelkommunikation (MGK), Unterföhring, is responsible for the technical assignment of broadcasting frequencies to the private radio and TV stations in Munich and Bavaria. The 'Münchner Kreis' (Munich circle); founded a decade ago, is an association for communication research. It is one of the most important institutions of this kind in Germany, organizes specialized conferences and conventions, and focuses and represents the interests of the telecommunication sector.

Events

A great number of events are held in the Munich area every year. These provide information on new developments in sub-sectors and offer an opportunity for meeting important protagonists of the media and telecommunication sector. These events include:

- 'Medientage München', one of the most important media-political conferences in Germany.
- 'Internationale Frühjahrsbuchwoche'.
- The associated event 'Werbegipfel München'.
- 'BLM Rundfunkkongress'.
- The 'Systems' trade fair.
- CINEC, previously known as ShowBIZ Europe, an international trade fair for film technology.
- 'Münchner Filmfest' held in summer every year. It is one of the leading festivals of Europe's film industry alongside Cannes and the biennial film festivals in Berlin and Venice.

Political frame conditions that help promote the media, multimedia and TIME industries

Prize awards demonstrate the attention and esteem bestowed on an actor, a product or a sphere of activity. In Munich, for example, the 'Bayerischer Filmpreis', the 'Bayerischer Fernsehpreis' and the 'Deutscher Videopreis' awards are granted by or with the support of the State of Bavaria. The City of Munich regularly awards various literature prizes.

Munich was slow to realize the importance of the media and telecommunication industry for the future economic development of the area and for years treated all innovative private media in a somewhat reserved manner. Recently, however, it has made great efforts to support and encourage activities in this sphere. The city of Munich for instance holds a 40 per cent share in the 'Internationale Münchner Filmwochen GmbH', which organizes the Munich film festival. The Bavarian State Government also sponsors the film industry. In 1980 it inaugurated a Bavarian film-sponsorship programme and established the 'FilmFernsehFonds Bayern' (film/ TV fund Bavaria), without which hardly any film project could be implemented in Munich.

'Bayern Online' is an initiative of the Bavarian State Government, which has 100 million DM to support telecommunication. The aim is to stimulate the use of modern telecommunication technologies and telematic services in Bavaria and to create or promote the use of the corresponding network structures and network capacities. Sixteen pilot projects have been designed to provide impulses for a speedy implementation and to intensify the use of telecommunication technologies and services.

The Bavarian State Government uses the 'Bayern Online' project to exert influence on industrial policy so as to speed up the introduction and dissemination of information and communication technological networks, services and applications in Bavaria. 'Bayern Online' presents itself as a programme opening the multimedia market, the targets of which are negotiated and stipulated between the representatives of industry, science, politics and administration largely without the participation of the public.

Summary

It can be stated that a comprehensive, broad media and telecommunication cluster which includes both the software and hardware sectors has crystallized in the Munich region. Technological, economic and political conditions have had a positive effect on the formation of this cluster. It is apparent that due to the entrepreneurial and infrastructural conditions prevailing in the

Munich area the multimedia sector (in its narrow sense) is going to expand and will gain even greater importance.

Recent technological developments (the expansion of digital information, communication and production technologies) and political decisions (liberalization/privatization of the media and telecommunication provider markets) support the integration of the media industry and the information and telecommunications industries into what is generally referred to as the TIME industry. Even if this is only discernible in outline, conditions are favourable for developing network-like interrelations between the protagonists and sub-segments of the 'multimedia sector' (in its broader sense).

The traditional borders between individual industries are blurring as new and pre-existing firms merge. The multimedia sector integrates traditional media industries (e.g. printing and publishing), the film industry, radio and TV with the electronics and telecommunication sector of the metal and electronics industries, the distribution sector for media technology and media products, and cultural production.

The stabilizing multimedia complex is becoming more and more attractive to external protagonists. To an extent hardly matched by any other agglomeration in Germany, the Munich area offers a range of advantages for the media and telecommunication protagonists. These include a flourishing urban environment and a creative working atmosphere, a subtly differentiated, broad range of qualifications, short distances for face-to-face contacts, and other favourable conditions. Many protagonists who have relocated their enterprise headquarters in the Munich area have at the same time enhanced the reputations of their enterprises. Sometimes this enhancement of reputation is the main reason for a move to the Munich area.

The multimedia cluster offers not only ephemeral but above all immediate material advantages, for example as regards the application of digital production and transmission technology against the background of a broad range of knowledge and experience in the micro-electronics and computer technology sectors at the location.

The media enterprises located in Munich are paying close attention to political initiatives in, for example, North Rhine-

Westphalia or the new Länder which aim to improve the innovation and location conditions for their (multi-)media industries. In so doing, they also point out that the past development of the media and telecommunication industries in Munich has for the most part been self-generated by the market without any support from economic policies.

The economic success of the media and telecommunication location in the Munich area has hitherto received political support mainly by means of establishing and safeguarding favourable infrastructural and 'climatic' conditions. State programmes have only recently been initiated by industrial and structural policies and used in a target-oriented manner to promote key projects of the media and telecommunication industries and speed up their implemen ration and distribution. These programmes include the FilmFörderungsFonds Bayern and 'Bayern Online'. It is not only the subsidizing of the media and telecommunication technologies that plays a role in this respect but also the efforts to enhance the position of Munich and Bavaria as compared to other national and international media centres.

Multimedia enterprises are somewhat sceptical about the 'Bayern Online' programme in particular. They do not have great expectations of the support of the multimedia sector by political measures. Small enterprises often gain no benefit from state-subsidized programmes. The market requirements facing the multimedia sector as regards speed and flexibility hardly correspond to the traditional political support instruments and procedures, which are felt to be rigid and slow. According to multimedia agencies, it would be useful if politics and administration were more flexible in adapting their own procedures to the ways of working prevailing in the multimedia sector and in the TIME industry.

5

Multimedia Clusters: Formulation and Sustainability

Introduction

Multimedia is generally related to the emerging fast-growing industrial activities based on new network technologies (e.g., Internet) and new products, processes and services integrating a variety of media (text, graphics, audio, pictures, animation, video, etc.), available in a digitized format that can be accessed interactively. These activities are perceived as the growth industries of the future and affect the concerns of a wide range of players, including network operators (for online multimedia), hardware producers (servers, computers, etc.), the media industry, service providers and content providers (entertainment industry, software producers, etc.). In this realm, new and established firms are active.

Not surprisingly, industrial policymakers from most countries or regions would like to have a strong, dynamic and long-term multimedia industry or capability that contributes centrally to the growth, employment and wealth creation in their countries or regions in short, a sustainable multimedia capability. Here, sustainability would not be merely an issue of presence, quantity and time. It would also be, fundamentally, an issue of quality and the harmonious integration of the activities which take place in a region. As such, we define sustainability as the ability to shape significantly the content, direction and dynamism of the long-term evolution of multimedia in a given region.

At the basic level the chapter asks whether such a process of clustering exists and whether there are strategic policies guiding its possible development towards sustainability. It defines the conditions for sustainability of a globally competitive cluster, and provides a framework to grasp and influence policy processes aimed at fostering cluster formation.

The main part of this chapter is organized in three sections which lay the theoretical foundations for the treatment of the clustering process and analyse the specific situation of Scotland in microelectronics and multimedia. The section on 'Clusters, networking and sociotechnical constituencies' begins by outlining the appeal of clustering as a policy instrument. It argues that knowledge networking is the fundamental characteristic of sustainable clusters. It introduces the sociotechnical constituencies (STC) approach, which assists understanding of how clusters work and how they are shaped in their purposiveness and potential sustainability. The process of cluster formation is here treated as a process of sociotechnical alignment fundamentally influenced and shaped by the governance or 'rules of the game' within which it unfolds.

The next section, 'A Scottish multimedia cluster', looks at the evidence of clustering processes in Scotland. Since multimedia is rather recent and the challenge is more how to stimulate multimedia clustering, this section approaches the problem by integrating insights from the better known electronics clustering process in Scotland, with particular emphasis on identifying governance features of direct relevance to other clustering processes such as multimedia. In the concluding section the chapter looks at policy options for multimedia clustering in Scotland. It argues that the constituency-building focuses policy in a purposeful way, and is necessary for public policy on clustering to achieve more of its desired goals.

Significance of clustering and networking

In recent years the idea of clustering and its relevance to economic growth has gained acceptance among academics and policymakers. This chapter will refer to various cluster-related policy themes such as spatiality, relationality, partnering and knowledge networking. These themes are all the subject of theoretical debate, and their balanced integration is required for holistic understanding and effective policy application.

Few would now accept a Marshallian view of clustering as resource-driven, or transactional-based 'agglomeration'. Clustering is now generally regarded as a technological and knowledge-based construction. It is not well understood as a construction, particularly in terms of the nature and balance between the various factors governing the emergence and evolution of a cluster. Are clusters market creations, or a result of networking? A central theme of this chapter is that the conscious (and unconscious) direction given by a constituency of players and interests moulds a cluster creation giving it purpose. It will be argued that cross-institutional networks deepen clustering, and that knowledge networking is the fundamental characteristic of sustainable clusters.

Issues of time and money feature prominently in debates around clustering: how much time, whose money, and at what (social) risk? Commonly, any plan for product or process development will analyse uncertainty and compute risk. Proposals for the investment of public and private funds, and social structures, might well do the same to enhance the chances of achieving a cluster. Policy processes that are founded on shared visions of clusters and invest time and money may play a forceful role in enhancing the prospects for success. However, there are great dangers in 'locking-into' trajectories which are not rewarded by the market, or which will not be sustained for an appropriate period. In this section, we shall demonstrate that the sociotechnical constituency tool helps to clarify the relevant questions.

Networking is an interorganizational perspective cementing the three other building blocks of the clustering concept: spatiality, relationality and knowledge. Network analysis has too often focused on classification of structures rather than on analysis. To be useful, network analysis must also avoid the functional determinism of outcome often found in systems theory. Carefully used, the STC approach we shall discuss below can avoid both these failings.

Commercial networks come in enormous varieties. Knowledge networks are a particularly complex area whose study involves analysis of resources, people and purposes that are dynamic and involve competition both within and between networks. Charles and Howells argue that cross-institutional linkages may be important at a pre-competitive Research, Development and Design (RD&D) stage of product development, but more spatially diverse global knowledge alliances seem to be more often used at later stages in new product development. Setting the domain of a network, identifying its purpose and dynamics, is a difficult but necessary pre-condition for analysis. This chapter argues that there is a spectrum of interorganizational relations whose quality is differentiated by the depth of the relationship (that is, how well the knowledge flows and common purposes interrelating organizations are integrated).

At the shallow end of the spectrum are non-value-adding inter-trading relations such as off-the-shelf technology supply, whereas at the deepest end are knowledge-partnering and knowledge-networking activities which most clearly characterize the sustainable dynamics of clustering processes.

Table 5.1 Examples of interorganizational relations by type and depth

Non-value-adding supply linkages	Off-the shelf market transaction such as standard screw purchases.
Value-added inter-trading	Improves delivery or information systems but without conscious intent; one-way learning; this may extend to industrial networking, for example local sourcing strategies.
Value-added (relational) inter-trading (partnering)	Two-way learning, but bounded, for example jointly developing a new machined part; 'tactical' rather than 'strategic' partnering.
Advocacy networking (narrow linkages)	No new knowledge generation; seeking to align institutional arrangements to suit a narrow constituency in competition with other constituencies within a spatial boundary.

Knowledge partnering	A strategic, long term and deep relationship, centrally featuring knowledge creation, but bilaterally based, for example 'corner engineering' and improving a sub-assembly or complex part.
Knowledge networking (wider relations)	Strategic multilateral knowledge networking, deepened by trust and previously successful joint knowledge development: a conscious knowledge generation and socialization within a network.
Sustainable cluster	A knowledge network capable of dynamically re-configuring to suit changing patterns of global demand; aligning the local mode of regulation with global regime of accumulation.

These categorizations are not intended to be exhaustive and should not be seen as having rigid borders. They may certainly be refined or added on but, for our purposes, the selection clearly indicates the existence of different depths in relationships between different organizations. A sustainable cluster is most likely to integrate all forms of relations into a dynamic process that aligns local and global patterns.

The issue for strategists and policymakers is how to approach practical processes of desired, potential or real cluster formation. It is important to grasp and assess the content and dynamics of these processes with a view to developing consistent policies for influencing and supporting their emergence and development. This is the role of the conceptual instrument provided by the framework of sociotechnical constituencies: it provides the metaphorical spectacles needed to see clearly the multidimensional processes involved in the depth, dynamics and shaping of a cluster.

Sociotechnical Constituencies

A rich analytical framework is necessary to analyse networking within a cluster or, more generally, the nature, state of development and dynamism of a cluster. A cluster is a large-scale sociotechnical constituency commonly consisting of broad fronts of sub-processes, involving a variety of specific and interrelated technical, organizational and commercial factors. The latter include, for example, agreements on standards.

In practice, the combination of these sub-processes will not only show a wide range of possible configurations; it will also manifest itself through various levels of operation from intracompany to standard-setting initiatives. The STC approach is an analytical method capable of dealing systematically with this complexity. It is an instrument of interorganizational analysis, a single process of interpenetration of technical, socioeconomic, political and cultural factors, that provides a snapshot of the dynamic creation of a technological artefact or system. It encapsulates relationships between organizations (and key decision-making groups) and varieties of organizations influencing the constituency.

Sociotechnical constituencies may be defined as dynamic ensembles of technical constituents (tools, machines, etc.) and social constituents (people and their values, interest groups, etc.), which interact and shape each other in the course of the creation, production and diffusion (including implementation) of specific technologies.

This approach puts technological processes at the centre of its analytical focus, and the meaning of technology (T) is not confined to a single specific product or process. It can be a product or, as is the concern of this chapter, a cluster. This focus means that STC is necessarily multidisciplinary. It also means that each constituency has a purpose for its members, though purposes may conflict and re-align over time. Indeed, players may take time to identify the hierarchy of goals each brings to the constituency. The types of interaction between different sets of social constituents are critical to the performance of sociotechnical constituencies. At both intra- and inter-institutional constituency-building levels, they may assume many forms (or combinations of forms). These may be, for instance, complementary, collaborative, competitive and so on.

Interactions may involve players of similar or of different types, and again this is valid at both intra- and inter-institutional constituency-building levels. At an intra-institutional level, for instance, interactions may be among engineers themselves, on the one hand, and among engineers, unskilled labour managers, and other personnel on the other. At an inter-institutional level (fourth circle from centre T), they may be among companies, on the one hand, and among companies and different institutions such as universities or government labs, on the other.

The third and fourth circles also show that the integration of resources inside a constituency building process is effected through the interaction of different intra- and inter-institutional constituents. Since these social constituents control the available resources (directly or indirectly and in varying proportions), they are able to influence the manner in which these resources are integrated. This allows them to shape the development of a given technology in accordance with their own interests, expertise, and generally with their relative weight and power within the constituency. In this respect, each STC entails power relations and, more generally, governance informing the relations between constituent actors who contribute towards the unknown but purposive outcome of the STC network.

Formal governance may differ from informal relations. there will be discourse within the constituency over how to achieve the desired outcomes. The knowledge and 'languaging' that junior members of the STC bring to this may give them a degree of intellectual power that allows them to shape outcomes to a greater extent than their physical input would otherwise entail. In this sense, STC easily incorporates specific cultural elements or the wider concept of 'habitus' into its analytical dimensions.

The development of a given technology is not simply the result of an insular, intra-constituency process. It is also the result of that sociotechnical constituency's interaction with other sociotechnical constituencies within its particular historical setting. It is influenced, for example, by legislation, regulation, technical and market standards, and trends; these are themselves the result of interaction between sociotechnical constituencies (i.e. an inter-constituency process). Thus, technical and market standards (trends) are not in fact exogenous to constituencies: sociotechnical constituencies themselves create and alter them according to the extent of their relative strengths, dynamism and growth.

These characteristics of STC enable a systematic integration of the micro-and macro-dimensions of technological processes. Moving from 'inner-to-outer,' or vice-versa, the same framework can be used at all levels of scoping. Thus, the constituency boundaries (key to the use of STC as an analytical device) can be narrowly drawn to understand the shape of particular products, or more broadly defined to understand the nature of a technology cluster or system. As this happens, every higher aggregate level of the constituency always contains or subsumes all previous levels. Thus, a specific product constituency becomes constituent of the broader cluster level and so on. The result is a transformation of context into content and vice-versa.

Finally, it must be noted that despite their perception of benefit, social constituents participating in a constituency do not invariably have a clear idea of where their specific interests lie in relation to a given technology. Nor does the development of this technology necessarily follow the intended path or yield the results expected by the constituents. Purposiveness is not a static well-defined ingredient and unpredictable and possibly unidentifiable factors have consequences which can lead to a change of direction or, indeed, make the difference between success and failure. Uncertainty is inherent in the technological process, particularly where constituents are trying to break completely new technical ground. This uncertainty factor figures prominently in new multimedia technologies, especially as they come to involve the development and integration of a broad front of innovations.

Clustering as intra- and inter-institutional processes of sociotechnical alignment

The emergence of a multimedia cluster can be treated as the intra and inter-institutional construction of competitive product constituencies through purposive processes of sociotechnical alignment. Sociotechnical alignment is what constituents engage in (however consciously, successfully, partially or imperfectly) when they are promoting the development of specific technologies either intra-organizationally, inter-organizationally, or even as industrial standards. It may be seen as the process of creation, adoption, accommodation (adaptation) and close or loose interaction (interrelation) of technical and social factors and actors which underlies the emergence and development of an identifiable constituency.

Alignment should not be seen as a mere accommodation of static available pieces as if they were parts of a jigsaw puzzle. Nor can it be considered as something complete and permanent, once achieved. For this reason, the term 'alignment' is well supplemented by those of 'mis-alignment' and 're-alignment' which express, on the one hand, situations of tension and disharmony and, on the other, changes or re-accommodations in the life of a constituency. Non-alignment best describes situations in which the parties have not come to each others' attention and in which it is thus less proper to talk of tensions or conflict. Also, alignment between people is not always simply a matter of consensus. 'Consensual alignment' is one possible form it may take, but there might also be, for instance, 'authoritarian' forms enforced by one party over another through sheer use of power.

In alignment the flow of influences is multidirectional. Indeed, as a sociotechnical process, the interrelations involved are not only among people and institutions but, simultaneously, among people, institutions and technical elements. Four types of alignment may be noted here. First, when two or more people or institutions come together (explicitly or implicitly) to pursue a common goal, we may talk of alignment between people or institutions. Second, when developers shape technologies in accordance with the specifications of potential users, we may talk of aligning technology to people. Third, when people have to learn new skills to be able to use a technology, we may talk of aligning people to technology. Finally, when technologies are shaped in accordance with the features of other technologies such as standards, we talk of aligning technology to technology.

In practice, all these elements are likely to be present in the development of a constituency at one time or another. Indeed, mis-alignment and re-alignment must also be included since practical constituency-building strategies may sometimes employ one or other of these alternatives in order, for instance, to generate space within an organization which has a strong competing constituency. The central task of a well-informed strategy is to identify these alternatives and ensure that the most appropriate combinations, emphases and changes are implemented during the life of a constituency.

In this respect, it is important to realize that the four types of alignment just mentioned are not necessarily complementary. Sometimes alignments in certain directions may actually produce mis-alignment in others. For instance, it is not uncommon for people to reach agreement (alignment) on the basis of expectations and specifications which then prove mis-aligned with what is actually feasible with the available resources and technology. This kind of mis-alignment may turn out to be very costly for a constituency and it may well be a major factor in the 'over-spending' that often bedevils technical projects.

When relations of power and authority exist among players, this may guide and even facilitate a process of alignment or decision-making. In large-scale clustering processes, however, no such clear source of decision-making is normally available. Organization, in terms of projects and of formal and informal working arrangements between players, is rather an outcome of the process of alignment: something to be created and shaped in a process of consensus and accommodation.

This task is large and complex. Although alignment may exist on a broad, non-operational goal such as the importance of Scottish capabilities on multimedia technology, the actual process generally starts from a situation of non-alignment or mis-alignment in both perceptions and specific operational goals. In addition, clusters can only start from what existing players bring with them, so the initial 'broad front' may not only be patchy but may also reflect narrower interests than desired. These are all aspects to be aware of as cluster strategies evolve towards long-term constituency-building goals.

It will be mainly the task of 'constituency-builders' and the policy structures embodying the broad clustering processes to provide vision, guidance, encouragement and reality to the integrated constituency-building efforts. Of course, it helps when resources are available to stimulate alignment. In this sense, the fact that multimedia technologies are becoming a major pre-occupation of Scottish policy is already a reflection of significant constituency-building. The truly complex part, however, is the gradual build up of constituencies which effectively realize the goal of sustainable Scottish strength and benefits relative to multimedia processes in other parts of the world. Obviously, given the increasingly global nature of markets, this goal will not be achieved in isolation. Scottish multimedia cluster capabilities must aim for a global presence and this will demand interactions on an equally global scale, with many non-Scottish institutions contributing to, as well as benefiting from, it. The measure of long-term sustainable success, however, will be a cluster relation of knowledge interdependence in which the Scottish voice is strong enough to shape events in the region as well as internationally.

For Scottish multimedia capabilities, this raises the issue of which players come to dominate the constituency-building process and what kind of technical strengths are effectively nurtured in Scotland. One has to take into account that, ultimately, clusters and sociotechnical constituencies only exist by virtue of being rooted in the sociotechnical fabric of specific countries and regions. Their presence and the specific way in which they are realized in given countries (through R&D, production, use, etc.) accounts for the kind of technological capabilities and the role played by these countries in the global development process of a given technology. The implications for Scotland are clear: if the region is to shape and reap the benefits of multimedia technologies with global market scope, it would do well to foster and maintain an influential presence and activity within the respective sociotechnical constituencies.

Diamond of Alignment

The complexity of the process of alignment involved in multimedia cluster formation is shown in more detail by the diamond of alignment. The quantity, quality and synergistic integration of these dimensions enables a detailed understanding and characterization of the depth, breadth, dynamism and purpose of any clustering process. The diamond distinguishes three integrated layers in the clustering process:

- Inner layer (a): intra-organizational layer of companies and other institutions.
- Middle layer (b): inter-organizational layer of projects and programmes that bring together 'value-chain' organizational players in purposive actions.
- Outer layer (c): layer of industrial and market clusters. Synergistic integration of the other two layers at this level is

required for global competitive positioning. Collaboration and competition is characteristic of this level.

As said earlier, each of the broader layers contains the inner ones and all of them are cut across by further dimensions. Dimensions I (a, b, c) and II (a, b, c) characterize the nature and state of development of the sociotechnical constituency and its technology from the intraorganizational to the clustering process.

Dimension I: Constituents' perceptions, goals, actions and resources

This relates to the present state of the sociotechnical constituency: the quantity and type of constituent organizations, people, material and financial resources, knowledge, expertise, experience and reputation. It also embraces other constituent elements such as current perceptions, goals, visions and strategies of the constituency. In short, what the constituency is at a given point in time.

Dimension II: Nature and maturity of the technology

This dimension relates to the importance of the nature and state of development (that is, the maturity) of the technology in the constituency-building process. The nature of the technologies involved is almost certain to affect the strategic limits and opportunities for its constituency-building process. It is a simple fact that the nature of telecommunications networks is different from that of biscuits or drugs, and a single 'universal' approach will not do. In the case of multimedia, at least three characteristics have critical strategic value: pioneering emerging technology; technologies with indirect network externalities; and consumer product. Pioneering emerging technology stresses innovation and the need to be first to market particular goods or services. This leads to high uncertainty and risk due to lack of precedents. The implication is a much greater need for market-fostering strategies aimed at aligning users with the technology. Indirect network externality stresses the dependence of the use-value of one product on the existence of another. For example, computers are useless without software and vice-versa; content is useless without delivery hardware. Consumer product highlights the fact that the ultimate adjudicators of success or failure are the people in the street. Dimensions 1 (a, b, c), 2 (a, b, c), 3 (a, b, c) and 4 (a, b, c) characterize the direction, dynamics, and depth of purpose of the process of constituency-building.

Dimension 1 (a, b, c): Governance

This dimension relates to the written and unwritten legislation that governs the behaviour, relations, interactions, calculations, transactions and conflict resolutions between all those involved in intra- and interorganizational constituency-building processes as well as inter-constituencies processes themselves. It includes cultural pre-dispositions and power relations between individual and collective players at intraorganizational, interorganizational and societal levels.

At intra and interorganizational level, effective constituency-building implies an alignment of the technology with the governance and strategic purpose of the organization, project or cluster. At project and cluster levels, arrangements for interorganizational governance are necessary to express, facilitate, stimulate and guide the alignment between different organizations. Mechanisms of collaboration, for instance, may include business alliances, second-source and market agreements, and many other forms. It is crucial for cluster strategies to acknowledge the existence and quality of these arrangements, either to align with them or to create or modify them to satisfy the needs of the constituency-building process.

Lack of attention to interorganizational governance may be the source of much mis-alignment and conflict. At the same time a careful approach is required to strike the right governance. After all, each institution is likely to have different blends of expertise, perceptions, imperatives and expectations, dictated by its history, current activities, industrial environment and possibly by its ethical stance as well as by idiosyncratic practices. One should stress that the flow of influence is not unidirectional, with the emerging constituency always having to align itself to existing governance. In fact, emerging constituencies may well have to challenge the prevailing governance as they develop, sometimes leading to adaptations, modifications and even major new features.

Dimension 2 (a, b, c): Nature of target problem

This dimension relates to the specific technical purpose and content of the constituency's technological activity (for example, a target activity of assembling rather than R & D and innovation). It thus also relates to the depth of clustering. At intra- and interorganizational level, effective constituency-building implies an alignment between the capabilities of the constituency and the technical demands involved in realizing the use-value of the technology (i.e., target functionality and cost). The literature of technology development is full of examples of failure to deliver what was promised: that is, of mis-alignment between the promise (expectation) and what could eventually be brought to the market. To avoid 'failure', the constituency must simply have the technical capacity to deliver the goods with the resources available at any given time. Capacity and resources, however, are dynamic, mutually influencing, factors and part of the capacity to deliver may imply an ability to expand the resources available.

Dimension 3 (a, b, c): Target constituents' perceptions and pursuits

This dimension relates to the people and organizations the constituency is seeking to enrol behind the purposive process, from intra-organizational constituency-building to market consumers. At intra- and interorganizational level it implies an alignment between the constituents and parties who are potential or target constituents (suppliers, individual consumers, and other relevant organizations such as independent software developers). The aim is for them to become members of the constituency. At cluster level, given the broader context, this alignment does not necessarily mean all parties working together across the board. Often, competing companies are involved (software developers, for example) and mis-alignments at certain levels are an unavoidable part of the constituency's make-up.

In practice, players will be aligned on the broad perception that the technology is worth the investment. At the same time they might be competitors or, indeed, collaborators who may differ on the ways to achieve certain specific aims. The entire process is most likely to involve manifold directions of alignment. These may include perception alignment between suppliers of different technical constituents (for example, hardware and software); alignment between technology suppliers and users; alignment of technology specifications to users preferences and requirements; alignment of users to new technology solutions; and alignment between interacting technologies.

Dimension 4 (a, b, c): Interacting technologies/constituencies

Commonly, a new constituency's technology will emerge in an environment populated by other technologies and constituencies. Some will be required to realize the emerging product (e.g., production technology), others may have a similar and even competing claim for resources. This dimension relates to the type of interaction and relations established with these other constituencies in the purposive process from intraorganizational to market constituency-building.

At intra- and inter-organizational level, effective constituency-building implies an alignment between the products of the emerging constituency and established technical and market trends and standards in the target industrial area (whether for mainstream or niche markets). Included in this alignment is a good understanding of the evolution, present strategies, and likely future actions of actual and potential competing constituencies. Since trends and specific solutions are dynamic mutually influencing factors, part of the capacity of a constituency to deliver may imply an ability to identify and generate new standards in areas not yet covered by existing standards.

At the broader cluster level, the boundaries between collaboration and competition, antagonistic and non-antagonistic relations are much more diffuse. Indeed, as with dimensions 3 (a, b, c) mis-alignments at certain levels are often unavoidable. Technologies may simultaneously collaborate and compete at different levels of the constituency, with the boundaries again very much a matter of players' perceptions, stances and, generally, strategic approaches to constituency-building.

Clearly, the process of constituency-building and sociotechnical alignment implied in product innovation will vary greatly in terms of complexity and conflict. Much will depend on the nature of the technology and its initial relationship to the various dimensions in the diamond of alignment. The diamond of alignment enables a systematic and holistic assessment of the multiple dimensions of constituency-building processes, including significant areas of alignment and mis-alignment at intra- and interorganizational layers (a) (b) (c). It also helps to identify the strength and degree of integration of the different layers, and their competitive performance at the industrial/market level. This knowledge is essential for the formulation of well-informed strategic targeting of future constituency-building actions and pursuits. In the following section, we look at the evidence of clustering processes in Scotland.

A Scottish multimedia cluster?

Scottish Enterprise (SE) the industrial agency of Scotland is considering the development of multimedia clustering as one of its strategic lines of action. Since multimedia is rather recent and the challenge is more how to stimulate multimedia clustering, this section approaches the problem by combining:

- Insights from the better known electronics clustering process in Scotland, with particular emphasis on identifying governance features of direct relevance to other clustering processes such as multimedia.
- Insights from the situation specific to the potential process of multimedia clustering in the region.

In electronics, Scottish Enterprise has worked for fifteen years to stimulate the creation of a microelectronics cluster in Scotland, apparently with major success. Financed by both foreign direct investment (FDI) and indigenous companies, electronics in central Scotland has grown at 14 per cent compound during this period, and currently accounts for 42 per cent of Scottish exports, with total annual sales of £6bn.

On closer examination, however, the depth and sustainability of the electronics cluster appears less impressive. In particular, FDI and indigenous manufacturers in the industry occupy separate networks. The indigenous company network benefits little in terms of trade, advocacy, or knowledge flows from the FDI network, and there is a low birth rate of new companies. In limited ways knowledge alliances are more frequent among the SMEs than between them and the foreign investors (FDIs); the latter network mainly with foreign suppliers and within their corporate network. Few companies have important connections with higher education institutions.

Overall, in electronics, it can be said that Scotland has re-shaped itself to the needs of FDIs in the global economy. Nevertheless, FDIs' added value and knowledge generation have largely remained abroad with suppliers, mother plants, or RD&D centres. Indeed, FDIs' spending in Scotland has tended to be upon lower value-added items: services, consumables, machined parts, and metal fabrication, with some turnkey sub-assembly and printed circuit boards (PCBs). This is consistent with an FDIs' strategic approach that has treated Scotland primarily as a lucrative manufacturing platform for the European market. The result has been a broadly scoped Scottish microelectronics cluster, covering most elements of the value chain, but lacking depth both in its conception and current operation. This demonstrates that inter-firm relations between FDI and indigenous firms have tended to remain at the lower levels of depth predominantly technology supply (shown in italics) and far from the deeper levels which would ensure the sustainability of the clustering process. It also draws attention (italics) to the presence of advocacy (cluster-representing) networking, although again this concerns mostly the FDI sector. This is not to say that the experience has not been valuable. Indeed, this cluster has had considerable impact on employment, capital inflow, and the upgrading of production techniques in the Scottish manufacturing base. But this does not alter the fact that it is a weak cluster with low local product demand, few backward value-adding linkages, exogenous knowledge generation, a limited perspective by public agency actors, a lack of endogenous knowledge networking, and little ability to influence its own development. The importance of this brief assessment for multimedia is that various of the broad factors operating in the Scottish economy and underpinning the weakness of the electronics cluster are also likely to influence the nature and development of a multimedia clustering process. In the following, we shall integrate these factors in the analysis of multimedia. Three recent studies have characterized different aspects of the state and dynamism of multimedia in Scotland. These provide a revealing overview of the development of the constituency at three levels:

- Scale of resources and degree and quality of interconnectedness between institutions in the Value chain' of multimedia clustering. This gives a sense of clustering presence and depth across the three layers of the diamond of alignment (dimension I (a, b, c)).
- General Scottish supply and demand infrastructure factors affecting the development of the constituency.
- Governance aspects underlying the dynamism (or lack of it) in the formation of a potential multimedia cluster in Scotland.

This stressed the elements of media mixes, interactivity and networking, including offline multimedia applications (such as CD-ROM, game stations) and online multimedia applications (including online services, web publishing, etc.) It was also mentioned that a variety of new and established firms are active in the field. These may be established firms moving into new business fields (development, production, marketing of new products and services and so on) or new emerging firms either producing new products and services or using them in a novel manner (including firms in the field of CD-ROM publications and Internet services). The latter group is the main concern of this chapter, since this has so far been the focus of the initial studies carried out in Scotland.

Thus, the Arthur D. Little study for Scottish Enterprise adopted a working definition of the multimedia industry with emphasis on the provision of interactive content such as corporate communications, entertainment, education and games. This is because interactive content is the element of the multimedia value chain with greatest value added and is expected to drive multimedia growth.

Overview of the state of development of the Scottishmultimedia constituency

The results of the studies reveal that the Scottish multimedia industry is small, fragmented and only at an early stage of development. Until recently, there was little interaction among established companies. Few links are evident between local companies or between companies at different stages of the value chain. The industry is so small that a company at one stage in the value chain, for example a packager or distributor, has no knowledge of companies at other stages. In addition, there is little informal networking to build relationships between the members of the Scottish multimedia community. The Arthur D. Little survey identified sixty-one small multimedia companies in Scotland, employing a total of 550 to 600 people. Most supplied only one or two product lines. These main types of content supply are:

- Animation/games typically for PCs, Sony Playstations, Nintendos and Sega Megadrives;
- Corporate communications;
- Solutions provision, typically interactive training packages;
- Internet consultancy, training and Web page authoring.

Here it is worth noting that, depending on how one defines multimedia, there are other potential players on the scene. For example, Scotland is host to a successful TV production company (STV), several small film producers, colleges of art and design, and software innovation centres. As yet, however, these organizations have not been at the forefront of interactive content production.

The picture of fragmentation gained from the Arthur D. Little survey is tempered somewhat by the existence of two significant groupings, in the areas of content for games and corporate communications. The largest and most substantial group is made up of seven games companies; the group of corporate communications companies has two significant players which have established long-term relationships and partnering across Europe on a small scale. These two groups stand out against the background of other small, sole-ownership multimedia companies and software companies that typically produce CD-ROMs for public agencies.

Business skills and growth-capital

Given the predominant small size and infancy of Scottish multimedia companies, it is not surprising that business skills and capital investment are not well developed. It was found that companies often lacked the management, marketing and finance skills necessary for effective business development.

This is reflected in difficulties in obtaining capital for growth, since venture capitalists want to see strong management teams, and the new companies often find it difficult to demonstrate this strength. This difficulty is compounded by the fact that interactive multimedia has a high-risk image in the UK venture capital market, something which is only reinforced by the characteristics of the small companies. As a result, the survey found that most of the companies had 100 per cent owner equity. The exceptions were the games companies and one corporate communications company.

It is also difficult to gain access to capital through large private sector contracts, simply because of small product ranges and lack of experience in tendering or in business and project management. Public sector projects are not conducive to growth since they tend to be small and very price competitive. Companies have also complained that procurement contracts are often poorly specified and managed, apparently because of a lack of relevant skills on the part of the public sector. Multimedia companies believe that public sector organizations do not understand the multimedia tools and techniques available, or their capabilities and benefits.

On the positive side, Scotland has potential catalysts of multimedia demand and supply in large multimedia projects such as the Millennium Commission-funded Scottish Cultural Resources Access Network (SCRAN). SCRAN aims to digitize Scottish cultural resources and could stimulate demand and encourage networking involving cultural institutions and local companies. The education sector is also looking to use multimedia more extensively in teaching and learning, especially in light of the Blair's government commitment to provide access to the Internet to all schools. As yet, however, this is a possibility waiting to materialize.

Cluster-representing Organizations

The small and fragmented state of the Scottish multimedia industry is reflected in the weakness of 'cluster-representing' industrial organizations such as associations or federations. Thus, the Interactive Media Association of Scotland (IMAS) has limited funding and no dedicated premises or administrative support. Board members carry out IMAS activities on a voluntary basis making it difficult to operate efficiently. A business plan is in preparation.

Effective interconnectedness is also affected by the existence of too many trade organizations. For instance, the Scottish Software Federation is planning to set up a multimedia interest group for its members that may overlap with the activities of the principal trade body, IMAS. The Scottish Internet Business Association, representing the distribution element of the value chain, does not appear to have links with IMAS. Other initiatives have little national impact.

Factors Affecting the Development of the Multimedia Constituency

The educational system in Scotland is well provided and computer science degree courses at the traditional universities such as Edinburgh, Glasgow and Strathclyde produce high quality graduates. There is concern, however, that the availability of staff with suitable technical skills could be a problem if the multimedia industry develops rapidly. Some graduates leave Scotland while the best of those who stay are absorbed by growth in the software industry and one or two multinational corporations.

In addition, the Scottish system does not compare well in terms of university-industry spin-offs and the commercialization of university-developed technologies. This seems to be a generic situation in Scotland and is also apparent in the workings of the electronics cluster. For instance, FDIs engage in little joint RD&D with Scottish universities, so that there are no significant knowledge flows between the FDIs and the universities.

Role of the Scottish Electronics Cluster

We have seen that the Scottish electronics industry is dominated by assembly operations and therefore lacks the innovative force that might stimulate synergies with the development and use of multimedia activities. Collinson also confirms that links and exchanges between incumbent electronics multinational corporations (MNCs) and multimedia SMEs in Scotland are limited. He notes, however, that personnel from MNCs do participate in informal networks, as do technical personnel from the large IT support departments of MNCs, including non-electronics companies (particularly from banks, finance and insurance firms, which have strong IT departments).

At the formal level, however, there are relatively few coincidences of interest between high-tech SMEs and MNCs, while there is a potential conflict of interest due to the overall shortage of software expertise currently affecting Scotland and most other industrial regions. There is a lack of interconnectedness and consequent synergies with the electronics sector in the Scottish multimedia situation. This is a major structural weakness when compared with other places where large and small companies interact through joint R & D initiatives, new product development alliances and frequent exchange of ideas and people in complementary and competing areas of technology.

Telecom Infrastructure

Scotland possesses a reasonably well-developed high-bandwidth communications infrastructure for multimedia. In particular, ISDN lines are available in the Central Belt and the Highlands and Islands, and three cable companies operate franchises in the Central Belt and Aberdeen. Also, the Eastman network interconnects most universities with a high capacity fibre optics infrastructure.

Governance in the formation of a Scottish multimedia cluster

Behind the static structural characteristics of multimedia cluster' development in Scotland are the governance factors underpinning the dynamics of this development. Governance factors at the three layers of the diamond of alignment tell us about the likely future of the multimedia cluster formation and about the difficulties of creating missing elements and, generally, overcoming present structural weaknesses. Three types of governance factors have been identified in the case of the Scottish microelectronics clustering process and they are also present in the case of multimedia in Scotland.

General Cultural Factors

Existing studies have pointed to the presence of a risk-averse culture as an important factor in the low birth-rate of businesses in Scotland. Social and financial rewards do not favour entrepreneurialism and risk taking. Entrepreneurs tend to have a relatively lower status than in the US, and employees are not encouraged to move jobs frequently or aspire to their own businesses. A comparison of new SMEs in Boston and Scotland found that more Scots entrepreneurs saw themselves as 'self-employed' or 'freelance', and more often viewed their attempted ventures as temporary activities in the absence of full-time employment. The same study concluded that the Scottish managers were less effective in their networking; they had a narrower range of networks overall and fewer relevant contacts, and were less able to transform these contacts into useful sources of business assistance. Clearly this situation is far from conducive to the entrepreneurial drive required for cluster sustainability.

Structural Positioning in the Global Economy

Scotland's structural positioning in the global economy (reflected in the predominantly assembling role of FDI in electronics) is also problematic for the establishment of a dynamic sustainable multimedia cluster in Scotland. The driving factors behind the FDI-financed electronics assembling cluster in Scotland are comparatively low wages, government grant incentives, a skilled workforce, English language and fears of European 'fortress' policies. As one FDI company put it: 'We came because we were worried about European barriers and Scotland was a low-cost corner from which to serve Europe effectively.'

Although this combination has helped to attract investment and create jobs, it has clearly failed to create a dynamic of wealth creation and competitiveness based on innovation, rising productivity and high added value. There is a significant flaw in the low-cost free market strategy of Scotland in that although wages may be lower than European or G7 levels, they are not in fact low in global terms. The Scottish cost structure is still significantly higher than that of the low-cost economies of the developing world such as Asia and Latin America. This means that FDI companies even if they want to embed themselves more fully in the local economy by substantially increasing local sourcing still face the fact that it is cheaper to buy parts from the global low-cost economies. Furthermore, in multimedia, it is critical to realize that the cost of labour is unlikely to be a determining factor, since the industry is at an emerging stage and demand for creative skills in innovative product and service applications is not easily satisfied. This means that Scotland cannot count on the previous low-cost free market strategy to attract FDI and stimulate an electronic-like clustering process in the area of multimedia.

In this context, the only possibility left at this initial stage is one of long-term positive local strategies and policies to stimulate constituency-building and capability formation, though this may include the role of FDI as one of its aspects. This, however, demands a strong degree of social consensus around a realistic vision and the commitment to persevere, which takes us back to the previous point as well as forward to the social consensus and the role of the policy instruments in Scotland.

Social Consensus and Policy Instruments

The governance factor has a dimension of general influence for clustering processes in Scotland, and also a dimension of more specific validity to the case of multimedia clustering. The general dimension can be extracted from the experience of the microelectronics cluster. This has shown that there appears to be little social consensus around a vision of an FDI-led cluster. Society in Scotland has welcomed FDI investment and the employment that accompanies it. It praises manufacturing, easily accepts an export orientation, and approves of skill training and non-conflictual human resource systems. On the other hand, in the context of market ideology, political commentators continually question the value-for-money aspect of FDI subsidy and the opportunity cost of support to innovative SMEs. In terms of policy instruments Scottish Enterprise is the key player. Its cluster vision, however, has not been informed by a holistic proactive constituency-building perspective. In microelectronics, its activity has primarily concentrated on attracting FDI to Scotland and interacting with the Scottish Electronics Forum (SEF) that largely represents the interests of FDI. Beyond this, Scottish Enterprise's role has been very limited. A number of points have been raised in this connection. One problem is that Scottish Enterprise is not a single unified body in charge of practical policies for the different regions in Scotland. This local focus is the responsibility of Local Enterprise Companies (LECs), who are related to Scottish Enterprise but have considerable autonomy. It has been noted that this local autonomous focus appears to encourage fragmentation of effort and ad hoc initiatives with no common Scottish goal or leadership. Ron Botham of Scottish Enterprise suggests that in this structure the organization sits uneasily with 'functional' and 'local' structures; the problem might be eased if multimedia clusters can work at LEG level, but there are no signs of this happening (personal communication with the author). Indeed, Botham argues that the organizational structure and mode of operation of Scottish Enterprise (in, for example, resource allocation) is not ideal, and he also points to the following governance elements as problematic:

- Scottish Enterprise's industry partners do not think in strategic clusters.
- Constituency-building is not the normal practice of the organization and is not part of its culture. It stimulates and provides incentives for FDI location in Scotland, but does not engage in mobilizing required players (such as academia) for a clustering process.

  This is reinforced by a number of elements which are quite contradictory to the needs of a long-term constituency-building paradigm:
- a predominantly short-term as opposed to long-term thinking
- simple cause and effect thinking as opposed to holistic and systemic thinking
- project-specific evaluation as opposed to strategic evaluation
- free-market flexibility as opposed to a strategy that is also driven by the supply side.

In sum, it is clear that there are deeply rooted cultural, structural and institutional aspects which require substantial changes if the most conducive environment for clustering is to be created. These governance issues must be faced squarely if policy efforts are either to engage in the long-term pursuit of more sustainable cluster dynamics than in the present situation. The alternative is to remain consciously inside the modest confines allowed by the present governance.

As far as the dimensions more specific to multimedia clustering are concerned, the picture is little better. It can be said that, at present, government policy instruments have a significant lack of direction or impact on the establishment of a dynamic process of multimedia cluster formation. This may be about to change with Scottish Enterprise's formation of a widely represented Scottish Multimedia Working Group (SMWG) which will have the purpose of developing and stimulating a coherent strategic approach to multimedia clustering in Scotland. The Arthur D. Little study on multimedia referred to in this chapter is part of the fact-finding exercise of this incipient process and, as we shall see, the study argues that there are ways in which government might play an important role in the fostering of a Scottish multimedia industry.

For the time being, however, Scottish Enterprise needs to begin to define its own long-term vision and the practical resource-aligned steps it must take if it seriously hopes to help move the infant industry towards the vision. In this process, the three types of governance factors identified above must be faced squarely, if these visions and actions are to be realistic. Otherwise, the vision is likely to become the centre of 'talking shops' and end in a great deal of disappointment. It seems clear that there are deeply rooted cultural and institutional elements which require substantial changes if the most conducive policy environment for long-term clustering in multimedia is to be created.

Conclusion

This study has examined the theoretical and practical nature of industrial clusters. It has identified the conditions for sustainability and has provided the sociotechnical constituencies framework to help understand and inform practical processes of cluster formation. Using this framework, it is possible to grasp and assess the content and dynamics (or lack thereof) of such processes, with a view to developing consistent policies for influencing and supporting their emergence and development. In this perspective, a cluster is a large-scale sociotechnical constituency. The discussion of clustering in Scotland has argued that there is no sustainable cluster in Scottish microelectronics, the most developed cluster process supported by Scottish Enterprise. Scottish Enterprise has helped to create a spatial concentration of microelectronics firms in central Scotland, but this concentration has no knowledge network and therefore little depth. The constituency-building process creating this concentration is narrowly constructed and has focused upon aligning institutional arrangements in Scotland to suit the needs of inwardly investing corporations. On the positive side, aspects of the lean production technological system have enjoyed diffusion by emulation into the indigenous sector, but there is little sign the constituency around microelectronics intends to establish a knowledge network to deepen the cluster. This cluster is stimulated to innovate by RD&D and value-adding suppliers abroad. The question is whether Scottish Enterprise could have consciously pursued a constituency-building model to improve sustainability. If so, the central aim of clustering microelectronics companies could have been more precisely defined to include and encourage knowledge networks amongst some FDIs and, particularly, with indigenous companies and Higher Education organizations. Such definition would have looked closely at the governance mechanisms at work in the Scottish context and would have faced up to the policy implications. In this respect, the value of a policy framework such as the sociotechnical constituencies model is that it helps to identify key issues and to pose the hard question of how these issues are to be faced by policy strategies. Will this happen with the policies intended to encourage multimedia clustering? The Arthur D. Little 1997 study has identified some areas of multimedia growth opportunities in Scotland such as Web authoring and Website hosting, network and online gaming, computer animations, and media-integrated call centres. It has also sought to stimulate debate by distinguishing three broad and potentially overlapping visions:

1 Develop a small self-sustaining industry meeting primarily local demand by producing largely bespoke, high quality, products and sourcing skills locally. Developing local demand, principally for multimedia products, will be important in all visions. It could also be stimulated in education. The impetus would come principally from public sector initiatives designed to create demand and develop the industry's competencies through, for example, demonstrator programmes. Practically, stimulating local demand could be the responsibility of a number of organizations. Scottish Enterprise and IMAS, for example, could produce demonstrator toolkits to show multimedia consumers and suppliers the benefits of state-of-the-art applications, building on the activities of the Department of Trade and Industry's (DTI) Information Society Initiative.

2 Develop global businesses in niche multimedia products such as games; a large niche product cluster would have global

players in selected multimedia sub-segments, high quality world-wide brands, and would be a recognized centre of excellence. Games seem to offer Scotland an opportunity to establish such niche clustering. The main intervention needed to support the niche products on a global scale is to provide, or encourage the provision of, risk capital to expand R&D activities and ultimately increase companies' product portfolios. This would make them less vulnerable and less dependent upon packagers and distributors. A self-sustaining and commercially operated Scottish Multimedia Fund (SMF), for example, would provide impetus for this strategy. Various organizations, such as Scottish Enterprise, universities and IMAS, could take responsibility for supporting financing and product development in established companies.

3 Develop a large, world-recognized, multimedia centre producing a complete range of multimedia products. As the cluster became recognized for high quality off-the-shelf products, the cluster would grow both in size and visibility throughout the world and this would encourage global players to locate in Scotland. Regions such as Victoria in Australia are aiming for this goal. The main requirement for this option is to have at least one major FDI multimedia company locating in Scotland. Potential investors could be encouraged through offering financial incentives, and marketing the skilled, flexible and competitively priced workforce, reputable education system and supply of competitively priced land.

The viability of each of these visions is subject to doubts, particularly, in the light of the findings of this study on the nature of clustering in Scotland and the trends towards globalization pervading every industry. There must be doubts, for instance, on the viability of vision one, propounding a small self-sustaining industry meeting primarily local demand. Stimulating local demand is indeed critical, but this does not amount to a vision of sustainability. Likewise, vision three will not automatically follow any possible success in locating FDI multimedia companies in Scotland. The experience of FDI in the microelectronics sector indicates that close attention to the depth of interrelations, including knowledge networking, will be necessary to sustain a multimedia centre producing a complete range of multimedia products.

Vision two can be construed as seeking to stimulate a variety of focused project- or programme-driven constituencies, potentially opening the way for wider cluster-type interrelations. In terms of the diamond of alignment, this would imply a great deal of activity starting from the middle-layer (b) and radiating to layers (a) and (c) of the diamond. This would identify and positively engage in focused action on Value chain' opportunities oriented towards internal and external demand. Here large projects such as SCRAN (Scottish Cultural Resources Access Network) may have the potential to stimulate demand and encourage value-chain networking focused, for instance, on education. Another example may be the new venture Scottish Knowledge with its intended university-networking programme focused on distance-learning exploitation of multimedia training courses.

Of course, the three visions may be combined. Whatever the options, however, the common challenge for all of them, separately or in combination, is to define and implement the practical process of constituency-building. Here the catalytic role is largely in the hands of government institutions who should stimulate the process, remaining within the confines of its own governance and resources, but with enough openness and innovativeness to question these constraints if this proves necessary and possible.

The support and effectiveness of Scottish Enterprise's Scottish Multimedia Working Group may offer a first test of the depth of commitment to stimulating multimedia constituency-building in Scotland. Scottish Enterprise has also recently decided to support the formation of a European Group aimed at enhancing Scottish participation in European information society projects. In principle, there should be substantial synergies between these two actions and others, such as the Scottish dimension of the UK Information Society Initiative (promoted by the UK DTI) supported by the Scottish Office and Scottish Enterprise.

In all instances, this emerging process will require identification of and access to 'value-chain' project opportunities focused on real demands. In this connection, a more precise mapping and assessment of the depth of relations in Scottish clustering processes should prove valuable. This would help identify strategic 'hot points' for implementation of targeted policies for both indigenous growth and sustainable FDI-based developments. It should also help to identify more precisely in which areas of the multimedia value-chain Scotland possesses real or potential competitive advantages for growth (for instance, knowledge creation, knowledge capture, programming, production, sales, servicing, etc.). Conversely, it would reveal weaker areas, in which Scotland might find it necessary or expedient to rely on others, or face the long-term challenge and difficulties of their generation if considered necessary and viable.

The gauntlet has been thrown down. Whether Scotland will succeed in generating a multimedia cluster only time will tell. The challenge of multimedia constituency-building is not easy and it is better to face it now, at the early stages of development of the industry. In constituency-building there are no straightforward mechanistic recipes, but a clear understanding of the nature of the complexities, factors, issues and alignment processes involved is a definite strength. This is what this chapter seeks to contribute to the challenge.

6

Models of Interaction and Designing

Introduction

Interaction can be mediated by different devices, speech, and natural language. Information can be presented in a complex mixture of image, sound, speech, and so forth. Furthermore, we interact within interfaces in virtual worlds, whereas in "ubiquitous" computing, the interface is distributed among various devices. In multisensory systems, the interface itself may not be a recognizable entity, as virtual environments become so realistic that we don't notice the computer. In ubiquitous computing, the interface may vanish in wearable computers. However, the design problem does not go away. To achieve effective and transparent interfaces we need to design interaction to fit with the user's expectation of action in the world.

Design could rely on guidelines and principles derived from psychology, but that doesn't help to plan dialogues and UI services in an integrated manner. To help integrate knowledge from psychology within the design process, a set of models describing interaction is proposed, to link the cognitive resources and design features required at different stages of interaction. The starting point is Norman's model of interaction that is already familiar to many and has served well as the underpinning for cognitive walkthrough methods for usability evaluation. Norman's model describes goal-directed action in general terms but it doesn't account for exploratory, opportunistic behavior that is commonplace in complex multisensory interfaces; it also does not describe behaviors in reaction to external stimuli. Hence an extended model is necessary, not only to deal with these aspects but also to link psychology to design so that we can predict the design features that should be required in a particular task context.

Ideally, theory should underpin all design. Although this has been a holy grail for HCI researchers, success in connecting theory and design has not been realized in the general case. This chapter is a modest contribution to this debate, so before embarking on an explanation of the theory, it is necessary to situate this endeavor within the wider field of HCI theoretical contributions.

Psychological theories of human-computer interaction are extensions of more general cognitive models of reasoning and problem solving. Preeminent among these is the ACT-R/PM model created and refined over a number of years by John Anderson and colleagues. ACT-R is a computational model of cognition that predicts how people reason and problem solve. It consists of components that model working memory, long-term memory, and reasoning, with an attention scheduling mechanism. Problems have to be described in a propositional form of facts and goals to be achieved. ACT-R will then predict learning and problem solving, including typical errors that people make when working memory's capacity is exceeded. Various cognitive phenomena such as the Stroop effect can be faithfully reproduced. The weakness of ACT-R is that all input had to be coded in propositional form. This has been partially alleviated by PM (Perceptual Motor extension), but that still requires preprocessed input. ACT-R/PM does not have an image, speech, or audio processor so configuring the model to process even a simple interface such as a menu takes considerable effort.

Other cognitive theories that model perceptual cognition, such as LICAI and EPIC, provide mechanisms for an architecture of perceptual and cognitive processors with rules that predict the user's attention, recognition, and understanding of UI features. However, these models also required propositional input, so dealing with complex multimedia UIs involves considerable effort in converting a UI into a detailed, abstract description. Inevitably, there are many subjective judgements involved in this process, so the theory may only predict behavior within the ambit of the input provided by the analyst.

Theoretically EPIC and ACT-R/PM might be able to answer questions about user behavior with multimedia applications, but they depend on preprocessing of complex multisensory input. The cognitive architecture has to be supplied with a list of objects attributed with perceptual properties to represent a computer display. The motivation to invest preprocessing effort will depend on the perceived payback in answering industrial-scale design questions. More effort may be expended in modeling the user than is justified by the benefits gained in predicting the affordances that should be designed.

Barnard has argued for families of theoretical models that address different aspects of users' cognition and interactive system designs with a means of exchanging knowledge between different theories and models. Modelers from cognitive, artificial intelligence, and software engineering backgrounds can contribute solutions to design prob lems from different perspectives using design rationale to summarize design issues and modeling recommendations; however, this study did not show how knowledge could be exchanged between models from separate academic traditions, although some progress has been made on linking cognitive and software engineering models. Unfortunately, design rationale has little to offer in organizing the semantics of knowledge exchange, so more rigorous definitions of HCI issues and arguments are required to create a lingua franca for designers and researchers. Barnard and May provided a partial answer in Transition Path Diagrams (TPDs), which are derived from running a computational cognitive theory (Barnard's ICS augmented with task or domain knowledge to create a Cognitive Task Model; CTM). TPDs represent snapshots of the user's mental model during interaction with a specific design created by a CTM analysis; however, understanding the design recommendations from TPDs still requires understanding the CTM analysis in some depth. In an attempt to escape from the trap of small-scope applications, this chapter follows Barnard's called for families of theories that address UI design, either by contributing to different aspects of the problem, or by connecting detailed cognitive mechanisms to more broadly-scoped models of interaction. The theory builds on an intermediate-level model of cognition proposed by Norman, and links this model to Barnard's Interacting Cognitive Subsystems. The following models are based on collaborative research with my graduate students who investigated cognitive resources for multimedia interaction and a theory of interaction in VEs. The models have been revised and extended in light of validation experiments and improved in subsequent research.

Modeling Multisensory Interaction

The theory of interaction predicts the resources the user will require and the features the design should contribute to enable successful interaction. Three components constitute the theory:

- A set of cognitive resources that the user contributes in solving the problem of interaction.
- A set of design features that the design should ideally contribute to facilitate solving the user's problem of interaction.
- A model of interaction that predicts the user's resources and design features that are necessary at each stage of interaction.

They facilitate design decisions by first indicating the design features that should be present for a usable interface, and suggest trade-offs between user abilities and design requirements, so that designs can be tailored for particular user requirements.

Models of Multimedia Interaction

I begin with multimedia to present a simplified model before progressing to the more complex theory that addresses VR and all multisensory interfaces. The action side of the model is not significantly different from Norman's original model that was extended to cover GUI interaction by adding a stage for locating appropriate controls and functions. However, because multimedia are frequently informationintensive systems, interaction can be interpreted from two viewpoints:

- Information retrieval in which the users' actions are primarily directed toward navigation and browsing through an information space.
- General task-directed interaction that is similar to other UIs.

At the start of the cycle, the user's resources are task and domain knowledge; the system features are clear metaphors for suggesting actions, followed by comprehensible prompts, cues, and icons for action specification. Information intensive multimedia systems make considerable demands on navigation so system features are required to represent a clear structure of the information content, possibly as a visual map. Navigation pathways are necessary to indicate where the user might locate the information he or she needs, with hints and prompts along the way, following the concepts of information scent proposed by. Other navigation support features are familiar in many interfaces, for example, waymarks (bookmarks in Web browsers). Controls such as the video player metaphor of fast forward, stop, and play help navigating in dynamic media streams; zoom, pan, and scroll controls support exploration in static media. Action execution requires that controls are easy to operate and within the normal human bounds of motor precision.

On the feedback side of the cycle, the picture is more complex. There are two possible contexts:

- Navigation and control Interpreting the effects of action.
- Information assimilation Interpreting the information supplied by the system as a consequence of user requests.

Navigation and control actions involve recognizing and interpreting the effect of action on objects and evaluating change in the context of the user's task. Interpretation and evaluation depend on the user's knowledge of the navigable space and how well the system indicates the user's location therein, for example, current position. When interpreting information feed' back, the user contributes domain and task knowledge to understand the perceived content, but the design needs to support the limitations in user attention or assimilating information, prevent working memory overload, and promote comprehension and learning. At the "recognize feedback" stage, the design should first ensure the user can perceive the feedback in an appropriate medium; for example, audio feedback cannot be heard in a noisy environment. Then the design should draw the user's attention to key facts and items within the content. Selective attention can be directed by judicious use of highlighting and emphasis in different media. At the next stage, information on different media streams has to be integrated to enable interpretation at the propositional level. The design should direct users' attention by making the reading and viewing sequence apparent so that users can recognize thematic links between different media. This is effected by highlighting and attention-directing effects between media to form contact points. Media integration also requires the design to deliver messages on appropriate media so that comprehension is efficient. Media selection and combination guidelines play a role at this stage. Finally, when the integrated message is evaluated in context, the role of content design becomes critical. The script and selection of content should be matched with the user's existing task and domain knowledge so that he or she incrementally builds up memory schema. In training and educational applications, this is often termed scaffolding. The new content fits into a topic or theme that the user already knows so he or she can incrementally develop his or her memory schema.

Multimedia Conversations

Our reaction to multimedia usually treats the content of presentation as information; however, when speech and images of people are used, something strange happens. We treat the computer as a person rather than a machine. This has been known ever since Eliza fooled people into talking to a computer as if it were a person. It appears that we context switch from receiving information and acting in the world to conversational interaction with another person, although we are still clearly communicating with a computer. The psychological reasons for this context switch are not well-understood; however, empirical evidence demonstrates we are very suggestible, so if a machine speaks to us we automatically grant it human-like status. Speech seems to be the most powerful trigger, so when we design multimedia with speech output and human image, the natural laws of dialogue have to be respected. There are still many interesting research questions about how robust this effect is; for example, the illusion of conversation rapidly disappears when the machine makes an error, and most of us are only too aware of voice-mediated telephone menu systems. Nevertheless, Reeves and Nass's experiments have demonstrated that people attribute computers with human properties although they will report that they deny consciously doing so. This has some important consequences for design.

This model approximates closely to human-human conversation. Indeed, if speech recognition and natural language generation or speech synthesis are available, in theory there should be no difference between human-human and human-computer conversation. In the current reality, natural language understanding and speech synthesis systems are far from perfect, although quality is improving. When encountering a multimedia UI, our reaction is governed by an automatic mode or context switch. Three decisions are possible:

- The other agent is clearly inanimate and we therefore treat it as a machine. Conventional user-system interaction with GUIs and most multimedia fall into this category.
- The agent has a human-like appearance (i.e., photograph or mannequin) and is manipulating objects, so we observe the agent acting and reason about any implications. This mode is dealt with in the section on VR.
- The agent communicates by speech and/or has a human-like presence for gesture-based communication. This switches us into conversation mode.

When speech or natural language output is received, we enter conversational mode and treat the other agent as a surrogate person. The laws of human dialogue apply and we expect a polite conversation following Grice's maxims.

First, we have to understand the speech output, possibly accompanied by gesture and nonverbal communication such as facial expressions. The next step, interpreting meaning, takes us into the semantics and pragmatics of natural language processing. First, we interpret meaning using linguistic, semantic knowledge, and then that meaning is refined with knowledge of the conversational context. This pragmatic knowledge consists of our awareness of whom we are conversing with, any previous history of interaction with that person, and the conversational setting and time that it is taking place. Thus, we interpret a reply to our question "How do I get to the railway station?" with knowledge about where we are (the starting point), what we can see (navigation cues), the time (how long it will take us to get to the station), and our assumptions about the person we asked. We will probably trust the reply of a friend more than that from a complete stranger. Conversational interaction is governed by pragmatic knowledge of the context, a shared common ground of understanding, and assumptions about a cooperative purpose. Conversations are built up by developing a shared common ground of understanding between the two parties. Dialogue progresses toward a common goal by an action ladder of stating propositions, explaining and clarifying the proposal, and leading to agreeing action. The design problem is how to communicate shared intent and how the system can understand the human user's goals. This is a difficult problem for artificial intelligence to solve, but it can be finessed by restricting the dialogue to a known domain.

When we plan our response, we employ pragmatic knowledge, and then articulate our response in language or action. If the system has natural language processing capabilities, it has the same problem of interpreting our utterance in context. This takes considerable common sense and specialized domain knowledge. Not surprisingly, machine capabilities for true multimodal communication are limited to narrow, domain'specific sublanguages where the interpretation problem is tractable.

In multimedia, we have an increasing ability to personalize computer conversations. This can be implemented in several ways. Video can show a person speaking to the user; a synthesized image or avatar can represent human presence with facial expressions and gestures; or speech may be used to talk to the user. To hold a real person's attention, we have to be polite, interesting, and helpful. Computers that adopt human properties are going to have to follow the rules of polite conversation. When we address another person, we look at them to make eye contact. Averting the gaze signals attention to another task and breaking off a conversation. At the beginning of an exchange, we show interest and give a subconscious greeting by raising eyebrows. Verbal greetings when we meet people and take our leave (hellos and goodbyes) should also follow the conventions of politeness. The content of speech can dramatically effect how we react to the content; for instance, praise from a computer will make us more favorably disposed to a following suggestion. Finally, we need to note that context switching is related to multitasking. From skill-based learning, we know that people can switch contexts rapidly when multitasking; swapping between conversing with a passenger while driving a car is a case in point. This review of multimedia interaction leads into the next stage where we consider multisensory interaction theory in more depth. First, the set of cognitive resources supplied by the user are described in more depth.

Cognitive Resources

These are divided into a set of knowledge structures the user should possess and a set of more general resources in which demands are made on interaction. The latter are better considered as limitations of human information processing that may lead to mistakes and errors if the design does not take them into account. Some cognitive resources are general requirements for interaction so they are not strongly associated with any particular interaction stage or context; however, other user knowledge resources can be associated with interactive contexts. Knowledge structures are memories employed by the user to solve the problem of interaction. Naturally, these will change with experience as the user becomes familiar with the system; furthermore, each knowledge structure will improve incrementally with experience. However, even experienced users may have partial models of some parts of a system so knowledge structures are rarely perfect. For design purposes, a stereotype simplification has to be assumed with novices possessing minimal knowledge and experts having richly developed memories. Knowledge structures are classified as follows:

- Task knowledge is composed of plans, procedures, and actions. A good description of task knowledge can be found in Johnson's Task Knowledge Structures. Briefly, tasks are composed of goals organized in a hierarchy. Upper-level goals form the task plan. Lower-level subgoals are decomposed into procedures that are in turn composed of actions organized in sequences with control constructs of alternatives (if-then-else) and iteration (do-while).

  Task knowledge is generally assumed to be well-developed in expert users, and represents the skill they bring to operating the system. Learning how to operate a system and to adapt to the design is a critical aspect of learning a new system. Task knowledge should integrate with device knowledge, so learning to use a system flows naturally as an extension of the known task.

- Domain knowledge is composed of objects organized in class hierarchies, with attributes describing objects and relations. Domain knowledge structures complement task knowledge as actions change the state of objects; however, domain knowledge will also include the user's spatial and episodic memory, as well as more abstract knowledge of the domain in categories and semantic networks. Novices (in device knowledge) may bring good domain knowledge to interaction, which the design should exploit by appropriate metaphors and representations of the domain in VEs.
- Device knowledge represents the knowledge the user has accumulated about the system. This, initially, will be nil or minimal, but increases as users learn the system. Device knowledge has the same components as task and domain knowledge: procedures, actions, objects, and so forth; indeed, it is an extension of both task and domain knowledge. When users learn to operate a new system, they extend their task knowledge to include procedures for operating the UI controls. In a perfectly designed VE, interaction would require no extension of task knowledge; the user just operates the virtual tool as a real-world one. Unfortunately, that is rarely the case in practice, and the designer's job is to minimize the amount of learning imposed on users. Although users will have little initial device knowledge, it is rarely nil. Most people transfer their experience of previous systems to a new UI. Unfortunately, we have adapted to certain styles of GUI interaction (e.g., menus, palettes, etc.) that may not transfer so well to multisensory UIs, so device knowledge may cause learning interference effects.
- Status knowledge is knowledge of the current state of interaction, so unlike the previous knowledge structures that are retrieved from long-term memory, status knowledge is held in working memory. It describes the user's current model of interaction and the interactive world, and where he or she is within it, and may be viewed as the subsets of task, domain,

and device knowledge recruited to working memory at a point in interaction.

- Motor skills coordinate precise action with multisensory feedback. Ideally, real-world skills should transfer into virtual worlds; however, lack of haptic feedback means that manipulation skills have to be relearned. Motor skills are an extension of device knowledge.

The system design should encourage the development of device knowledge, easy maintenance, and update of status knowledge. Design has a paradoxical role; on one hand, device knowledge needs to be mini' mized so that the computer becomes invisible, but on the other hand, technology may change the way we work for the better, in which case the design has to be explicit and help the user learn new actions and procedures. In tutorial applications, the design'actually needs to impart domain and task knowledge to the user. In this case, although the device knowledge should be easy to learn, the role of the design may need to make learning effortful to be effective, because active problem solving helps depth of encoding. The second set of resources are the general cognitive facilities required by the user during interaction. These are subdivided into perceptual resources for receiving input, cognitive resources that will utilize knowledge structures in memory, and action resources necessary for the user to act on the world or communicate with others. Cognitive theories like ICS can be interrogated as "tools for thought" with different scenarios or snapshots of interaction to determine which subset of the following list of cognitive resources will be necessary. The appropriate component of the ICS model with the resources is given in parentheses and are identified as follows (the first list consists of perceptual resources, the second list consists of cognitive resources, and the third list consists of action resources):

- Vision The ability not only to recognize but also interpret the image (Vis, Obj).
- Audio Hearing and sound interpretation (Aud).
- Speech recognition (Morph).
- Tactile ability to detect properties of surfaces and temperature (BS).
- Proprioceptive sense of balance and muscle tone for posture (BS).

- Selective attention The automatic control of perceptual resources between competing stimuli.
- Working memory to hold status knowledge and subsets of task, domain, and device knowledge.
- Language processing ability to understand the content of spoken or written language (Prop).
- Comprehension to interpret change in visual and other sensory inputs and make sense of the integrated input (Obj, Prop).
- Problem-solving abilities Understanding the causation of perceived events and reasoning (Implic).
- Panning The ability to organize and rehearse future action and communication (Implic).
- Attention and concentration The ability to continue problem solving and learning how to interact without becoming distracted or giving up.
- Motivation Internal volition which underlies attention and concentration.
- Planning movement in detail (Implic, Prop).
- Locomotion The ability to move (Lim).
- Manipulation of objects grip, hand, and limb movements (Lim).
- Speech generation (Artie).
- Gesture A generation of gestures with head, arms, and body, including facial expressions (motor).

The combination of resources used will depend on the user's experience and level of knowledge. Experienced users need a combination of perceptual and action resources but they do not have to exercise conscious control over them because they run as precompiled skills. In contrast, novice users have to actively analyze perceptual input and control motor output at a higher knowledgeor rule-based level. This requires more cognitive processor resource at the implication and prepositional level, which makes interaction slower and more error prone. This is taken from a tutorial sequence that explains how cancer cells divide and invade other tissues. The design aims to increase the user's domain knowledge about human biology by giving a causal explanation. The cognitive resources (using ICS subsystems) are understanding the image (Vis>Obj>Prop), making sense of the speech track that accompanies it (AudA>Morph>Prop), and then integrating the message on both modalities (Prop>Implic). At the basic resource level, the design does not seem to present any problems; however, when the role of attention is considered, a potential problem arises. First, animation is used selectively for some parts of the explanation. The sequence should have transferred the following domain knowledge:

- Cancer cells multiply in the epidermis (skin).
- Cancer cells invade the body by chemically attacking the basal lamina and entering blood vessels.
- Cancer cells are transported through the vascular system.
- Cancer cells invade the liver and other tissues by dissolving cell walls.

Animation focuses the user's attention on the movement part of the explanation (cells invade liver via blood vessels) to the detriment of other key facts (chemical attack) that appear only in the speech track. Hence, the (Prop>Implic) cycle will be unlikely to integrate all the information that was presented. The concept that cancer cells invade by chemical attack is less likely to be learned. Besides the role of attention, the use of visual and audio (speech) media will reinforce the explanation of cell movement because two media streams come together with a single proposition for the movement sequence (skin>blood ves selsmother organs). The user's mental model of the explanation is not constructed effectively because the necessary background information is not given to describe how the cancer cells invade other organs. A more effective strategy would have been to establish the cancer cells' means of attack first (by chemical assault on other cells) and then build the explanation while visually cross-referencing where the attacks take place (on the basal lamina, blood cell walls, and liver membrane). One may argue that this omission was a failing in content selection or pedagogical design by the authors, and indeed that may be true. However, the point of modeling is to make that omission explicit.

In the gulf of execution parts of the Norman cycle (Plan-SpecifyExecute), the ICS processes transform plans as implications to propositions and then to limb and detailed motor actions. In the gulf of evaluation side (Recognize to Evaluate), sensory input is transformed in the opposite direction from multisensory input into propositions and implications. Sensory and motor skill resources are needed in the Execute and Recognize stages; long-term and working memory are necessary for other stages. Attention is a necessary resource throughout the cycle; however, it is more critical in the Specify-Execute-Recognize-Interpret stages where slips and lapse errors result from attentional failure.

The user has to find out how to alter the position of the drawing board. In reality, there are several controls that change angle and tilt, but in VR, only one is active so the user receives inconsistent feedback from trying affordances. Thus, the user's domain knowledge does not transfer to the virtual world device knowledge. Because the rule that a device which suggests action (an affordance) will respond to manipulation is not generally applicable, either the user has to substitute the impaired domain knowledge by testing all or possibly some interactive objects, or the design should indicate which objects are active by visual cues. Imposing the sampling load on the user overloads working memory and attention resources. First, working memory is strained by the need to remember which objects should be and have been sampled; this distracts attention from the user's task, and hinders planning. Memorizing which specific objects are active does not allow any general rule to be learned, so the user's device knowledge will only increase slowly. Learning interaction by a few general rules is easy, whereas devices with many specialized rules impose a worse memory burden, as demonstrated by TAG.

Even if the system did signal that the object was active, when manipulation was attempted the lack of haptic feedback would create two contradictory input channels: (Vis>Obj>Prop) indicates an affordance for action whereas (BS>Prop) does not give a sense of touching a handle because no tactile feedback is built into the system; hence the user is forced into concentrating on visual control of manipulation. This shows how the user's resources and knowledge structures can be integrated with the ICS model to analyze potential usability problems; however, we can refine this analysis by considering models of interaction.

Interaction Models

The model is composed of three cycles or submodels. The most important cycle is task'based activity, when the user is trying to achieve a goal. Subordinate to this cycle is navigation and exploration, when the user's intention is simply to find his or her way around the VE. In some cases, exploration may become a task goal in its own right. We distinguish between goal-directed exploration and serendipitous browsing in which the user's goal is not clearly formed. The third cycle describes system initiative when the user's role is to interpret actions taken by the system and respond to them when initiative is returned, or interrupt and seize initiative from the system if necessary. System initiative may be a manifestation of action by other users represented as avatars in collaborative VEs; and multiparty interaction in shared virtual worlds. The models describe behavior during normal interaction. Errors occur when the necessary cognitive and system resources are not present at any particular stage of interaction. Errors introduce a behavior subcycle of error recognition, diagnosis, and remediation that may occur at any stage when users make mistakes.

Task-Action Model

The task-action cycle is driven by the goals in the user's task model. There are two loops: an outer one which starts with goal formation from which the user forms an intention to achieve a task goal or subgoal and retrieves the appropriate procedure from memory; and an inner one that runs through each action in the procedure. Procedures are scripts of actions that achieve the task goal, so the user will commence interaction with an intention to carry out the first action in the procedure. The first step is to scan the immediate environment for any affordances for action. Affordances are any design feature that matches the user's intention and suggests how to act; for instance, a handle on a coffee cup indicates that it can be picked up. If the objects necessary for the first task-action are not visible, then the user has to search the environment for them. This leads into the navigation subcycle and exploration until the necessary objects are found or the user gives up. The next step is to specify action. How an action is specified depends on the modality choice available to the user. Modality selection depends on the ease with which the modality or device matches the user's goal. Speech may be efficient for commands and invoking automated procedures, but for movement and precise manipulation, physical interaction will be necessary. Modality choice may also be influenced by habit. We are used to interacting physically with computers, so swapping to speech can be inhibited unless users are trained to use speech in particular circumstances.

Assuming that manipulation has been chosen and a familiar part of the VE is found with the necessary objects, then the user has to locate the objects, approach, and orient his or her self-representation in the correct position for interaction. This may invoke movement for the preparatory action. With simple shapes and large objects in an uncluttered environment, this step may not be necessary. For traditional GUI features, the action specification step is simplified to finding the appropriate control or UI feature that triggers an action.

Specifying action is followed by executing action. Actions may be simple controls, manipulating objects in virtual worlds, or operating virtual tools. Actions that involve movement to a target become progressively more difficult as the size and proximity of the target decrease. This relation is expressed in Pitt's Law. Actions are followed by feedback from the environment, or the effects of tools on the environment. In continuous actions, manipulation and feedback are interleaved as the user may adjust action in light of feedback. First, the user must receive and recognize the feedback and then interpret the change. Problems may arise if the change is not immediately perceivable; for example, feedback may be given in an inappropriate modality or in a location not expected by the user. Interpreting and evaluating change involves making sense of the perceived input (ICS prepositional and implicational level). Once an action is complete, the user may continue to the next specify-action by loading the next action from procedural memory. However, if interaction has caused change in the VE that obscured the necessary objects, then the user may have to search for affordances, reorient, and approach again. Alternatively, if the end of a procedure has been reached, then the user proceeds to the next task goal and the cycle resumes.

Specification of action may be determined by retrieving task procedures from memory or by problem solving in response to the environment. Action specification is shaped by what is available via display-based cognition, in which the user's perceptions of affordances shape action. Hence, the task model stage is not completely sequential: location, intention, and action specification may overlap. The main connotation of the procedure-driven versus display-based cognition is that the VE needs to shape intention and action more directly. Because there is considerable evidence that users specify action using environment cues, by following menu cues and graphical icons, display-based interaction is likely to be the dominant mode in VEs.

Pathways through the model will change with experience. Novice users will progress through each stage under conscious (knowledge-based processing) control. This will invoke longer resource cycles in the ICS model chaining from the top implication level to action and back up to implication as feedback is interpreted. The chain of processing for novices and experts with shortcuts in the task-action model.

Skilled knowledge short circuits the cycle between interpret change and specify action. The user simply checks that the effect of action conforms to the expectation of the procedure (see script and procedural memory) and then continues with the next action In highly skilled procedures, action may become an unconscious activity that loops between recognize feedback and execute action. The disadvantage of skill is that slip errors can occur. When the user is familiar with the device, procedural memory has been laid down that specifies the necessary action, so simple memory-fetches shortcut the need for implicational processing. Once the task commences in response to an event trigger, the appropriate rules and procedures are retrieved from memory. The degree of automation will depend on the detail of the user's procedural memory. In a perfect case, the user memory contains the location of actions and their specification, thus leading directly to execution.

However, if some aspect of the environment does not accord with memory (e.g., an object has been moved), then conscious rule-based processing intervenes for approach and orient. Similarly, skilled action may relegate feedback recognition to an automatic process so that interpretation and evaluation are not necessary. Unfortunately, although skilled operation is cognitively efficient, it can easily lead to errors from slips in attention or failure to recognize unexpected feedback.

System Initiative Model

Reacting to events and behavior of other agents in VEs, or when the system takes control, is described in the system initiative cycle. The importance of reactive behavior was highlighted by Suchman, who made the case for considering most user behavior as reactive or situated action; however, the proportion of reactive behavior depends on the task and application. In some domains, planning and task-driven interaction will be the norm; in others (e.g., games), situated action will predominate. Reactive or opportunistic behavior may either require reasoning at the knowledge-based level if the stimulus and its context are unfamiliar; or, if it has been encountered before, a preplanned automatic response can be triggered.

System initiative may occur at any stage in task-action when an event interrupts the user's action. If the system initiative is communicated by speech, or action involves human-like presences in the virtual world, then we will switch into conversational mode. In conversational systems this cycle may become the dominant mode of interaction as the user monitors the behavior of other agents (or their avatars) and then responds to their messages. Behavior in this subcycle reverses the task-action cycle. First, change is observed, evaluated and interpreted, and then action is planned in response. Planning may involve deciding what to do by reasoning at the knowledge level if the situation is unfamiliar or retrieving procedures from memory and running these precompiled responses. The user may allow the system to retain the initiative until the action sequence terminates, or to interrupt. In the former case, the observe-interpret loop continues until the system action ceases, when the user plans a response and carries it out. If the user decides to interrupt and regain the initiative, action is specified and executed, and the subsequent effects will be recognized and evaluated to determine success. Action may then transfer back to the task-action cycle; however, in groupware applications, interaction will continue as an interlinked set of conversational turns between different users, each taking the system initiative. Expert behavior depends on possessing memory of the triggering stimulus and the appropriate response, whereas novices have first to analyze the implication of the system's behavior and then actively plan a response.

Exploration and Navigation

System exploration is frequently embedded within task-action or system initiative cycles when the user needs to find information or discover parts of the interactive world. Exploration has two main modes. In serendipitous exploration, the user has no specific goal in mind, so interaction is composed of a series of scan environmentA>specify direction >navigate>recognize and interpret change loops. If interesting objects or information are encountered, these may be memorized for subsequent use or explored further by manipulation, which is modeled as goal-directed exploration. The main difference between goal-directed and serendipitous exploration lies in the interpretation and evaluation part of the cycle.

In goal-directed exploration, the user decides what to find and then forms a plan about how to find it. If the environment affords no clues about where to look for the search target, the user may resort to guesswork. Interaction proceeds by a loop of scan>navigate>interpret; the interpretation is whether the user has found, or is closer to, his or her goal. Serendipitous exploration follows the same cycle but omits planning as the user follows cues that look interesting. Interpretation may be cursory if the new location does not evoke interest; however, if it is does, then further exploration cycles may be invoked. The dividing line between goal-directed and serendipitous exploration is finally one of degree. Hints of interest encountered during browsing may lead to goal-directed navigation; locating a target object may stimulate exploration of its immediate environment. Exploration reverts to the task-action cycle when the appropriate part of the environment is found and evaluated to be relevant. In some applications, goal-directed exploration is the main user task, so interaction may reside primarily within this subcycle.

Novice-expert differences are reflected in different pathways through this cycle. Complete expertise is interpreted as the user knowing the desired location and going directly to it; for example, direct access facilities help expert users by navigating directly to an address. Other interpretations of partial expertise range from some knowledge of the search environment, so that the user does not need to form a plan or scan the environment for cues, to knowledge of search strategies but with little knowledge of the environment. This case is closer to novice behaviors where navigation becomes a conscious planned process. The models of interaction are general descriptions of how user action should occur for a novice user. With expert users, stages in the cycle will become increasingly automated and unconscious, so navigation becomes a closely coupled loop of action interleaved with feedback.

Context Switching

The theory proposes that we act and react in virtual worlds in different modes. The link between these modes will not be consciously recognized, so if users are asked to think aloud while interacting in VEs, they are unlikely to report any perceived change between navigating and task action. Nevertheless, modes have powerful effects on how we act. This is because we load different goals and knowledge into working memory when we make the transition across a mode boundary.

The first mode switch is between immersed and nonimmersed interaction. This is not dealt with explicitly in the models because it is a property of display. Immersive interaction with head mounted displays or CAVE technology fills our peripheral vision with the virtual world. We are less aware of the computer and its interface, hence the virtual world becomes the context for interaction. In contrast, desktop VR presents us with two contexts, one virtual world displayed by the computer and the external world. Our sense of presence is reduced and the illusion of acting in the virtual world is not so powerful.

The second mode switch is between conversational and traditional interaction. Transitions across this boundary are mediated by speech and display of human image. This mode has a powerful effect on our interpretation of the information communicated by the other party. When conversation is generated by people and mediated by computers, as in chat rooms, MUDS, MOOs (multiuser dungeons, multiuser object oriented systems) and virtual world implementations thereof, the interface should become invisible because interaction is governed by the laws of human discourse. When faced with speaking avatars, we react according to our expectations of humanhuman discourse and treat the avatar as a person, irrespective of whether it is visibly a computer agent. This mode exerts a powerful effect because we load very different assumptions into working memory when we converse as opposed to when we act.

The boundary between exploration and task-action is rarely noticed, as we often have to investigate objects and explore virtual worlds to achieve task goals. Although we can switch rapidly between these modes, there is still a cognitive effort in context switching while we refocus attention on task goals in working memory. The switch between task-exploration and reactive mode is more dramatic and noticeable. This is because the flow of reasoning is reversed. In task-action and explore mode we are engaged in a plan-act-interpret cycle (Implic>Prop>Lim>motor in ICS terms); whereas in reactive mode, the flow is switched to interpret-plan-react (ObjA>MorphA>Prop>Implic>Prop>Lim). Sometimes when we are deeply engaged in a task or exploration, we fail to notice messages and don't make the appropriate switch to reactive mode.

Design Features

UI design features are the third component of the theory. Because these change as technology advances, generalized usability requirements are specified. These are called GDPs: Generalized Design Properties, which can be mapped to more concrete design components that implement them. To effect this mapping, the knowledge representation schema of claims analysis and the task-artifact theory may be used.

GDPs are organized into groups motivated by general design issues in VR and multimedia, and usability support requirements implied in the interaction models. The first and second groups record general usability requirements. The third group involves supporting action planning and specification, and facilitates user navigation in its various forms. The fourth group supports execution of action and interpreting feedback, and the final group supports reactive behavior. The GDPs selected for an application depend on the communication modality, user's knowledge, task, and the naturalness constraints imposed by the domain. For example, in multimedia systems, facilities for navigating through complex information structures are necessary and these may be manifest as maps, metaphors, and visualizations of classification structures. In contrast, for a VR training application, a realistic representation of the domain will be necessary so that the user can encounter all aspects of the system although some features may not be easy to learn. In many VR applications, the need for natural representation may override adding artificial features that could improve usability (e.g., wayfinding maps). Appendix B describes GDPs with correspondence rules linking them to appropriate stages in each cycle.

Design features put in place the third component of the theory. The next step is to integrate the models, cognitive resources, and design features to produce a model of design requirements for normal interaction, and then to explore errors that result from any departures from the normative model.

Integrating Resources and Action

Knowledge sources, design features, and user behavior are integrated by rules that predict the requirements for successful interaction. The theory balances the cognitive resources possessed by the users with the facilities that should be supplied by the system. Some cognitive resources are general throughout interaction (such as working memory limitations); however, knowledge resources change. Users start as novices with little device knowledge but become experts with comprehensive device knowledge. As users learn the system, their needs for support change. To deal with the problem of adaptivity, the theory adopts the stereotype solution of proposing two rule sets, one for novices and one for experts.

Experts will share some system features with novices but new ones will be necessary such as power effects, and ability to change and customize interaction. Rules are instantiated to predict novice requirements for more supportive and error-preventing design features; in contrast, experts require more powerful features with less support. Departures from the expected expert (or novice) profile will result in a usability problem, and this theme is taken up in the "Error Diagnosis and Recovery" section. The current section deals with normal interaction. Application of GDPs has to be judged in light of HCI principles; for instance, in VEs the naturalness principle overrides GDPs that recommend system initiative to help the user. Indeed, there is a more general trade-off between helping the user by representation, metaphor, and affordances, in contrast to system initiative, wizards, and assistive agents. GDPs do not apply exclusively to a single stage, but may be inherited by subsequent stages. For instance, GDPs that support goal formation will usually be relevant to the locate command-function stage, and possibly to the action specification stage. The rules recommend when GDPs should be deployed during the interaction cycle; however, when they are removed depends on the designer's judgment. In most designs, GDPs in the goal to action side of the cycle (i.e., gulf of execution) will be replaced by a different set for feedback in the gulf of evaluation.

GDPs specify the requirements for usability. In some cases they recommend specific design features, but more usually the general requirements have to be interpreted by the designer in the context of the application. Each rule indicates one or more GDPs so the designer still has to interpret the theory's predictions in light of the task and domain requirements. For instance, one filter is to eliminate GDPs that recommend intrusive design features, when naturalness of the VE is required by the task. Another limitation on GDPs is the ability to analyze the user's task and intentions accurately. If the user's intentions cannot be captured, then plan-related or system initiative GDPs cannot be deployed. Listing rules can make for laborious reading, so the working of the model will be illustrated by two scenario walkthroughs: one for a multimedia system and one for a VE.

Multimedia Interaction

Interaction with multimedia systems is simpler in terms of action but involves complex navigation and evaluation. The user's task is to make a reservation to see a play by Shakespeare, so the application involves information searching and then transaction processing to make a booking.

At the planning stage, the user has to decide how to search for a play. The user has good domain knowledge about Shakespeare's plays and knows what he or she wants. Task knowledge for searching and making a booking is not complex and can be considered to be complete. However, because we assume a novice user, device knowledge will be low. The system should provide one or more of the goal formation GDPs, such as task-related cues and feature hints. The system gives two options, search by browsing a time line of what is coming in the next few months, or search the theater's catalogue for current and future productions. Appropriate commands are listed in a top-level menu so that interaction can proceed.

The user has to locate the play he or she wants, and the interface needs to provide GDPs to help the user locate the appropriate search function. This is supported by GDPs (clear prompts, information scent) that recommend search facilities to find information, as well as browsing along a time line display that adopts an appropriate metaphor for the underlying information. This gets the user to the decide direction stage. The user decides to select a play from the time line, which supports the action specification, followed by action-execution stages. The system highlights the play and the duration of its run (recognize and interpret the feedback stages) and provides highlighting and feedback GDPs to implement perceivable effects of change, and structures the plays in a time line schedule to ensure that changes match task and domain knowledge.

The user progresses to the next goal in his or her task, making a booking. The first subgoal is to establish the prices and availability of seats. The system supports this by a menu option (GDP feature hints) that the user selects; this leads to display of a seating plan (GDP appropriate media for the message) highlighting the available seats according to the selected date (GDP direct attention to key information). The user chooses a date, then selects a seat leading to a system response of displaying the price but also showing the viewpoint of the stage from that location (GDP augmented viewpoints). The user selects the seat and the dialogue continues with payment and confirmation of the booking; these steps are dealt with by a standard form-filling dialogue that will not be described further.

Virtual Reality Walkthrough

The application is an exploratory VR that demonstrates the facilities of buildings in a business park; however, embedded within the exploration are discrete tasks where the user has to operate virtual equipment to assess its suitability.

Task-Action Cycle. The user's task in this case is to operate a virtual drawing board in an architect's office. The links between action-cycle stages, user knowledge with index numbers that point to the more detailed description.

This cycle commences with retrieving the appropriate procedure from memory for the current task goal. Two problems may arise at this stage: user memory failure or inadequate task knowledge. This can be alleviated by GDPs for task maps that provide a browsable aide-memoire or a searchable task list. In the next step, form intention, the user loads a goal into working memory to execute the procedure. This could be supported by a status indicator to remind the user which subgoal is currently active. In the next stage, the user needs device knowledge to locate the control. To help the user, GDPs are suggested for clear structure, consistent layout, and meaningful labels, familiar advice from HCI guidelines; however, system initiative may also be deployed to actively suggest appropriate controls for the user's current task goal or to initiate the appropriate tool. However, the application demands naturalness because the user is assessing the usability of a real design in a VE, so no GDPs are added beyond natural representation of the domain.

Action specification involves detailed planning about how to act, and draws on the user's device knowledge. GDPs are for clear operational metaphors and perceivable affordances. Design of affordances depends on mapping from past experience and features that suggest specific actions (e.g., door handles that indicate push rather than pull; tool grips that suggest twisting operations). At this stage, if power tools are available they need to be explained to the user because such effects cannot be predicted from task-domain knowledge. In VR applications, preparatory actions may be necessary to approach and orient the user's self-representation into a position to operate a control. GDPs in this stage are for accessible controls and snap-to effects to help orientation without haptic feedback. Execution of action should be supported by visible controls that do not make above average demands on human sensio-motor coordination. The effect of action should be signaled by precise feedback and mapped to the physical forces expended, for example, visual feedback for contact and force; the demands of naturalness may inhibit adding these GDPs to the design. Only one control is active to tilt the table and this is not clearly indicated; other control features are located underneath the table and are hard to access. The design, therefore, does not supply GDPs clear affordances and consistent controls.

To recognize and interpret feedback, users need domain knowledge. The GDPs recommend locatable and perceivable feedback. This may be a problem when the effect takes place in a remote part of the virtual world, where the user is unaware of it. In these circumstances, active notification by speech or audio may be necessary. The locus of objects that have changed should be portrayed in sufficient detail to allow the change to be interpreted and feedback messages should be meaningful. The evaluation of change relies on the user's task and domain knowledge; however, deficiencies may be remedied by active explanation of changes and facilities so that before and after effects can be compared. The final stage of determining whether the task is complete can be helped by the aide-memoire status indicators, and then the cycle continues if more actions and goals are present. Changes in the position of the drawing table reflect manipulations in the real world but without any haptic feedback to represent the force exerted on the surface. The GDP modal substitution recommends use of visual feedback to signal touch and force. In the real application, usability errors were observed because this GDP design feature was absent.

Navigation-Exploration Cycle

In this example, the user's goal is to explore the buildings in the virtual world and test electrical equipment contained within the building. The task is goal-directed navigation, so the first step is to select the navigation strategy. The user has little domain knowledge of the buildings and their layout, or necessary task knowledge for operating switches. Task knowledge for searching is assumed, e.g., sampling strategies, random search, and so forth. The sequence of navigation cycle stages, user knowledge. The GDPs that the system should provide at the select navigation strategy stage follow:

- Clear metaphor and system structure.
- Guided tours.
- Overview map.
- Reusable searches.
- Explanation of the navigation controls.

In this case, the virtual world is based on the real world, so the first and third GDPs do not apply. If the representation of the building is a reasonably faithful rendering of the real world, then navigation strategy selection can rely on the user's task knowledge; e.g., search each building systematically, random sample, and so forth. Note that if the user's knowledge is deficient, then system initiative GDPs may be deployed to compensate. For instance, the system could propose strategies for navigation, or take the user on a guided tour, or provide reusable histories of previous searches. A systematic search is adopted to visit each building in turn.

The next stage, scan environment, only requires that the VE is visible and has sufficient detail to be discriminable. The ability to change the user's viewpoint could help scanning. This is followed by select cue that should be implemented by highlighting appropriate cues, landmarks, and indications of pathways. If the user's knowledge is poor, the interface can compensate with directions to the search targets depicted as highlighted pathways and landmarks, but this assumes that the user's knowledge of the domain can be captured beforehand. The naturalness compromise and lack of knowledge about the user's intentions inhibits explicit design of these features for this application. Decide direction is based on the user's perception and interpretation of cues with domain knowledge. GDPs in this stage recommend indication at the current location as well as pathways and landmarks for course setting. In this case, commonsense knowledge of doors indicates the direction and pathway for entering the building and rooms within it. At the specify navigation action stage, the user changes from domain to device knowledge. The user has to translate the desired direction and speed into action using the available navigation devices. These may be gestures with a virtual hand, operating controls on a 3D mouse, or selecting a hypertext link. Execute movement will follow, assuming that the control is visible, easy to use, and gives precise control.

Once motion is underway, it needs to be tuned with feedback to adjust course and speed until the destination is reached. Movement, recognizing, and interpreting change in location become a closely coupled loop that should be supported by perceivable and incremental feedback, clear representation of the self position, movement history where appropriate, and meaningful messages from the system. In the buildings example, feedback accords with the natural sense of motion through the virtual world as objects become closer or recede during the user's progress through the building. Domain knowledge is vital for interpreting feedback. If the user's knowledge is poor, some help can be given by explanation of any hidden states, modes, and objects within the new context. For example, as the user approaches the electric switches, hover text labels explain their properties and operation.

System Initiative Cycle

The GDPs selected for system initiative are influenced by the nature of the initiating event. If it represents communication from another user or an intelligent software agent masquerading as a person, then the response will follow the conversational mode. The GDPs invoked in this path support understanding, planning, and generating a natural language dialogue. If the event signals a possibly dangerous state from the environment, then interpretation and planning response actions are more important The event may signal a change in system initiative, in which case the user has to interpret whether this is acceptable.

The cycle is initiated by the stimulus event that may signal that the system has taken the initiative, or it may be an external event from the environment or communication from another user or automated agent. The GDPs at this state indicate that the design should make the event clear and ensure it is perceived as a warning if it signals danger. For "recognize change" the user employs domain knowledge to identify the event and understand its content. The GDPs point out that the event should be locatable and perceivable and that active notification may be necessary for hidden events. Interpretation attaches significance to the event using domain knowledge to infer a causal explanation about why the event occurred. Planning a response will be necessary if the event or situation is unfamiliar and diagnosis of the implications of the event precedes the response decision. In safety critical systems, this gets into a considerable debate about allocating automated or human mediated responses.

Alternatively, if the event emanated from a human-like agent, then it is interpreted as a communicative act and this invokes different

GDPs to supply information about the identity of the originating agent, their role, character, and intentions. The decision whether to react builds on the causal and intentional analysis of the speech act, but it also requires more information about the history of the conversation and status, role and authority of the sender agent. Planning a response to an agent requires knowledge of the agent's personality. In the absence of specific information, people attribute artificial agents with human properties; for instance, they trust older personalities more than younger ones. Locate control and specify action depend on the available communication modality: speech, gesture, or movement response.

Planning a response depends on the user's prior experience of similar events and their context. For conversational dialogue, this depends on knowledge of the sender agent, so planning is usually conscious at the knowledge-based level. For events originating in the environment and system initiative signals, explanation of the event's implications and context may be necessary, as well as access to any appropriate preplanned responses. This stage draws on the user's task and domain knowledge for proceduralized responses. If these are minimal, the system may have to take the initiative in responding automatically to hazardous events. A specialization of this is to initiate an automatic response with a user override. Alternatively, a list of appropriate preplanned responses could be provided from which the user could choose.

The next three stages have GDPs shared with the other cycles, although "locating controls" has additional GDPs for selecting the modality for response, which is important for conversational interaction; automatic selection or suggestion of controls may follow from a preplanned response. Having integrated the models, GDPs and resources, we can now put the theory to work in design and usability evaluation. The next section describes prediction of user errors and usability problems with the models.

Error Diagnosis and Recovery

Usability problems will arise if user resources or design features are inadequate. Errors are predicted when one or more contributions for successful interaction are absent, so the rules can be used to predict errors:

IF user knowledge or system feature is not present THEN ActionStage(x) may fail.

Errors may be the responsibility of the design or the user. Design errors are manifest as usability problems during interaction, but the dividing line between user and designer's responsibility can be fine. If one user in a population experiences an error but all the others encounter no problems, then the user is probably (but not always) at fault, and training to increase device knowledge may be the cure. In contrast, if several users experience the same problem and sufficient training has been given, then the designer is responsible.

The causes of human error described in chapter 2 are revisited in the context of models of interaction. Classification of user errors follows Reason's categorization of slips, failures in attention that can be quickly corrected; and mistakes that arise from incorrect plans and errors in knowledge-based reasoning. Slips and mistakes are refined into error types that help diagnosis of usability problems by forming a bridge from observation of users' problems in interaction to pinpointing their cause in a UI design feature. However, the function may be present but not visible to the user. In complex interfaces, access paths have to be provided to functions so cues support user navigation to locate the function. If preparatory actions are necessary, problems may arise from inaccessible objects and inability to navigate and orient the user presence into the appropriate position. Action execution has to take account of the limitations of human sensorymotor coordination. Controls that are poorly tuned or make excessive demands on human coordination cause problems at this stage. In the feedback stages, design-induced errors will arise from inadequate or missing feedback, and presentation of feedback in a manner that does not make sense in the user's context. Sometimes observation of a problem is not located with the cause. This is common in mode errors when the user's mental model is not consistent with the system state. An example is being puzzled when graphical objects automatically align themselves, a consequence of not being aware of the "snap-to" autoalignment mode. This error has three possible causes: lack of user device knowledge of the snap-to option, a working memory error in having forgotten the mode setting, or a design error in not giving mode status.

Slips are more likely to occur at the action execution and recognize feedback stages. In contrast, mistakes are more probable in the intention formation and action specification stages, when faulty memory may result in the user applying the wrong rule to carry out a task, or applying a correct rule in the wrong circumstance. The latter is caused by a recognition error and failure to correctly analyze the current task context. Slip-errors are manifest in action execution and feedback recognition stages, when failure of attention may result in omitted or incomplete action, and failure to perceive feedback. Mistakes make their appearance again in interpretation and evaluation of feedback, where inadequate domain or device knowledge and reasoning failures may lead to users jumping to false conclusions.

The system initiative cycle is prone to mistakes when the original event is misinterpreted. This is common when the intentions of other agents are not clear, or false assumptions are drawn. Inadequate knowledge of the domain and status knowledge of the other party may be to blame, but inappropriate responses may also play a part. For instance, when we are unfamiliar with a system and it uses speech, we tend to attribute human-like qualities to computers and give apparently mistaken responses. Mistakes may also be present in planning responses if domain and task knowledge are poor. Slips are more likely when the event first occurs and the response invokes an automated procedure. It may be missed or ignored if our attention is distracted.

In the navigation exploration cycle, mistakes are possible in panning the search and in interpreting the change of location and feedback. Goal-directed navigation will be more prone to mistake-errors because the user has to undertake more knowledge-based planning. Slips will happen during navigation and feedback perception, especially if there are distracting stimuli in the environment and features are missed.

In the feedback stages, design-induced errors will arise from inadequate or missing feedback, and presentation of feedback in a manner that does not make sense in the user's context (i.e., disorientation). These errors, and techniques to discover them from observation of user's problems when interacting with multisensory interfaces.

Conclusion

This chapter introduced a theory of multisensory interaction. The theory comprises three components: models of interaction, cognitive resources, and design contributions to successful interaction that were expressed as usability requirements or GDPs. Three interacting submodels were described: one for planned task-action, one for reactive behavior to events, and one for opportunistic exploration and navigation. The models elaborate Norman's theory of action. The models describe generalized stages for action or reaction in a plan-specify action-interpret change cycle. The model stages provide the context in which user cognitive resources and system facilities are recruited to ensure usability for each stage in interaction. Cognitive resources are divided into general resource limitations of human information processing and knowledge sources which users need for successful interaction. Differences in complexity of domain, task, and device knowledge reflect novice and expert user profiles. GDPs were proposed for design requirements to support effective interaction at each model stage. Two rule sets, one for experts, the other for novices, link the contributions that the users should make with design requirements (GDPs) for successful interaction. Errors, mistakes, and slips are associated with human failings at each stage and design requirements are needed to counteract them.

7

Multimedia and Industrial Restructuring

Introduction

The Asian model of economic growth have only recently been punctured by a widespread series of unsettling news of currency turmoil and looming recession. World markets are currently buzzing with conjectures that the global economic forces that have brought investment and prosperity to countries like Japan and Korea are now threatening to take them elsewhere.

Amid news flashes of strikes, galloping deficits, bad-debt problems, corruption, infrastructure bottlenecks and overheating, Asia's miracle economies that have grown fat on annual growth rates of more than eight per cent are ill-prepared for leaner times. While Japan continues in slow recovery mode, other Asian economies such as Malaysia and Singapore are restructuring to beat labour shortages and the World Trade Organization deadlines for liberalization. More specifically, concerns over falling growth rates have spurred Singapore to make sweeping changes in work orientation and infrastructures, both soft and hard.

Broadly, this study aims to focus on current restructuring strategies in Singapore as it moves from a newly industrialized (NIE) to a fully developed economy. In particular, attention will centre on the strategic importance of information technology (IT) and its subset, multimedia. Like the rest of the industrially advanced economies, Singapore is targeting IT not only to deliver a healthy recovery but to act as the primary infrastructure and export product for the 21st century. In launching Communicate Asia/Broadcast Asia '96 and Network Asia '96, the Minister of Communications spoke of Singapore One. He emphasized that:

Rapid technological advances in recent years, coupled with the convergence of the telecommunication computing and broadcasting industries, have resulted in the advent of new leading industries based on high performance multimedia communication. The multimedia industry alone is envisaged to grow and become the leading industry in the 21st century. Singapore must nurture this industry now as it will form the heart of the new industrial structure.

Key Thrusts of Restructuring

The past three and a half decades since political independence in 1965 have seen Singapore's economic growth rates advance at more than eight per cent annually from 1960s to 1995. The policy centrepiece driving this growth is the global orientation of Singapore, as expressed in multinational-corporation-based manufacturing using export-orientated industries, combined with a free trade regime and lavish use of immigrant labour at both the high- and low-end skill levels. Ironically this policy, which was forced on Singapore due to resource deficiency and lack of a sizable market during the early years of industrialization, has in hindsight ensured Singapore a competitive edge in an increasingly global economy.

Since the first serious crisis of 1985, which rocked Singapore with a threatening one per cent growth, an array of new goals and strategies have been put on track to shift the economy up the technological scale. To attack rising labour costs and shortages, the state has put together a policy package to help Singapore adapt to the challenge of world competition.

Sectoral Transformation

The basic goal of restructuring is to maintain the manufacturing sector at twenty-five per cent of the Gross National Product (GNP) in the medium and long term. Manufacturing is seen as an essential base to support a plethora of other industries such as services. It is also hoped that Singapore will gain new appeal by casting itself as the business services gateway to the region. Realization of this goal can already be seen in a range of developments: the rapid expansion of financial services; the establishment of Singapore as tourism hub; the number of operational headquarters located there; its role as a centre for logistics distribution and media telecommunications hub for the Asia Pacific rim.

In thirty-five years of sparkling growth rates, the Singapore economy faced only one short recessionary spell in 1985 (commonly labelled the 'Oil Crisis'). However, this period sent interesting signals about the underlying structural shift which witnessed the beginning of a process of capital exodus.

By 1995, the total cumulative stock of outward FDI amounted to $46.24 billion which is equivalent to 38.1 per cent of GNP. Trying to mitigate this trend, Singapore attempted to keep back as many business activities as possible by providing generous incentives, for example, in R&D. The increasing capital outflow, however, has still not led to a hollowing out of the industrial sector. This could be due to two factors. First, the state actively enters joint ventures with foreign partners to increase the rate of investments in selected industries, including those requiring massive amounts of capital or those requiring long-term investments. Second, the booming Asian market has drawn in a massive flow of FDI. By offering Singapore as a tentative first stop, the state was able to divert selective parts of this flow for its own purpose of shifting the economic landscape to a high-tech one. A third strategy is designed for the uninitiated and smaller investors who do not want to be hassled by dealing with the uncertainties of emerging economies such as China, Vietnam and Burma. Singapore has planned to export its system of governance by building safe industrial parks in these most unpredictable business environments. Investors are thus freed to concentrate on the actual business of production while the park managers work diligently to untangle and diffuse the element of precariousness that operating in such environments entail.

New Management Orientation

It was envisaged that with the creation of the new industrial economy, the management of human resources will also need to be revamped. The aim is to replace monetary incentives as a motivational force with psychological instruments such as group identification that comes from teamwork and a heightened sense of shared vulnerability.

Table 7.1 Outward foreign direct investment by Singapore-based firms, 1976-94

Year	Cumulative stock of direct foreign investment (S$mn)*	As % of GDP	No. of companies which invested abroad
1976	1,427.6	9.8	n.a
1980	2,493.9	10.3	n.a
1990	16,877.9	25.3	2,391
1991	18,607.5	25.2	2,721
1992	22,442.5	27.9	2,954
1993	28,900.4	31.0	3,764
1994	37,319.3	35.6	4,295

The constant portrayal of national vulnerability and insecurity in the mass media has caused anxiety amongst Singapore's population. Both print and electronic media have succeeded in nurturing a sense of national insecurity which in turn provides the motivation for hard work, thrift and a general compliance with particular types of behaviour necessary for the enhancement of national competitiveness. One strategy is to set the country's ranking along internationally-created scales of performance. A regular ranking system was deployed by Business Environment Risk Intelligence which placed Singapore second world-wide in terms of profit opportunity. This ensured a conducive climate and the easy mobilization of human effort in the current restructuring exercise.

Human Resource Supply and Development

The state, with the help of EDB (Economic Development Board, lead investment agency), works closely with tertiary and training institutions to ensure the development of adequate manpower for the restructuring of the economy. Various specialist manpower programmes have been established to churn out the new skills required by industries targeted for special development. These include:

- Specialist Manpower Programme in Wafer Fabrication, Disk Media and IC Packaging.
- R F Engineers Development Programme.
- Analogue IC Designer Programme.
- Precision Engineering Manpower Programme.
- Specialist Mould Designer Development Programme.
- Broadcasting and Production Training.

Apart from these initiatives, the Board has programmes to assist Singapore-based companies to recruit international talents in order to broaden the local manpower pool. Since 1992, more than eighty private companies and public organizations have benefitted from EDB recruitment facilitation. Finally, an EDB immigration facilitation programme has enabled more than 4,000 foreign professionals and skilled workers annually to take up employment in Singapore.

The development of manpower in Singapore has been subjected more to overall political considerations rather than to the workings of the market. The main focus of attention and financing was on the education of elites; education policies were conceived within a conservative framework aimed at reproducing a new generation of conforming workers accustomed to strong rule from the top.

It was only in 1997, driven by economic imperatives, that a third university was allowed to be established by the private sector. School and university curricula were revised to ensure a broad-based education so that graduates will be more creative and effective in the now flexible and intensely competitive business environment. Alongside this, to ensure that students learn to love the nation and its leaders, local history was made a mandatory subject for schools and universities. Obviously, government needed to ensure both an efficient force of creative surplus producers and, at the same time, docile subjects.

Technologies for Competitiveness

Popular expectations aside, it is increasingly recognized that telecommunication technologies are perceived as the 'competitive edge weapons' for advancement into the information age. Starting from the 1990s, action in this direction has been transformed to a well-coordinated, concerted and more ambitious drive to build an all-embracing information network to nurture multimedia content industries and a national information infrastructure.

IT Infrastructure Phase 1 (1980)

Science and technology were only seriously expected to take off in the 1990s but the institutional foundations were laid in the 1980s. These early initiatives include the establishment of the National Computer Board (NCB), generally to promote computerization and IT industry development. More specifically, NCB's initial role was to spearhead the deployment of IT in the public sector through the Civil Service Computerization Programme thus effectively making the government the lead user of computer technology. Other specific functions of the NCB include the coordination and promotion of computer education and training and the nurturing of a software export industry. The latter task, jointly carried out with the Economic Development Board, was aimed at attracting IT vendors the world over to use Singapore as their business (marketing and technical support) and production/ development base.

The 1985 recession had crystallized deep concerns over the need to accelerate transformation of the economy. Singapore from that year onwards witnessed a rapid proliferation of initiatives and institution building to promote technological development. Apart from the National IT Plan which was formulated in mid-1985 under the aegis of NCB to promote IT development in Singapore, a plethora of other institutions were also set-up, including the Technology Institute, the Information Institute of Singapore, and the Japan Singapore Artificial Intelligence Centre. Countless ad hoc promotional programmes mushroomed at that time including the Small Enterprise Computerization Programme, the Programme for IT training of office workers, and grants for advanced IT manpower training. Public awareness and mobilization was sustained by annual events such as the National IT Award, National IT Week, and Software competition.

Phase 2 (1990 to year 2000)

The realization that Singapore's competitive position was in grave danger of being eroded by the emergence of regional successes in the 1990s provided added urgency to questions of technological upgrading. This momentum was given a huge push by the 1992 IT 2000 Report; A Vision of an Intelligent Island which had been in the making under the NCB since January 1991.

IT 2000

Whereas the National IT plan focused on computation, the IT 2000 was more ambitious, extending its goals to include the development of a more advanced all-embracing information network, the nurturing of multimedia content industries and a national information infrastructure. 'The essence of IT 2000 is the synergistic development of a well integrated and extensive national information infrastructure based on advanced information technology'. This will allow for the storing and sharing of information on a national basis. Thus the IT 2000 plan could be perceived as proposing a '3C' dimension of IT: Compute, Conduit and Content. Efforts at building a national information infrastructure (NII) are centred on conceptualizing and designing an NII backbone and a multimedia broadband network. Projects involving new media technologies such as cable networks and wireless networks are also being explored.

The NII will not be built from a vacuum. The National IT Plan launched in 1986 has created the strategic framework and positive environment for both private and public sectors to collaborate in exploiting IT for enhancing productivity. A first rate telecommunication infrastructure, continuously upgraded, already exists. When the IT 2000 Plan was mooted in 1992, additional services like the Teleview videotex system, narrow-band integrated services, digital networks and cellular phones already existed.

A plethora of electronic data interchange networks was also on offer to the business community. These include Trade Net, Medinet, Lawnet and other sectoral networks. By 1990, the IT industry (excluding hardware manufacturing and telecommunication services) had grown to $2.15 billion. IT R&D capacity was expanded within the public sector by establishing new institutes such as the Information Technology Institute and Institute of System Science, and upgrading facilities at the universities, Singapore Telecom and the Ministry of Defence. Emphasis was also given to IT manpower development and the training of IT specialists. Communication software engineers are educated by the Information Communication Institute of Singapore, knowledge engineers by the Institute of System Sciences and the Japan-Singapore Artificial Intelligence Centre, and computer integrated manufacturing (CIM) engineers by GINTIC Institute of CIM.

The first phase implementing the high-speed network infrastructure involves linking up network providers, data hubs and government networks by the end of 1996. The completion of this phase would facilitate the provision of common services such as e-mail, universal directory and information exchange to the public. In the meantime, the infrastructure for electronic identification (public key) will be implemented to ensure security for transactions in electronic commerce (National Computer Board 1995-6:27).

Singapore One, total electronic link up

Singapore One constitutes the key component of IT 2000. It is spearheaded by the Multimedia Broadband Network Project and TAS. The NCB is responsible for development of applications on the network. The National Science and Technology Board (NSTB) and its research institutes (such as Institute of Systems Science and Information Technology Institute), together with the Telecommunication Authority of Singapore, will provide technical leadership in the network architecture and the development of advanced multimedia applications. The project is also supported by the EDB and Singapore Broadcasting Authority. It was launched in 1996 with the aim of transforming Singapore into an intelligent island. This multimedia broadband will possess three elements:

- Digitization to enable the information infrastructures to carry and route a mix of voice, data, graphics and video.
- Abundant network capacity by means of data compression technologies, high capacity fibre-based networks and digitized transmission.
- Personalized services that can be accessed through PCs, personal mobile communications and personalized interactive services such as electronic commerce and video on demand.

The technology deployed will allow the network to be tailored to suit individual bandwidth or speed requirements. A hybrid fibre-coaxial network, Singapore One will provide the telecommunication infrastructure that will enable the whole population to be wired up via a broadband network which will deliver a whole suite of broadband multimedia services. The government will invest $82 million into the system which will allow users to send e-mail, carry out video-conferencing, surf the Internet faster, shop safely online, study, watch movies and even pay their bills. Companies will be able to serve their customers directly in their homes and offices. As of April 1997, seventeen companies have pledged a total of $115 million into the project to develop services and technology for purposes ranging from entertainment to travel and banking. Participating companies include Microsoft Corp., IBM, NEC Corp., HP Co., Reuters Holdings PLC, Sun Microsystems Inc. and Yahoo! Inc.

The purpose was to project Singapore One as the launching pad for new multimedia contents, hardware and software platforms, and applications and services in the Asia Pacific. It will not only serve as a pilot project site but also as a platform to develop new innovations. This multimedia computer network is to have about one hundred applications, from training and instruction to information services and entertainment.

By February 1997, 40 per cent of all residences in Singapore had been wired. 24,000 homes are provided with cable connections a month as part of a nation wide project costing $50 million. The target completion date is 1998. Satellite links are available in Singapore to all major regional and international satellites such as Palapa B2P, Apstar 1, Pan Am Sat 4, 2 and the Pas-four whose footprint covers 120 countries. In August 1998, Singapore launched its US$240 million satellite jointly owned with Taiwan.

Telecommunications and the media

Singapore's recent ascent to affluence can surely be attributed to its strategic geographical position combined with excellent infrastructures. This not only allows speedy movement at entry and exit points but also provides an efficient telecommunications system. This was a fact despite the monopoly of Singapore Telecoms.

New features are continuously being added to help upgrade existing IT infra-structures. For instance, two high-speed Internet links were recently installed at a cost of $80 million to be spent over three years. The first T3 link was recently installed (2 May 1997) to speed up Internet connections (quadrupling the current speed) and to allow for smoother access to world-wide sites. Each T3 is a forty-five megabits per second (mbps) network connection to the global Internet backbone in the US and can transmit data at 5.6 million characters per second, equivalent to 2,240 A4-sized pages of text. This can be compared to the current 4 million characters per second or 1,600 pages of text. The current connection from Singapore to the US is thirty-one mbps. With the two new links completed, this would increase four-fold to 121 mbps. Singapore is the first country in Asia outside Japan to have such a facility.

Excellent communication infrastructure, however, does not ensure unconstrained free flow of information. The state maintains a tight grip over both the print and media electronic industry. Practically all local dailies are published by the Singapore Press Holdings (SPH) which is closely linked to the state via rules regarding the ownership of paper publishers. The Singapore Broadcasting Corporation (SBC) has a monopoly over terrestrial broadcasting (three TV and radio stations). No public cable TV or satellite broadcast receiving dishes are permitted. Where political dissent and suppression of human rights are seen as synonymous with stability, it is not surprising that IT development is channelled primarily into enhancing training and business goals. Despite these narrow and focused goals for IT development, much care is also taken to prevent the liberating' potential of IT to take hold.

Publishing

Booming economies of the Asian region have triggered demand for the commodification of knowledge and information. In business terms this has translated into a vibrant publishing sector expanding at an annual rate of 12 per cent in Singapore. Currently, 100 local and foreign companies (including multinationals like Springer Verlag, Time Life Asia, Hofer, the Viacom group of which Simon Schuster is a member, and specialist publishers such as Reed Elsevier, Pearson, and Imperial College Press) have made their home in Singapore, either for original publishing (in both print and electronic formats) and distribution or as regional headquarters for their newly launched Asian publishing programme (as in the case of Springer Verlag).

Furthermore, led by the increasing emphasis on education, training and higher education in the region, the printing industry is set to experience an unprecedented expansion over the next decade. The publishing and printing industry in Singapore alone is worth $2.5 billion. The Managing Director of International Thompson Publishing Asia (ITP), whose company is involved in the publishing of professional and high technology books and expanding its CD-ROM capability, when interviewed in 1995 said:

We foresee a rising demand of Asian language books in the region and this is the market niche we are aiming at. Singapore is the ideal location for coordinating all these activities (publishing centre and regional headquarters) and for our business expansion, with its good supporting infrastructure, talented people and high quality colour separation and printing services.

Mass Media and Broadcasting Hub

Fast becoming the regional satellite broadcasting hub, Singapore is now the regional headquarters of Home Box Office, the largest and oldest pay-TV company in the US. The company is also the cable programming and marketing subsidiary of Time Warner Inc. and the first English movie subscription service in Asia. The move, according to Chairman and CEO M. Fuchs, is designed to grab a slice of the subscription television industry in Asia which is at its nascent stage of development. 'We want to gain entry into the key Asian markets and Singapore will be central to our regional expansion plans' which includes establishing a pan-Asia distribution network and the sourcing of locally and regionally produced and orientated programmes, developing additional programmes (especially those in the Chinese language), and introducing subtitling in other Asian languages. The company's service is uplinked from Singapore to the Palapa satellite (whose footprint service area extends to some sixteen Asian countries with a potential reach of 420 million people).

Asia Business News

Asia's first business news satellite television channel, is also located here and broadcasts from the Palapa satellite to key South-East Asian countries. It is jointly owned by Singapore-based SIM Ventures Pte Ltd (10 per cent), Dow Jones and Co Inc. (29.5 per cent),

Television New Zealand Ltd (29.5 per cent), and Telecommunications Inc. (29.5 per cent)).

Singapore has increasingly been drawing broadcast and media multinationals. ESPN, MTV, Walt Disney Television, Discovery Channel, Sony Entertainment TV, JET TV, Channel KTV and Golden Eagle Communications are amongst the companies which have set up bases here. There are several reasons for this. First, excellent uplink and downlink satellite communications, global optic-fibre connectivity and international air transport linkages enable programmers to receive incoming programming feeds and material, and to distribute them to the region through their channels with a high level of confidence.

Nikkei Group President and CEO A. Arai, when launching the printing of the Asian edition of its flagship newspaper, Nihon Keizai Shimbun, said that Singapore was chosen as the focus of the company's regional expansion because of its developed information services. Managing Director P. Job of Reuters Asia, which has been operating in Singapore since 1868, noted on Reuter's move to relocate their South-East Asian headquarters from Hong Kong: 'we recognize it as a leader in information technology, as a major Asian financial centre, and as the hub for a dynamic and expanding region'. Reuters was granted OHQ status by the EDB in 1988. It recently moved into its $40 million new quarters at the Science Park which house Asia-wide research and development units, training facilities and administrative staff. M.D. Weetman said, 'Singapore has a growing hub of international fibre circuits essential for the Reuters global networks'.

Finally, Singapore's multi-ethnic and multicultural population offers companies servicing the region a workforce fluent in a variety of regional languages (such as Mandarin, Malay and Tamil) and English. Moreover, the stress on continuous education has bred workers who are always ready psychologically for upgrading and continuous learning.

Singapore's Infant Multimedia Industry

Information for this section was gathered from personnel of eight multimedia firms involved in multimedia applications for entertainment (games and movies), operational multimedia (databases with multimedia interface), corporate presentations, interactive learning, advertising (virtual shopping) and IT based products and services (client-server solutions, Internet/Intranet solutions, data communication). All of the eight firms studied were less than three years old.

Multimedia is a single neat slogan referring to a more elusive bundle of elements which would rightly belong elsewhere. As it stands, the industry encompasses such a variety of production sectors that it defies definition. The recentness of the industry as it continues to emerge from the computing, media and telecommunications sectors may well account for why the industry has such as nebulous appearance. In Singapore particularly, where the industry is still at the very initial phase of its evolution, it actually straddles the hardware, software and content industries even though the content sector is the most active and generates most business opportunities, along with other supporting companies associated with the production of multimedia products and services.

The manpower situation in multimedia also reflects the diversity of origins that characterizes firms operating in this sector. In Singapore, the industry is characterized by a rather young workforce, with substantial numbers from backgrounds in engineering, information systems and the graphic arts. After all, multimedia is a computing technology capable of processing and delivering a range of existing media such as text, graphics, sound and video as a single experience. Most of the professionals interviewed admitted their training in multimedia was at the practical level and on the job, meaning that they were good enough to pick up these skills as they move from project to project.

The School of Design offered a whole module in multimedia in 1996 whereas previously, multimedia was offered only as a sub-module. Under these circumstances, it can be concluded that state preparation for generating engineering and information system skills has enabled operators to pick up multimedia skills. But since these skills per se have yet to be taught widely in academic institutions, there is an urgent need for facilities producing them. This shortage is now only being addressed by the establishment of courses at polytechnics and art schools. However, due to the volatility of the sector (in essence, multimedia has the reputation of becoming anything), even if one were equipped with multimedia skills, one would still require flexibility and innovativeness so as constantly to acquire new tools and improvise new ways of using old applications creatively. As the range of possibilities for manipulation of applications is so wide, it allows and, in fact, encourages behaviour that searches continually for more creative ways of constituting unique products. Moreover, due to the rapid rate of obsolescence of software and hardware in the sector, workers are a self-selected group always eager to experiment and try out new ways of doing things.

For instance, engineer Ng, who is a software analyst, picked up animation design and graphics skills on his first multimedia job. He now owns a multimedia enterprise which specializes in programming interfaces. Another example is graphic designer Yen who only took a sub-module in multimedia at art school. He then went on to perfect these skills while working on more projects. It is commonplace that learning and relearning occurs in every project one is involved in. Much of what is used in everyday practice, according to those interviewed, cannot be taught systematically in schools. Instead, it is picked up and accumulated as one's own collection of integrated skills.

Industry Structure

Skill deficiencies and the volatility that is so characteristic of the multimedia sector actually contribute to its inherent structure of thick network relationships that are both formal and informal, contractual and non-contractual. Networks of production groups within firms (including freelances) contribute to a particular project as firms come together out of necessity to complement and supplement the skills and resources needed to customize a product required by the market.

Multimedia production units actually started as departments of large firms in a related business that was discerning enough to seize the growing opportunity when clients requested a related service. Instead of handling these requests in-house or rejecting the client outright, such firms may pass on these business opportunities to another firm and thus earn a commission. Due to the great assortment of skills needed to customize a particular project, it is especially difficult for small firms to handle a whole project on their own. Consequently, firms get tied into all kinds of partnerships with others. Alliance with others also serves the purpose of allowing smaller firms to compete with larger companies when tendering for larger projects. Besides, smaller firms with friendly ties to large firms can ensure their continued existence because of jobs sub-contracted out to them by overloaded larger firms.

Initiation of multimedia firms is very much dependent on networks of friends and relatives. Initial capital for starting a multimedia firm can range from $20,000 to $200,000 depending on the sophistication of equipment and the location of firm. For all the firms questioned, this initial sum was collected substantially from relatives and friends. One father invested $40,000. For all the rhetoric of the state about nurturing this industry, none of the companies received any subsidy at the outset. The reason given was their small size and lack of track record. Neither were loans sourced from banks whose cumulative interest could quickly cripple a new firm just struggling to get on its feet. One production house estimated that a fully-equipped post-production studio would cost around $6 million, a sum only a mature firm could afford. Firms with such facilities are rare at this stage of development of the industry apart from the studios owned by the state. In fact, sophisticated production and editing of films is currently mostly done overseas.

Business is roaring in the multimedia sector, which is expanding rapidly. The multiplication of firms from around twenty (content providers) in 1995 to more than double that figure in 1998 indicates the robust state of the sector. These opportunities for expansion offer clear examples of the significance of social networks in facilitating economic transactions. The expansion of firms has been funded by sale of stocks to friends and to a lesser extent, to kin. Since many friends (old boys/girls) share similar technical backgrounds, they also serve as interested and capable advisors, whereas kin normally only contribute in terms of financial resources. By limiting financial sourcing to selected friendly investors, entrepreneurs try to ensure that control remains in their own hands.

The idea of stock options for workers has been widely bandied about, but with little effect, owing to the need for bosses to keep control in their hands. Giving stock options to workers may lead to awkwardness as stockholders have a right to sit on the Board of

Directors. Only one firm interviewed offers shares to workers (who are on the whole also friends of the director). What is so remarkable is that the initial group of employees included like-minded friends who shared the same ideals as the entrepreneurs, including classmates at college. The entrepreneurs thus felt a sense of obligation to them for helping out when the company was in dire need. For instance, the company could not have employed such workers at market rates. Some worker-friends could not be paid for the first few months because the firm could not yet make enough to meet its cost, yet they have continued working faithfully, hoping for better times to come. Hence the pressure felt by owners to share the fruits with their loyal worker-friends. On the part of the workers, offers of stock options have been turned down because they plan to start their own companies or to leave for greener pastures.

All entrepreneurs interviewed agreed that state activities have indeed stimulated business in this sector. Foucault's description of the power agent actively organizing to constitute its subjects as consumers (e.g. of hospital services) and as political subjects aptly describes the Singapore state, which is an avid consumer of multimedia applications. In fact, holding an account from a state agency in one's portfolio can be considered one measure of a company's size and significance in the multimedia industry. The numerous public campaigns generated each year to encourage courtesy, marriage, speaking mandarin etc. are all backed by multimedia spiels.

The billions of dollars of public money poured into the communications infrastructure through institutions such as Singapore One and the IT infrastructure for schools and institutions of higher learning have also been greeted with cheers by the multimedia sector. Such moves not only generate demand within the state sector but also have a multiplier effect, triggering the use of multimedia by individuals and companies across the board. In addition, workers trained in multimedia subsidiaries of government-linked companies have gone on to form their own companies. Simply by playing the conventional state role of providing the infrastructure (partly subsidizing its initial foundation), the state reaps long-term benefits such as higher tax revenue and possibilities for more extensive control over its constituents.

The privatization of some state activities such as broadcasting and telecommunications has also created opportunities for new firms in this sector. In fact, one of the production houses interviewed is owned by a former staff member of the SBC. With long years of working experience garnered from work with the SBC, he was able to start (albeit on a very humble scale) a production house which today has grown enough for him to think of applying for a state subsidy which is normally given to firms with a credible and successful track record. The progress of such firms has been held back by a lack of capital to purchase sophisticated post-production machinery such as the non-linear digital editing equipment.

Social Design of Technology

This section aims to provide a non-technical social orientation to the understanding of IT strategy in Singapore's restructuring. The analysis will primarily be based on the early ideas of Habermas that considered how the dynamics of capitalism were interrelated and explored the ideological function of science and technology in reducing political normative questions to simple technical problems which can be solved by specialists. This makes it possible to distinguish between the basic structure of modern technology as such and the specific way in which this basic structure is actualized under capitalist conditions, in other words, how it is directed by economic and political pressures and subjected to the imperatives of the capitalist accumulation process.

Institutional Shaping of IT

More specifically, borrowing the idea of 'institutional tissues' from Hudson, one can clearly relate the implementation of IT in Singapore to the authoritarian structure of Singapore politics. IT in Singapore is chiefly state-led (hierarchy) rather than market oriented, despite the current liberalization of telecommunications by the WTO. Superficially, it would appear that the Singapore government, like governments of other countries, will try to separate the regulatory and operational functions of state monopoly telecommunication providers. In theory, it will oversee regulation as a government function but privatize operations, and bring in other providers to compete with the former monopolies. In fact, however, the market dominated by state monopolies has been transformed to one resembling more that of an oligopoly.

Singapore Telecoms (S Tel), the national PTT, was privatized in 1993. Although several new companies were allowed to operate, they include some of the largest GLCs (government-linked companies with significant state-owned shares) such as the Singapore Technology Group, Sembawang Group, Keppel Group and Singapore Press Holdings. In effect, this has raised the question whether with this mode of privatization, the monopoly previously held by S Tel is being replaced by an oligopoly involving a few telecommunications and media giants that control production and distribution of content and conduit.

A good example is the provision of Internet services. The state decided to allocate licences to three large domestic firms (GLCs): S Tel, Sembawang Corporation (by the transfer of a government-developed scientific network) and Singapore Press Holdings. AT&T, the foreign competitor, lost the bid even though its bid was the lowest. The inefficiency of this oligopoly was recently highlighted by letters to the press. Another suggestive indication of the influence of the authoritarian political structures can be found by looking at the choice of products offered to Singapore consumers. Direct satellite broadcast reception dishes continue to be banned for general households although business corporations are allowed access for data communications. In addition, even though cable TV was reluctantly introduced, its availability was only reluctantly accelerated to pre-empt demand for satellite broadcasting as neighbouring countries such as Indonesia and Malaysia announced the provision of these pleasures to their residents. Perhaps the state believed it could exercise greater control over the content of cable TV rather than satellite broadcasting. The area of implementation is also affected by political considerations. The Internet and the World Wide Web have unexpectedly opened up immense possibilities for user-to-user distribution instead of the conventional distribution mode from provider to user. In reality, however, the model of NII (National Information Infrastructure) is that of interactive TV and commercial online services, such as Pacific Net (a privatized Internet service provided by a consortium of GLC subsidiaries including Sembawang Corp., Sembawang Media, Singapore Technologies, ST

Computer Systems and SIM) and Singnet provided by S Tel. These are based on the gateway-model, with control over content and distribution resting with the service providers who bundle content and distribute it through their own conduit. Despite wishful thinking by optimists like Toffler that the new technology of IT could heighten the trend towards democratization, the model of NII that most countries have adopted is that of the gateway, where providers could in theory put an end to lovely fantasies promised by liberalization of pleasures. Under the guise of restructuring, GLCs have quickly seized the opportunities offered for feverish expansion. More GLCs have also been spawned to cope with the implementation of IT 2000. For instance, the national broadcasting corporation, Singapore Broadcasting Corporation, was privatized in October 1994. In its place, a holding company Singapore International Media (SIM) was born with four subsidiaries:

- Television Corporation of Singapore (TCS) allotted two public broadcast channels.
- TV Twelve also allotted two channels.
- Radio Corporation (RCS) responsible for existing radio stations of SBC.
- SIM Communications tasked for Cable TV and Multimedia.

Singapore Cable Vision (SCV), a joint venture between SBC and SIM, offers three subscription TV channels via free-to-air broadcasting. In July 1994, a new consortium with $500 million to invest, (comprising SIM, two GLCs Singapore Technologies and Singapore Press Holdings and US-based Continental Cablevision Inc.) was established to provide cable TV access to all Singapore homes in 1998. SCV then contracted to connect its to-the-home coaxial cables with S Tels optical fibre networks to the curb. SCV also holds the future option to apply for a licence to provide interactive multimedia services to the home via PC or TV.

The common-carrier peer-to-peer model as illustrated by the Internet in the USA and Minitel in France was rejected as unsuitable. Yet, after an initial fright when users began extending the boundaries of the permissible, both subjects and authorities found that total control of the Internet was never plausible. Finally, the speed of implementation of the NII could be attributed to the penetrative presence of the state in the economy and society. More than 80 per cent of the population live in state-organized housing under the governance of the state-regulated Housing Development Board (HDB). This huge reservoir of households was therefore easily made available for fibre-optic wiring to access the cable. 20,000 HDB homes could be wired per month. The first point put in was also subsidized by the HDB. On the other hand, private houses could only be wired at a rate of 4,000 per month.

Future Trends

The innovative nature of multimedia jobs and the quirky requirements of clients catering to ever changing post-modernist tastebuds of consumers tend to translate into a premium on improvisation skills and creativity. The question frequently asked is whether the politics of Singapore will now give way to the economic imperative to restructure with multimedia?

Democracy and Inclusiveness

As part of its goal of shifting Singapore to a more cultivated and mature society, state-initiated pólitical discourse has recently even included the radical idea of public participation:

We must change the mind set that only a few leaders at the top of the system need to think and take responsibility for social and national issues, while the rest of society can simply mind their own business and go about their daily lives.

There could be some degree of decentralization as a result of IT implementation. For instance, 18,053 out of 22,000 teachers now have Internet accounts. Teachers can now access the Teacher-On-Online facility to bring their queries or comments directly to the Ministry of Education, instead of having to go through their respective principals. This can be said to be an advance, because a study has identified bosses as the second most stressful element in their working lives after heavy work loads. Principals now no longer have the monopoly over information emanating from or flowing to policy makers. In this way, both teachers and principals can be made more accountable for their actions. More important, however, is how feedback is used to improve the system. The rapid rise in the salaries of teachers shows that dissatisfaction and the problem of a high turnover have yet to be addressed. Instead of allowing more room for decision making, monetary incentives continue to be used to quell dissension, a line of action much in tune with general developmental trends in Singapore society.

On the other hand, the fact that IT is being implemented not to enhance the intrinsic social nature of the human species but for commercial reasons has triggered a clash between the intrinsic inclusive quality of IT and the exclusive nature of commercial markets. There is no doubt that the cost of information and its technologies have been in constant decline. Yet, artificial barriers have been erected and reinforced by the state to exclude from the market those possessing few resources. The role of the state enforcing legal mechanisms for the private appropriation of value copyright and patents points to tensions between private property and democratic communication.

Film piracy in the Asia Pacific region costs the industry more than US$530 million annually (a quarter of world-wide losses), according to the Motion Picture Association (MPA) and Singapore has the worst incidence of film piracy in this region. Street operators in Singapore are selling pirated VCDs, usually for $15 a piece. MPA Vice-President and director of anti-piracy operations in the region, L. Strong, had alleged that since VCDs and DVDs are small and easy to conceal and there are enormous profits to be made, it is virtually impossible to stamp out the trade totally. While appearing to enforce the law (operators caught can be charged in Court), enforcement is not always stringent as the losses incurred do not fall on the state. Moreover, the low median wage of the workforce would totally exclude them from the multimedia market if these copyright rules were strictly imposed. So, as Strong concedes, the piracy problem in Singapore is manageable. Such an equilibrium satisfies both political constituents and foreign investors.

Production of Consumption

WTO agreements threatened to prise open the markets which had been in the grip of state monopolies, thus leading to privatization of these high-tech monopolies. One obvious effect has been the multiplication of media alliances (with foreign providers) that enhance even further the capacity of domestic elites to intensify hedonistic consumption. The multimedia corridor thus formed constitutes a rich matrix for consumers to live out their lifestyle dreams, while design and marketing agents manoeuvre to construct and project goods into ethereal images and ministers move to maximize their own ambitions.

In reality the low level of median income prevents consumers from playing out their indulgences. Teenagers who want more may work long hours at fast food restaurants to accumulate their store of Versace jeans or turn to crime to access designer goods. For adults, the state had to act to regulate an over-rapid expansion of credit card use and rising debts. In expanding the virtual market, the state had thus to contend with issues of higher wage demands and growing numbers of bankruptcy cases. This is not to say that IT has not also been deployed to legitimize the existing system.

Production of Consent

Singapore's problem with the potential subversive influence of IT is not peculiar to this island nation. It is experienced by other authoritarian governments in the region whose path to capitalist industrialization has not been accompanied by rationalization of other areas of life. Yet, as emerging Asian economies struggle to restructure their failing economies, they all need to develop IT, both as a tool and a product to survive the global onslaught brought on by WTO agreements. In launching JET TV (the first Japanese broadcaster based in Singapore), Yeo, the Minister of Information and the Arts, gave the assurance: 'We must always remain pro-business. Whatever censorship is necessary must be carried out sensitively and selectively, and with a light touch'.

He took the growing number of media companies to indicate that Singapore has achieved a good balance between laissez-faire and regulation. In reality, the government's 'light touch' saw the ban of the July 1997 issue of Vogue (UK) because it contained an article condoning and promoting drug use. The month before, the publication permit of IS, a fortnightly entertainment magazine, was not renewed because it exploited sex to raise its circulation and encouraged undesirable lifestyles. However the permit was renewed on appeal in July because IS agreed to drop their columns of personal advertisements. Around July 1997 too, Asiaweek (Hong Kong) was allowed to raise its circulation from 15,000 to 18,000 copies (The publication previously had a restricted circulation, only 500 copies in October 1987, because it was deemed to have interfered with domestic politics). At the same time, the Far Eastern Economic Review (Hong Kong), another restricted publication, had its circulation increased from 6,000 to 8,000 copies as of 1 July, 1997.

Apart from such clumsy and costly attempts at keeping its subjects docile, Singapore is also making efforts at the global level to expand its capacity for government action. Singapore International Television (SITV) was launched through Indonesia's Palapa B2P satellite to viewers from Surabaya (Indonesia) to Shanghai, Port Moresby to the Maldives. The aim is to provide a window an Singapore for non-Singaporean viewers. To Singaporeans abroad, SITV aims to help 'maintain links with their country'. Though multimedia firms could live with censorship of pornographic and political content, this is an inhibiting factor that could cramp both style and flair. On the other hand, the current development of hardware and the emphasis on engineering skills and education and training have served to channel multimedia production from entertainment products towards more technical and neutral contents such as interactive learning and engineering software where higher profits maybe made.

8

Designing of Multimedia User Interface

Introduction

This chapter deals with the multimedia subset of multisensory UIs. Multimedia raises special problems because most applications are information intensive, so design needs to focus on information presentation. That is not to say that multimedia systems are not interactive; indeed, the converse is the case. However, the dialogue design problems can be treated as an extension of standard GUI interaction.

Multimedia applications have significant markets in education and training; however, many systems just use text and graphics with a restricted dialogue for drill and quiz interaction and simple navigation. This approach is oversimplified; for effective training and education, interactive simulations and microworlds are more effective. These necessitate more sophisticated approaches to dialogue design, which will be briefly introduced in this chapter. Multimedia has been used extensively in task-based applications in process control and safety critical systems; however, most transaction processing applications are currently treated as standard GUIs rather than using the potential of multimedia in design. With the advent of the Internet and e-commerce, this view may change.

Multimedia design involves several specialisms that are technical subjects in their own right. For instance, design of text is the science (or art) of calligraphy that has developed new fonts over many years; visualization design encompasses calligraphy but also considers design of images either drawn or captured as photographs. Design of moving images, cartoons, video, and film are further specializations, as are musical composition and design of sound effects. Many of these design specializations are taught in arts degree courses that teach skill by example, case study, and mentoring. This approach encourages creative and aesthetic design; in contrast, com' puter science encourages a systematic, engineering'based approach. Consequently, multimedia design lies on an interesting cultural boundary between the creative artistic community and science-based engineering. Although I do not intend to address the debate between these communities, I reflect on some of the tensions between them. One implication of this cultural collision (or rather, one hopes, synthesis) is that "within media" design, that is, guidelines for design of one particular medium such as animation and film, are not dealt with in depth. Successful multimedia design often requires teams of specialists who contribute from their own disciplines. Management of such teams and how they communicate is a vexed problem for further research.

The distinguishing characteristics of multimedia applications are that they are information intensive and have a complex design space for presenting information to people. Design, therefore, has to start by modeling information requirements, a topic that is not covered by most software engineering or HCI methods. This chapter starts with an information analysis then progresses to deal with issues of media selection and integration. The background to the design method presented in this chapter can be found in several publications. Other sources are the media taxonomies of Bernsen and Heller and Martin, design principles, user-centered design process for multimedia, and studies of usability engineering for hypermedia. Pragmatic graphical and multimedia design guidelines based on experience have also influenced some of the following recommendations, which have been incorporated in the ISO 14915 standard: Multimedia User Interface Design: Part 3, Media Combination and Integration. First an overview of the method and its stages is given, followed by more detailed description of each stage.

Design Method Overview

The agenda which the method addresses is the creation of a task model incorporating specification of information requirements, followed by designing a coherent presentation that directs the user's attention to extract required information at the appropriate level of detail. In doing so, the design method makes designers aware of the cognitive issues underlying a multimedia presentation such as selective attention, persistence of information, concurrency, and limited cognitive resources such as working memory.

The method starts by requirements and task-information analysis to establish the necessary content and communication goals of the application. It then progresses to domain and user characteristic analysis to establish a profile of the user and the system environment. The output from these stages feeds into media selection and integration that match the logical specification of the content to available media resources. Design then progresses to thematic integration of the user's reading and viewing sequence and dialogue design. The method can be tailored to fit different development approaches. For instance, in rapid applications development, storyboards, prototypes, and iterative build and evaluate cycles would be used. The guidelines in this case are applied both in design and evaluation. On the other hand, in a more systematic, software engineering approach, more detailed specifications and scripts will be produced before design commences. Notations such as UML for object-oriented design can be adopted to fit within software engineering approaches. Although the method is described as a sequence, in practice the stages are interleaved and iterated; however, requirements, information modeling, and media selection should be carried out before the media and attentional design stages can commence. Design approaches in multimedia tend to be interactive and user-centered. The time-to-market pressure gives little incentive for systematic design, so at first reading a complex method may seem to conflict with the commercial drivers of development. However, methods don't work by being followed as a rigorous cookbook. Maybe for the first few times the method steps and guidelines do have to be followed by referring to the manual (or this book), but thereafter the knowledge becomes internalized and the designer selects and integrates media without having to consciously think about a guideline. However, not all design is automatic. Many trade-offs have to be consciously evaluated during design, and the method's duty is to make these choices clear.

Design Approach and Technology

Design should always be user-centered as a cycle of requirements capture, prototyping, and evaluation. The important point is that users should be involved continuously. The prototype-evaluation cycle should be iterated several times, but only too often a design is tested once and then rushed to market. This approach just clutters the market with unusable products. Design needs to be based on the psychology of multimedia information processing. For example, we learn more effectively from interactive multimedia because active engagement encourages problem solving and this leads to the formation of richer memory schema. Consequently, tutorial multimedia should be designed where possible as interactive microworlds. Furthermore, we can apply the same principles to the design process. Requirements analysis and design refinement is an interactive process, hence interactive prototypes, simulations, and mock-ups all help. The method emphasizes specification for designers, especially software engineers; however, specifications should be developed in tandem with prototypes for user testing, because concrete examples of design stimulate reasoning. Some variations on design realizations follow:

- Storyboards are a well-known means of informal modeling in multimedia design. Originating from animation and cartoon design, storyboards are a set of images that represent key steps in a design. Translated to software, storyboards depict key stages in interaction with a product. Storyboards can be made semiinteractive by conducting walkthroughs to explain what happens at each stage, but this is still a passive representation. Allowing the users to edit storyboards and giving them a construction kit to build their own encourages active engagement. This is the essence of the PICTIVE method. Other researchers are trying to extend the flexibility of storyboards toward "paper prototypes" that give a construction kit so that rough-and-ready sketches can be scanned into a computer and then linked in a script to create a limited animation. This approach converges with building concept demonstrators using standard multimedia or hypermedia authoring tools (e.g., Macromedia.Director) to rapidly develop semi-interactive early prototypes.

- Wizard of Oz simulations One computer has a simulated interface of the application which is connected to another computer controlled by the human "wizard" who mimics more complex aspects of functionality that have not been implemented. This approach is useful for speech-based multimedia where the human mimics the intelligent agent. The user interacts with the simulation and should be unaware that part of it is still human.
- Concept demonstrators are active simulations that can be played or run. The simulation follows a script and exhibits behavior, but departure from the preset sequence is not allowed. The advantage of simulations is that they engage human reasoning more effectively, because we are challenged to interpret what we see. Also, several variations can be run to support comparison; however, the user experience is still mainly passive, as there is little opportunity to interact.
- Interactive prototypes These are active and also interactive, so users can test them by running different commands or functions. The degree of interactivity depends on the implementation cost. At the low end, a set of scripts is provided which simulates a small number of commands. More expensive are narrow, in-depth prototypes in which functionality is fully implemented but only in a restricted subsystem, or broader, shallower prototypes that have functionality partially implemented throughout the system. Cost increases as prototypes converge with a fully functional product.

All these design realizations employ interactive media that engage our attention and thereby help requirements analysis.

Requirements and User Modeling

First, the requirements for the application need to be established. It is not the purpose of this book to cover requirements analysis methods; however, a brief introduction to multimedia-centric requirements analysis will be given. Requirements are expressed as goals that represent the users' intentions for the new system. These are elicited by a task analysis that develops requirements goals in task models of the user's current work and then translates this into a model of how the new system should work. However, requirements for multimedia also need to capture the designer's communication goals, as well as an outline of the necessary content. Three issues need to be analyzed:

- The communication goals of the application are specified in light of the domain, for example, to entertain users the communication goal might be to excite and stimulate, whereas for safety critical applications, the goals should be to warn the users and provide appropriate information for responsive planning. High-level application goals may be to educate or train; in this case, the learning outcomes need to be specified.
- Nonfunctional requirements (NFRs) are performance and quality of service parameters that will become benchmarks against which a design can be tested; hence, they need to be specified as measurable criteria. Some NFRs that have implications for multimedia are learnability, for which an example benchmark might be "Concepts x, y, z will be learned by 90% of the users so they can recall the information with 5% errors after 5 hr instruction." Other NFRs are security, privacy, accuracy of information, response time, clarity of presentation, and reliability.
- Users' information needs may be related to their task or requirements in their own right, as in information retrieval systems, or the goal may be information provision in kiosk applications. Information may be required on different topics, levels of accuracy, at a certain cost, and so forth.

Requirements are listed and categorized into information, task-related, and nonfunctional classes. These will be expanded in subsequent analyzes.

User Characteristics

It is important to get a profile of the target user population to guide media selection. There are three motivations for user analysis:

- Choice of modalities This is important for disabilities, but also for user preferences. Some people prefer verbal-linguistic material to image, and this may be linked to a gender difference.
- Tuning the content presented to the level of existing knowledge held by users. This is particularly important for training and educational applications.
- Capturing the users' experience with multimedia and other computer systems.

Acquiring information about the level of experience possessed by the potential user population is important for adaptation. Users start by being novices, but they rapidly become skilled. Unfortunately, the design has to accommodate a heterogeneous population of users, some of whom will be novices, others experts. The design solution is to provide individualization and adaptation facilities so that the user can tailor the sophistication of the interface and the information presented by preference files linked to their log-on ID. User profiles can be used to design training applications to ensure that the right level of tutorial support is provided, and to assess the users' domain knowledge so that appropriate media can be selected. This is particularly important when symbols, designed image, and diagrammatic notations may be involved. The role and background of users will have an important bearing on design. For example, marketing applications will need simple focused content and more aesthetic design, whereas tutorial systems need to deliver detailed content. Analysis of user motivation also plays an important role. For marketing, the link to motivation is obvious; however, motivation is important for learning applications as well. A well-motivated participant will learn more effectively, so questions directed toward why users want to leam may lead to useful insights for design. A key question at this stage is whether the purpose of the system is to just deliver information or to ensure comprehension and learning. The difference may not be clear-cut. Information kiosk applications need to provide information as do task-based applications, but decision support and persuasive systems also need to ensure users comprehend messages. There may be several user groups or stakeholders in a population, so the role, background, and information requirements need to be recorded for each group. Design variants may then be targeted on each stakeholder group. The following user characteristics are gathered by interviews or questionnaire:

- General abilities May be captured from educational qualifications, job descriptions, or aptitude tests and used to assess the level of tutorial support in training applications.
- Computer experience To determine if computer familiarization is necessary.
- Domain knowledge Users may be novices or experts in the application area. Their knowledge of conventions, symbols, and terminology in the domain should be ascertained. Novices will require more complete information.
- Preferences for media Some people prefer visual presentation, others are happier with language and text. This information may become. part of a preference file that controls media selection.
- User motivation People will have differing levels of curiosity, need for self esteem, power, and so on. Motivation is not easy to analyze because people may be unaware of their motivations or hide them. Questionnaire techniques that analyze motivations indirectly will be more effective than overt questions

More sophisticated data can be captured by use of psychological inventories that contain lists of questions to elicit personality characteristics. These inventories will be too complex for most design requirements; however, one scale that does have a direct bearing on multimedia is the visualizerverbalizer preference. This can be used to adjust media selection preferences for individual profiles.

Domain Modeling

The context and environment of a system can have an important bearing on design. For example, tourist information systems in outdoor public domains will experience a wide range of lighting conditions that make image and text hard to read. High levels of ambient noise in public places or factory floors can make audio and speech useless. Hence, it is important to gather information about the system environment and context of use. For example, see the following:

- Location of use Office, factory floor, public or private space, hazardous locations.
- Usage conditions Single user, shared use, broadcast, projected image for shared use.
- Environmental variables that are pertinent at the location: range of ambient light, noise levels, temperature.
- Technology Distributed system, client-server architectures, and network support.
- Expected change in location Change in environment, country, and culture; choice of language, icon conventions, interpretation of diagrams, and choice of content all have a bearing on design of international UIs.

As well as gathering general information about the system's context of use, domain modeling can prove useful for creating the system metaphor. A sketch of the user's workplace, recording spatial layout of artifacts, documents, and information, can be translated into a virtual world to help users find the information and services they need. Structural metaphors for organizing information and operational metaphors for controls and devices have their origins in domain analysis. Domain models are recorded as sketches of the work environment showing the layout and location of significant objects and artifacts, accompanied by lists of environmental factors.

Finally, the target technology needs to be analyzed. This can be difficult in Web-based multimedia, so estimates based on surveys may have to suffice. The target technology imposes constraints on design. If most users have low capacity PCs, there is no point in designing a sophisticated application with video and high-resolution graphics. Technology analysis needs to establish the characteristics of the hardware and software platform that can be expected, and network bandwidth for distributed multimedia. This part of the domain model will constrain media selection and choice of interaction.

Task and Information Modeling

Task analysis focuses on the goals the user wants to achieve. However, user goals need to be supported by the design so requirements should describe how the system will help the users achieve their tasks. For the information-searching example, a user's requirements might be the following:

- The system shall show the user the available databases that might be searched (supports goal of find resources).
- The system shall indicate the relevance rating of retrieved documents (supports goal of evaluate results).

A useful alternative view of behavior is provided by use cases in objectoriented development. Use cases focus on interaction between agents and describe the patterns of events or messages that flow between two or more agents. Use case sequence diagrams model interaction and hence can complement task-oriented views. Requirements are also apparent in use cases, as each step in a sequence diagram implies the need for user support. The circles identify information requirements as follows:

1. User information need or goal, available events or plays.
2. Articulate the need as search keywords.
3. Summarize search results (available plays) in a table or graph.
4. Prices of tickets, seats available.
   The system and human agents are represented by vertical bars, with events
5. Link views to seat position.
6. Input and validate reservation.

Tasks and use cases are captured by a combination of interviewing and observing users' work in the real world. Interviews are suitable for gathering user requirements, and task descriptions of activity and domain knowledge for understanding how user activity is actually carried out and where it is located. Cross-checking interviews against observations frequently illuminates discrepancies between the way people say they carry out activities and the way they actually do things.

Scenarios of use are another effective way to gain information about the user's task. Asking the user to talk through "a typical day in the office" forms useful input to task analysis. This approach is also useful for discovering information needs by asking users about the documents and information they employ in the current system. Scenarios are a useful complement to task analysis because they give specific stories of use from which requirements can be extracted.

Scenarios also provide concrete examples from which more generalized task models can be derived. Space precludes a detailed description of requirements analysis techniques; for more detail, contextual inquiry gives plenty of advice.

Information Types

Unless design is based on the premise that the presentation content should be specified in logical terms before media are selected, ad hoc ineffective interfaces will be the result. Only when the "amodal" specification of content has been produced should media selection and design proceed. The approach is to carry out a task analysis and then augment the task model with the necessary information content. In tutorial multimedia, when the task is teaching or learning (for the user), task analysis is replaced with scripting the information content to achieve the user's learning goals.

To form the Task Information Model, the initial task-goal hierarchy is elaborated by attaching information types, which specify the content to be communicated to the user. The resulting model should allow the designer to answer the following question: "What information content does the user need for this task subgoal or input-output interaction?"

Information types are amodal, conceptual descriptions of information components that elaborate the content definition. The analyst progresses through the use case task model in a walkthrough, asking questions about information needs. This can be integrated with data modeling (or objectclass modeling) so that the information in objects and attributes can be categorized by the following types, although one object will usually contain several different logical information types. Information typing extends data models to help the process of media selection. A finer grained classification enables more finely tuned media selection decisions, but at a cost of more analysis effort. The following definitions are based on those in the Task-Based Information Analysis Method and ISO 14915, part 3. Components are classified using the decision tree and the following questions:

- Is the information contained in the component physical or conceptual?
- Is the information static or dynamic, that is, does it relate to change?

- Which type in the terminal branch of the tree does the information component belong to?

The first two questions guide the user toward subsets of the types; the third question identifies the individual type. The decision tree gives a set of ontological categories that expand on type definitions commonly found in software engineering specifications. It is important to note that one component may be classified with more than one type; for instance, instructions on how to get to the railway station may contain procedural information (the instructions "turn left, straight ahead, " etc.), and spatial or descriptive information (the station is in the corner of the square, painted blue). The information types are "tools for thought" which can be used either to classify specifications of content or be used to consider what content may be necessary. To illustrate, for the task "navigate to the railway station, " the content may be minimally specified as "instructions how to get there, " in which case the information types function as questions in the following form: "What sort of information does the user need to fulfill the task or user goal?" Content can be organized as a thematic outline or as a scenario, for instance directions, waymarks to recognize, and description of the target location. In the latter, case the information types may be used to segment the scenario into components. The granularity of components is a matter for the designer's choice and will depend on the level of detail demanded by the application. To illustrate the analysis, see the following:

Communication goalExplain how to assemble a bookshelf from ready-made parts. Information Component 1: Parts of the bookshelf, sides, back, shelves, connecting screws Mapping to information types: Physical-Static-Descriptive; parts of the bookshelf are tangible, don't change and need to be described Physical-Static-Spatial; dimensions of the parts, how they are organized Physical-Static-Relationship; to describe which parts fit together

Information Component 2: How to assemble parts instructions Mapping to information types:

Physical-Dynamic-Discrete action Physical-Dynamic-Procedure Physical-Static-State; to show final assembled bookshelf.

Information Analysis

At each step the level of the required information is assessed, although the quantity and quality of information may need to be modified in light of the user's domain knowledge. For instance, trained users will require little knowledge whereas novices may need considerable knowledge as prompts and instructions. The following questions help in eliciting information requirements in a walkthrough.

For each input from an external agent to the system and vice versa:

- What information does the user need to carry out the action manually?
- What information should the user supply to the computer as input?
- What supporting information should the computer supply to help the user complete an action?

For decision support and action steps:

- What information does the user require for decisions?
- What information is required to support execution of human activity and how should that be presented?

Other information may be required throughout the task; for instance, continuous monitoring of data, or knowledge about how to carry out the activity. The information types are annotated on the task model to denote information required. If the application does not have a strong task model, the information content can be organized by other criteria, for example, see the following:

- Historical or time sequence Where the content is structured by time or in the order of its development discovery. Access points are specified for time points or to address significant events in a history.
- User preference Where the structure is arranged in the order which conforms to the user's model of the content, for example, by importance, frequency of use, or individual viewpoints.
- Alphabetical order Where the content is alphabetically structured based on an index of meaningful descriptors.
- Data model-based Where the content structure is determined by a data model, for example, in categories, entities, aggregation of attributes, objects, or classes.

Information structures are used to plan navigation and access dialogues as well as forming the basis for media selection. This analysis describes the information requirements of the task; however, if tutorial applications are being developed, task information will constitute the content that has to be taught. The teaching task has to be added as the pedagogical strategies to deliver the material and encourage students' learning. The task itself becomes the domain knowledge content and this necessitates further analysis of learning goals. Learning goals are established, then the delivery of knowledge is planned to incrementally develop the student's understanding. For instance, to teach students about the fresh water ecology of a pond, the learning goals (or outcomes) might be the following:

- Understand the roles of plants, herbivores, carnivores, and decomposers in an ecosystem.
- Be able to explain the concept of a food chain and dependencies between populations of plants and animals.
- Appreciate that pollution can upset the ecological balance and the reasons why.

The basic grounding knowledge that students will need before they can start will be facts about the objects, agents, and structures in the domain; for instance, fish, insects, pondweed, tadpoles, the pond, and its environment. Note that the quantity and quality of the grounding knowledge will be informed by the user profile analysis. The knowledge to be imparted is scripted in explanatory sequences; for example, the classification of pondweed as plants, tadpoles as herbivores, and so forth; the causal explanation that plants derive energy from the sun (photosynthesis) and are eaten by herbivores, which in turn are eaten by carnivores; with more advanced causal explanations for the effects of pollution either killing animals or encouraging excess growth of plants and so on.

Explanatory scripts, however, are a static presentation. As learning is encouraged by active engagement, specification of interactive microworlds should be considered, from domain analysis of content and causal explanation to encourage discovery-based learning (e.g., effects of adding pollutants, more herbivores to the ecosystem). A range of different pedagogical strategies should also be considered, such as teaching by examples, counter examples, and use of analogy. A good implementation based on the aforementioned domain is the Pondworld system.

Media Selection and Combination

Media classifications have had many interpretations. Most have proposed commonsense definitions of categories such as text, image, animation, and speech. Bernsen's modality theory is more complex because it distinguishes among a modality of communication (vision, hearing, touch); an information encoding dimension, either realistic (analogue) or symbolic; and discrete or continuous media. The following classification focuses on the psychological properties of the representations rather than the physical nature of the medium (e.g., digital or analogue encoding in video). Note that these definitions are combined to describe any specific medium, so speech is classified as an audio, linguistic medium, whereas a cartoon is classified as a nonrealistic (designed) moving image. The approach to classifying media uses the decision tree with the following questions that reflect the facets of the classification:

- Is the medium perceived to be realistic? Media resources captured directly from the real world will usually be realistic, for example, photographs of landscapes, bird song sound recordings. However, the boundary case that challenges the category is a realistic painting of a landscape.
- Does the medium change over time? The boundary case here is the rate of change, particularly in animations where some people might judge 10 frames per sec to be still a video, whereas five slides shown in a 1-min Microsoft PowerPoint presentation is seen as a sequence of static images.
- of static images. Which modality does the resource belong to? In this case, the categories are orthogonal, although one resource may exhibit two modalities, for example, a film with a sound track communicates in both visual and audio modalities.

The classification may be used from different viewpoints; for example, a film of a professor illustrating a diagram may be classified as a realistic, moving image medium portraying a nonrealistic, still image medium. Classification of media resources facilitates mapping of information types to media resources; however, the process of selection may also guide the acquisition or creation of appropriate media resources. Thus, if the selection process indicates the need for a resource that is not in the media resource library, the classification guides the necessary acquisition or creation. Cost trade-offs will naturally be considered in this process. Finally, the classification provides a mechanism for indexing media resource libraries.

Media Selection Guidelines

Task and user characteristics influence media choice; for instance, verbal media are more appropriate to language-based and logical reasoning tasks; visual media are suitable for spatial tasks involving moving, positioning, and orienting objects. Some users may prefer visual media, whereas image is of little use for blind users. In some circumstances, the information model may specify content for which no existing media resource is available, so the costs of capturing or purchasing media resources have to be considered. If existing media can be edited and reused, this is usually preferable to creating new media from scratch. Graphical images can be particularly expensive to draw, whereas capture of images by scanning is usually quick and cheap. The mappings are used in multiple passes; for example, when a procedure for explaining a physical task is required, first realistic image media will be selected, then a series of images and text. The guidelines that differentiate physical from abstract information are used first followed by the other guidelines. The summary mappings in Table 8.2 are described in more detail in the following guidelines:

- Physical information For physical information, visual media (e.g., realistic still or moving image) are preferred, unless user or task characteristics override this choice, for example, a photograph is used to portray the landscape in a national park. When physical details need to be communicated precisely, such as the dimensions of a building, captions may be overlaid on an image. When a partial abstraction of physical information is desired, a nonrealistic image may be used (e.g., sketch or diagram).
- Conceptual information Linguistic media, e.g. text or speech, are preferred for abstract or conceptual information, e.g. to convey sales objectives and commentary on the market

strategy choose text bullet points or speech for the commentary. Abstract information with complex relationships may be shown by non-realistic images (graphs, sketches, diagrams) or by graphical images with embedded text; for instance, categories of animals can be placed in a tree diagram, or a flowchart used to portray the functions of a chemical process, with speech to describe the functions in detail.

- Descriptive information Linguistic media (text, speech) are preferred for information describing the properties of objects, agents, or the domain, for example, narrative text describes the properties of a chemical compound such as salt. When describing objects and agents with physical attributes, language may be combined with an image.
- Visual-spatial information Still images are used for visual-spatial information, for example, the location of cargo on a ship is shown by a diagram; someone's face is portrayed in a photograph. Spatial, detailed information may be presented in a realistic image, for example, photographs. Spatial information that involves complex pathways may be conveyed by a moving image, for example, animating a pathway.
- Value information Numeric text and tables represent numeric values and quantitative information, for example, the height and weight of a person is given as 1.8 m, 75 kg. Graphs and charts can be combined with captions and tables to summarize trends, differences, and categories in quantitative data. Speech is not effective for values because they usually need to be inspected during a task, so a persistent medium is advised.
- Relationships in value information A nonrealistic image (e.g., charts, graphs) represents relations within and between sets of values or conceptual relations between objects and agents, for example, the values for rainfall in London for each month are displayed using a histogram.
- Discrete action information Simple or discrete actions map to still image media, for example, an image of the coffee machine showing a person performing the action illustrates filling a coffee percolator with water. Use of still image media for discrete actions allows the relation among the action, the

object acted on, and the agent performing the action to be inspected. Abstract actions, for example, mental processes, are described using speech or text.

- Continuous action information Complex or continuous actions map to moving image media, for example, turning while skiing is illustrated with a video. Complex physical action may be better illustrated with nonrealistic media (animation) so the coordination of motor actions can be inspected.
- Event or temporal information For significant events and warnings, sound or speech help to alert the user, for example, the outbreak of a fire is conveyed by sounding an alarm followed by a red marker on a diagram of the building to show the fire's location. Abstract events may have to be explained in language. Temporal information may be illustrated in sequence as lists, text, or graphical images such as time lines.
- State information For states, still image or linguistic media are preferred, for example, the state of the weather is shown by a photograph of a sunny day. Abstract states, such as a person's belief, may be explained in linguistic media or described in diagrams. If a sequence of discrete states is required, then an animation or a series of still images may be used as a slide show.
- Causal information To explain causality, still and moving image media need to be combined with linguistic media, for example, the cause of a flood is explained by text describing excessive rainfall with an animation of the river level rising and overflowing its banks. Causal explanations of physical phenomena may be given by introducing the topic using linguistic media, showing the cause and effect by a combination of still image and linguistic media for commentary; integrate the message by moving image with voice commentary and providing a bullet point text summary.
- Procedural information A series of images with text captions are preferred for procedural information, for example, instructions for assembling a bookshelf from a kit are given as a set of images for each step, with text captions. To explain procedures, a richer combination of media may be necessary,

such as a still image sequence with text, followed by an animation of the whole sequence, Nonphysical procedures may be displayed as formatted text, for example, bullet points or numbered steps.

The end point of media selection is media integration: one or more media will be selected for each information group to present complementary aspects of the topic or object. Some examples of media combination that amplify the basic selection guidelines are given in This illustrates media allocation for the browsing task in which the customer inspects the forthcoming program and other publicity material. Other information types are used in the reservation task (not discussed here). Note that information may often have multiple types; for instance, the players have descriptions in their biographies that are conceptual, but they also have physical identities. Integration Heuristics. The media combination and selection guidelines are augmented with a set of heuristics that warn the designer about undesirable consequences of media combination. The design principles described in can also be employed in this role:

- Memorisation of content from dynamic media (animation, speech, sound) is generally worse than from static media. Key facts and important messages are conveyed more effectively by static media (text, still image) because users will generally acquire only high-level gist memory from dynamic media.
- Dynamic media will attract the user's attention more than static media, so motion and stimuli which change, for example, animated captions, are hard to ignore. Beware distracting the user with superfluous animation. Dynamic media can be displayed concurrently with static media, although the user's attention will be diverted while the video or speech is playing. If dynamic media need to be integrated with other media, then provide controls to allow replay.
- Information presented in one medium can have a priming effect and help the user to understand following information in another medium. For example, text or speech can introduce an idea and should be presented before visual media to "set the scene" and direct the user's attention to information within the image.

- When speech and text are combined, the same wording should be used, unless speech is referring to a visual attribute of the text or preceding it as an instruction. Speech and text compete for language processing resources so they should not be used concurrently apart from language-learning applications.

Media Selection Patterns. For larger chunks of information, such as causal explanations and procedures, single rules cannot specify the appropriate combination of media, so media selection is better expressed as templates or patterns. The following list is not exhaustive, but illustrates the concept. Classification explains how instances of objects, agents, events, and so forth, belong to general categories. First the category is introduced, and then examples of well-formed members are given, followed by poor examples and members of related categories. The pattern concludes by summarizing the classification rules. Media selection will be different for conceptual and physical phenomena, and the following pattern is for the latter:

- Text introduces the category, its attributes, and its position in a large taxonomy (possibly augmented by a diagram).
- Image is used to explain a good member (text if conceptual), with captions and speech to point out the member's features that agree with the category's attributes.
- Image is used to explain a related category member or counterexample.
- Text is used to summarize the classification rules, supplemented with a class diagram for the large taxonomy.

The pattern of composition (whole or parts) explains the composition of a physical object in terms of its components and how they fit together. The pattern can be specialized to illustrate decomposition rather than composition.

- Image is used to introduce the whole object with speech and text to describe its role or function.
- Image then shows its parts in an exploded part diagram with captions to label the parts.
- A slide show sequence of still images is used to illustrate the composition or aggregation sequence from parts to substructures and the whole.
- The object and its parts are summarized using image and text captions to point out major subcomponents.

Regarding task based (how to do it) presentation, the physical task sequence will be specialized for abstract cognitive tasks. The sequence should be organized to first provide the task goal (purpose), and then give details of its procedure, followed by a summary.

- Text is used to introduce the overall plan and explain the task goal. This may be accompanied by a diagram of the plan.
- Preconditions are described by text and image.
- Procedure steps are given with speech and a sequence of still images.
- A moving image of the procedure is used to reinforce the message and integrate the actions.
- Text bullet points summarize, with an image to show the postconditions for task completion.

Regarding causal (why or how it works) presentation, this starts with an explanation of the domain, important objects and concepts, then the causal model is explained, followed by background knowledge to back up why the events happen. A summary concludes with key events and their causal explanation.

- There is text to introduce the domain and important objects, illustrated with a diagram.
- The sequence of cause and effect is presented by diagrams and speech, using text captions to explain key facts and background knowledge.
- Animation of the sequence reinforces the message.
- There is summarization by a diagram and text captions for key events and causal explanation.

Each pattern has a generalized script describing the presentation sequence. Dialogue controls are added to make the presentation interactive, so a sequence can be replayed, paused at each step, played in reverse order, and so forth. Further development of a library of media combination patterns to suit generalized information and task requirements may be developed in the patterns community which has started to address UI problems.

Aesthetic Motivations

The aforementioned guidelines are oriented to a task-driven view of media. Media selection, however, can also be motivated by aesthetic choice, which is important in Web-based multimedia. These considerations may contradict some of the selection rules stated earlier because the design objective is to please the user and capture his or her attention rather than deliver information effectively. Guidelines for aesthetic design are not easy to find because this aspect of design is either acquired by experience or taught in the graphics arts design courses that emphasize example-based learning, rather than generalizing knowledge as guidelines. In spite of these limitations, some advice can be given. First, a health warning should be noted: the old saying, "beauty is in the eye of the beholder, " has good foundation. Judgments of aesthetic quality suffer from considerable individual differences. A person's reaction to a design is a function of their motivation, individual preferences, knowledge of the domain, and exposure to similar examples, to say nothing of peer opinion and "fashion. " Furthermore, aesthetic judgment is often more about content than the choice of media or presentation format. Hence, the following heuristics of media selection are rules of thumb that should be interpreted with care and their design manifestations tested with users:

- Dynamic media, especially video, have an arousing effect and attract attention; hence, video and animation are useful in improving the attractiveness of presentations. However, animation must be used with care as gratuitous video that cannot be turned off quickly offends.
- Speech engages attention because we naturally listen to conversation. Choice of voice depends on the application: female voices for more restful and information effects; male voices to suggest authority and respect.
- Image needs to be selected with careful consideration of content. Images may be selected with a background for aesthetic motivations, to provide a restful setting for more important foreground information. Background in half shades and low saturation color provides more depth and interest in an image.
- Music has an important emotive appeal, but it needs to be used with care. Classical music may be counterproductive for a younger audience; older listeners will not find heavy metal or pop attractive.

- Natural sounds such as running water, wind in trees, bird song, and waves on the seashore have restful properties.

Media integration rules may also be broken for aesthetic reasons. If information transfer is not at a premium, use of two concurrent video streams might be arousing for a younger audience, as MTV (Music Television) and pop videos indicate. Multiple audio and speech tracks can give the impression of complex, busy, and interesting environments.

Image, Media Personality, and Identity. Design of image for motivation is a complex area in its own right. Some effects are general, such as use of a faint background image to suggest depth and hold interest once the foreground image has been absorbed. The overlay of background and foreground image needs to avoid clashes in color and context between the layers. Content can have a more salient effect, especially through brands and logos. The image of the brand owner is projected first through the graphical icon that identifies the brand and then publicity that attaches attributes to the brand; for example, Sir Richard Branson's Virgin brand logo has become identified with an informal but modern company, from its origins in the music industry.

Human identity can have an important effect on user motivation. Simple photographs can personalize a Web site by indicating that real people are present to help. More complex interactive animations (talking heads or full body mannequins) also have an attractive effect. We appear to ascribe human properties to computers when interfaces portray human-like visual cues; however, the use of talking heads and human mannequins in animations requires careful design to be effective. A list of some of the problems follows:

- Synchronization of lips and speech generally has to be within 0.02 sec to avoid the dubbed film effect. This can be solved by predesigned canned presentations, but at the sacrifice of flexibility in responding to user actions and questions.
- Facial expression and other nonverbal communication—We use a variety of facial expressions to signal attention and reinforce speech. For example, raised eyebrows show attention, head nods signal affirmatives, and eye contact is used in managing turn-taking. It is difficult to program these

responses into virtual people, although research prototypes are becoming more natural. Talking agents without facial expressions distract attention because they look unnatural.

- Choice of the characters' appearance and voice—This is complex because we modify our reactions according to our knowledge, or assumptions about, the other agent's intention, role, group identification, and culture. For example, reactions to a military mannequin will be very different from those to the representation of a parson. Trust and power assumptions vary widely between different professional identities. People tend to trust scientists more than politicians and journalists. Male voices tend to be treated as having more authority than female voices.

Use of human-like forms is feasible with prerecorded video and photographs; however, the need depends on the application. Video representation of lecturers adds little to the content of their presentations, although video image does help in interactive question and answer dialogue.

Attention in conversations is governed by linguistic cues and by proximity, so when human image and speech are being used, designers have to bear in mind the conversational context that is invoked. People manage personal space in meetings and pay attention to others who are close by and facing them. Images of virtual humans in multimedia need to be in a foreground shot for a normal size computer screen. In human-human conversation, we approach to within 0.5 m and look at the other person. This translates into a foreground face filling circa 50% of a 50 cm monitor at a normal viewing distance of 0.25 m. The size of a human image depends on projection technology and we react adversely to larger than life human forms with "big brother" connotations, so projecting a close-up of a face on an IMAX screen will not facilitate normal conversation.

Although it might seem to be gratuitous for a computer to say thank you and goodbye, politeness, in fact, does engender a more positive user attitude toward computer conversation. We all like to be flattered, and computers can fulfill this role, too. Praising the user has a positive effect on attitude, so in persuasive computing, the application is obvious. Criticism is more difficult. We generally react badly to criticism that is unjustified and has no constructive content.

Criticism from experts tends to be taken more seriously than from novices. These reactions can be embedded in a computer critic's conversations: start with some praise, then make the criticism constructive, justify the assertion, and sound confident to project an expert image.

We all attend to stimulating speakers. A good speaker holds our attention by a variety of tricks, such as maintaining eye contact, varying voice tone, using simple and concise language, as well as delivering an interest ing message. These are still general effects, but they can be reinforced by the projected personality. We respect dominant personalities, leaders, and experts, more than submissive people. Friendly people are preferred over colder, more hostile individuals. TV announcers, who tend to be mid die-aged, confident, but avuncular characters, have been selected to optimize the attention-drawing power of a dominant yet friendly personality. However, the preference has a gender effect. Men and women both prefer the dominant, friendly leader; and whereas both sexes pay attention to extrovert, young personalities, the male preference for beautiful young women is a particularly strong effect. These traits have been exploited by advertisers for a long time. There are lessons here for multimedia designs as the Internet and interactive TV converge.

Although the bounds of media selection are only set by the creative imagination of the designer, some fundamentals don't change: design still needs to be motivated by goals, even if it is to entertain; and testing with users is still essential.

Presentation Scripting

Once media resources have been selected, storyboards will be created and tested with users to gain further feedback on the design. In rapid application development, the design will proceed by developing concept demonstrators and early prototypes. In a software engineering approach, design will proceed with more detailed specification. Storyboards should illustrate the high-level dialogue design that is addressed in the next section, and show a set of snapshots of the application following a scenario of use. For instance, the theater booking system goes through a set of images that illustrate how the user selects a play, then makes a reservation.

Only a few dialogue controls are shown, in particular those relevant to the explanatory script. The story is walked through with the user to explain the choices and information available at each step. At this stage, it is also possible to develop concept demonstrators or early prototypes in authoring tools such as Director. Concept demonstrators follow a scripted scenario like a storyboard, but real media can be presented to provide a more realistic demonstration of the design. The task information model should give the approximate order for the presentation; however, decisions still have to be taken about concurrent versus sequential presentation and windows management.

Concurrent or Sequential Presentation

Generally, dynamic media enforce sequential presentation except when speech or sound and video share the same theme; in contrast, several static media can be presented concurrently. Maximizing concurrent presentation helps users by increasing visibility of information and reducing the burden on working memory. If users can scan a VDU for all the necessary information, this saves actions for manipulating windows and reduces the chance that the user will forget key facts. However, concurrent display should not be achieved at the expense of legibility. Reducing text font size or shrinking images to fit onto one screen can make detail difficult to perceive; furthermore, more detail increases the user's search time. Planning concurrent media presentations is therefore a trade-off between the available screen size, the demands of the task, and the user's preferences.

Window Management

Concurrent displays need to be planned for their spatial organization. For instance, each medium may be given equal screen area in a tiled display or placed in overlapping windows. If tiled windows are being used, the layout should be planned using a grid to allocate areas to each window and ensure windows do not depart from the golden mean of breadth: length. Long thin or short fat windows look strange, disrupt attention unnecessarily, and hinder reading or viewing image content. Consideration of legibility and level of detail informs the decision about how much screen space to give each medium. For text media, density metrics given by Tullis can be used to assess readability; however, generalizing these to multimedia is difficult because the cognitive process of viewing images is very different. User testing of images is advisable to make sure they are not too small for effective viewing. The user's task can also be important. For example, comparative tasks that require two or more media to be viewed should be placed in adjacent displays, whereas tasks involving sequential or time series information (e.g., event histories, procedures) suggest a linear layout. Further guidelines follow:

- Juxtaposed windows can help to relate detail to a more general context with side-by-side display for comparison.
- Avoid overlapping windows where possible because of the effort in manipulating windows to find information and the burden on working memory if information has to be compared between windows, although the technique may be useful for multitasking when foreground or background displays are needed.
- Center-embedded displays can be used for foreground detail overlaid on background context for image media; however, center embedding of dynamic media in windows containing static media is nothing more than a gimmick.

When visual media need to be closely integrated, windows get in the way. Putting content in a window imposes a psychological isolation. The window boundary sets up an arbitrary dividing line between related information, which can be difficult to overcome. Unfortunately, GUI operating systems encourage window proliferation and mapping single media resources to individual windows. The designer can counteract this effect but at the cost of doing more media design. Thus, if text and image need to be integrated, place them together within one document with captions pointing to image components. This overcomes the isolating effect of two windows: one with the image and one with the text.

Screen navigation maps, or draft site maps for Internet applications, can help to provide an overview of the major presentation components in a system, organized to reflect the hierarchy of content. This may be supplemented by a time line view of scripts illustrated by bar charts to show the sequence, duration, and overlap of media segments. The presentation script in the theater booking system after allocation of media types to information types. This illustrates media presentation scripts for three option subgoals of the browsing task in which the customer may either inspect the forthcoming program, promotions, or other publicity material. The duration and order of presentation are indicated by the user's task. The bar chart illustrates which media should be presented when the user selects a task option. Decisions on timing also depend on the content of the media resource, for example, length of a video clip or frame display rate.

Scripting raises issues of synchronization between dynamic media. When speech and video are being played simultaneously and the speaker is visible, then close synchronization of 0.2 msec between the speaker's lips and the onset of speech is necessary. We are very sensitive to lip synchronization, as dubbing foreign language films demonstrates. A longer synchronization gap may be tolerated (circa 0.5 sec) for natural sound and action, for example, bird song and video of a bird singing; however, people find presentation unnatural when action is not associated with sound within a few seconds. When there is little expectation that sound and action should be linked (e.g., film of a whale swimming while vocalizing), then synchronization is less important.

One final point to bear in mind is that, generally, it helps to present linguistic media before image media to provide background information. Giving language first activates relevant memories and cues the user to search for appropriate information in the following images, thereby providing a framework for building comprehension.

Navigation and Control

Task analysis provides the basis for dialogue design. Navigational and control dialogues enable flexible access to the multimedia content, and give users ability to control how media are played. Dialogue design may also involve specifying how users interact with tools, agents, and objects in interactive microworlds.

The first question to be resolved is whether the UI is to support a single dedicated task or a range of tasks. If the application supports many different tasks, then the interface design has to enable task switching. This implies an outer layer of dialogue that supports user access to appropriate task support functions with status indicators and aide-memoire displays to remind the user which system functions are active and where they are within a task sequence. If the application needs to support one or two well-structured tasks, the dialogue and screen sequence will follow the steps (goals or procedures) in the task model. Screen navigation diagrams are created from the task model sequence of subgoals and procedures, then storyboards are developed to illustrate key task steps, and they are validated with users. If multitasking is required with less well-structured tasks, then a high-level access dialogue will be necessary. Each task fragment (i.e., subgoal) is analyzed and storyboard minisequences planned as before. Commands are placed into task- or functionally-related groups and access dialogues specified. In simple cases, this will involve menu design; however, in more complex cases, commands may be organized by structural metaphors, for example, palettes in paint and drawing programs. Determining the requirements for multitask working and the user's need to cross-reference between tasks helps to plan how many dialogues and windows may need to be active at once.

Hypermedia Dialogues

In information intensive multimedia where access to content is the main design goal, hypermedia dialogues link content segments. Hypermedia enables browsing a network along all the possible pathways between segments that the user may need. Studies of user interaction with hypertext systems have shown different user search strategies:

- Random — No particular order is observable.
- Scanning — Users sample different parts of the hypertext without systematically exploring any part in depth.
- Spike exploration — The user follows link pathways, although the search may not be directed to any specific goal, and sidetracks are evident in the trace of the user's search.
- Searching — Exploration follows pathways in a directed manner toward an information-seeking goal. Fewer diversions down sidetracks occur in searching.

Link structures and overview maps for scanning can be planned with these strategies in mind. Unfortunately, hypermedia systems assume a fixed database and link structure. This can be made more flexible by branch points in scripts, but the user is still ultimately limited to the pathways provided by the designer. More open-ended hypertext environments provide links with scripts and query facilities so users can access databases as well as browse the hypertext network. Preformed queries can be attached to hotspots in images or nodes in hypertext documents. These are more flexible because queries attached to links can provide access paths to a wider variety of data compared to static links. In this case, the division between hypertext links and database query languages becomes blurred.

Good hypertext design is a matter of sound information analysis to specify the pathways between related items, and use of cues to show the structure of the information space to the user. In document-based hypermedia (e.g., HTML and the Internet) links can only access the whole media resource rather than pointing to components within a document. Design advice on hypermedia Web interfaces is already swamping the bookshelves, so I will restrict myself to a synopsis drawn from Nielsen and Spool, Scanlon, Snyder, Schroeder and De Angelo. The design issues are to plan the overall structure, segment complex structures into a hierarchy of subnetworks, and then plan the connectivity in each subnetwork. The access structure of most hypermedia will be hierarchical, organized according to the information model and categorization of content, for example, information grouped by functional, organizational, task, or user preference. This shows a hierarchical access structure, with limited network links within content pages to view more information or to access related documents elsewhere. Restricting network links within the site and creating a page for network links outside the site help to preserve a clear navigation structure. Return to home and exit pathways are always accessible. Navigation controls can be implemented as side bar menus, but it is also advisable to place these controls at the bottom of pages. Too many links within content pages can disrupt reading or viewing the medium, so a separate outlink or Web resources page containing links outside the site is preferable to embedding too many links within contents pages.

Overall, constructing good hypertext is based on translating the user's model of the information space into a hypertext graph.

Unfortunately, individual users have different models, so this may not be an easy task. Too many links will make the system too complex and increase the chance of the user getting lost. Too few links will frustrate a user who cannot find what he or she wants.

One problem with large hypermedia systems is that users get lost in them. Navigation cues, waymarks, and minimap overviews can help to counter the effects of disorientation. Minimaps provide an overview of the hypertext area while another display shows the local part of the network. This gives the user a reference context for where he or she is in large networks. Filters or user views for part of the network can also help to reduce complexity by showing only a subset of nodes and links in which the user is interested. Having typed links helps filtering views because the user can guess the information content from the link type, for example, reference, example, source, related work, and so forth. Other facilities for user navigation are visit lists containing a history of nodes traversed in a session. The user can backtrack using the visit list as a trace pathway. Nodes in visit lists can be tagged with the date they were accessed so that users can find out where they have been in a particular part of the hypertext and when. Another navigation problem is not knowing where to get started. Guided tours can help to solve this problem by taking the user on a preset exploration of the hypertext. However, guided tours do militate against the spirit of free exploration in hypertext because they enforce a particular pathway. Once the structure has been designed, link cues need to be located within media resources, so the appropriateness of the cue needs to be considered within each medium. For example, see the following:

- Text media—The Web convention is to highlight and underline text in a consistent color, for example, blue or purple.
- Images—Link cues can be set as stand-alone icons or as active components in images. Icons need to be tested with users because the designer's assumed meaning might be ambiguous. Active components should signal the link by captions or pop-up "hover text" so the user can inspect a link before deciding whether to follow it.
- Moving images—Links from animation and film are difficult to design because the medium is dynamic; however, link buttons can be placed below the movie window. Active

components within a moving image are technically more challenging although overlaid buttons can provide the answer. Buttons may also be timed to pop up at appropriate times during the video.

- Sound and speech make link origins difficult for the same reason as with moving images. Solutions are to use visual cues, possible synchronized with the sound or speech track. If speech recognition is available, then voice commands can act as links, but these commands need to be explained to the user. Automatic links can also be used, but if these are embedded within the speech or sound medium, then user controls to activate preset links before playing will be necessary.

Navigation Controls

The motivation of navigation controls is to give the user access to the logical content of multimedia resources. However, access to logical components may be constrained by limitations of physical media resources. For example, a movie may be logically composed of several scenes, but it can only be accessed by a timer set to the beginning of the whole film. Worse still, a video clip may only be playable as a single segment making implementation of navigation requirements impossible.

Specifying Media Controls

In many cases, controls will be provided by the media-rendering device, for example, the video player. If controls have to be implemented from scratch, then for static media there are size and scale controls to zoom and pan, page access if the medium has page segmentation as in text and diagrams, and the ability to change attributes such as color and display resolution, font type, and size in text. For dynamic media, the familiar video controls are stop, start, play, pause, fast forward, and rewind, along with the ability to address a particular point or event in the media stream by a time marker or an index, for example, "go to" component or marker.

As well as navigation controls, dialogue controls will be necessary for the information that the user has to input into the system, and the commands the user needs to give to invoke automated functions. These become the available command options; however, sometimes the boundary between a command and input data can be hard to define, for example, a dial metaphor used to set a temperature level on a thermostat may be considered as an input and a command, that is, system commands that implement automated or semiautomated actions in the task model. The final step is to select standard UI components (e.g., buttons, dialogue boxes, menus, icons, sliders) to implement user actions and controls. Most multimedia controls and data entry dialogues will employ standard UI techniques, that is, form filling, dialogue boxes, and selection menus.

Designing the Reading or Viewing Sequence

Having selected the media resources, the designer must now ensure that the user will extract the appropriate information. Visual media in particular may contain detailed information and, in the absence of specific directions, users will only extract high-level overview or gist. Presentation design is primarily concerned with visual media, as the user's viewing sequence is unpredictable; however, the design should also make important information salient in speech and sound. Another important consideration is to link the thread of a message across several different media. The need for focus shifts between information components are identified and attention-directing techniques are selected to implement the desired effect. This section addresses design to direct the user's attention across several media so the overall theme is delivered as a coherent whole.

Media Integration and Design for Attention

Recommendations on planning the user's reading or viewing sequence are specialized for presentation sequences, hypermedia dialogues, and navigation controls. The essential differences are timing and user control. In presentation design, the reading or viewing sequence and timing are set by the designer; whereas the reading or viewing sequence in hypertext and interactive dialogues is under user control.Presentation techniques help to direct the user's attention to important information and specify the desired order of reading or viewing. Key information items are annotated onto presentation bar charts when planning the sequence and duration of media delivery. The design issues follow:

- It is necessary to plan the overall thematic thread of the message through the presentation or dialogue.
- One must draw the user's attention to important information.
- One must establish a clear viewing or reading sequence.
- It is necessary to provide clear links when the theme crosses from one medium to another.

Design for attention is particularly important for images. User attention to time-varying media is determined by the medium itself, that is, we have little choice but to listen to speech or to view animations in the order in which they are presented. The reading sequence is directed by the layout of text, although this is culturally dependent; for example, Western languages read left to right, Arabic languages read in the opposite direction. However, viewing order in images is unpredictable unless the design specifically directs the user's attention.

Directing the user's reading or viewing sequence helps the thread of a message to be perceived more easily. In some cases, a common topic may be sufficient; however, when the thread is important or hard to follow, designed effects for attention are necessary to aid the user's perception. The term contact point refers to a reference from one medium to another and comes from the experimental work of Mary Hegarty, who demonstrated that comprehension is improved by reinforcing the links between information in different media. Two types of contact point are distinguished:

- Direct contact points—Attention- directing effects implemented in both the source and destination medium; for example, in the text an instruction is given such as, " while the component is highlighted. Direct contact points create a strong cross reference between two media.
- Indirect contact points—Attention-directing effects implemented only in the source, or less frequently the destination, medium; for example, "In Figure 1, the assembly process is shown" is spoken, with no highlighting being used in the image. Indirect contact points have less attention-directing force and work by temporal sequencing or spatial juxtapositoning.

In most cases, the attentional effect in a direct contact point will be actuated in sequence, although occasionally both effects may be presented concurrently if the order of the association is not important. In hypermedia implementations, direct contact points become a link cue in the source medium and a highlight anchor in the destination medium.

A direct contact point should be used if the connection between information in two different media is important. Implementation depends on the selected media; for instance, speech directs the user to the object in the image while highlighting the object that is being spoken about: "Look at the map; the road to London is (highlight)"; or a text caption is revealed with an arrow pointing to the road. Direct contact points emphasize the links between media but can become intrusive if overused.

Indirect contact points are used when the connection between information in two media is necessary but perception of the destination components is less important, speaking about an object while displaying the image; freeze frame video while describing objects. Indirect contact points are less intrusive, so they may be used more frequently without becoming disruptive.

Multiple contact points can direct the user's attention to follow the theme and connect a thread of topics. For instance, inabiology tutorial, explaining parts of a cell is organized with interleaved speech segments and a diagram describing the cell's components from top to bottom, left to right. Highlighting techniques locate each component in turn, following the order of the spoken explanation. The contact points have been made explicit as buttons that jump to the start of a video segment that was related to the text. An alternative implementation would have been to highlight the text and pause the video clip at the start of the appropriate scene. The attention-directing techniques described in the following section are used for implementing contact points.

Salience Effects in Single Media

In larger development teams, within-media design is carried out by specialists, for example, video and animation designers, graphics and calligraphic specialists. However, in smaller teams, such experts may not be available; furthermore, novice designers still require advice. In this section, the principal design concern is making important parts of the content salient. Aesthetic and motivational issues are not addressed.

Still Image Media. Extraction of information from images depends on domain knowledge, what people know about the components, the task, motivation (which govern how much they want to find information within an image), and design of the medium. The design problem is how to direct the user's attention to the appropriate information at the correct level of detail. Regular layout grids help design composite images and encourage a consistent layout in image sets. Users will tend initially to extract information from images at the scene level, that is, major objects will be identified but with very little descriptive detail. A list of the key components that the user needs to focus on and an estimate of the facts that should be extracted from the image are prerequisites for this stage.

Generally, users will focus on components that change or move, are brighter in color, set apart from other objects, larger in size, shown in more detail, sharper in focus, or nearer the front of the scene. If the key components have none of these properties, then a highlighting technique may be necessary. Alternatively, the window frame can be set to control which parts of an image are viewed. Larger window frames will be attended to before smaller areas. If a particular object needs to be located accurately, then mark it with a salient icon. This will act as a landmark, which will help to locate components more accurately and improve memorization of proximal objects.

A common highlighting technique will pick out spatially distributed objects, for example, change all the objects to the same color; co-located objects can be grouped by using a common color or texture for their background or drawing a box around them. The highlighted area will set the granularity of the user's attention. Captions linked to objects in an image are another useful means of drawing attention and providing supplementary information (e.g., identity). Dynamic revealing of captions is particularly effective and can be used to direct the user's viewing sequence. Sequential highlighting is also useful for showing the pathways or navigational instructions.

Moving image Media. Directing attention to components within moving images is difficult because of the dynamic nature of the medium. Design of film and video is an extensive subject in its own right, so treatment here is necessarily brief. The design advice is based on Hochberg. First, the content needs to be structured into scenes that correspond to the information script. Scene boundaries structure animation sequences, and so a cut, wipe, or dissolve can be used to emphasize that a change in the content structure has taken place. Cuts, wipes, and dissolve effects will reset the user's attention and make the initial part of the following scene more salient. However, cuts should be used with care because continuity must be maintained between the two action sequences if they are to be integrated. Continuity maintains the same viewpoint and subject matter in the shot. Change in background or action, for example, a person walking left in one clip and walking right in the next, is quickly noticed as a discontinuity. The objects involved in the motion should be identifiable across the cut and the ground over which the action takes place should be stable. If the change in sequence required is large, then a wipe or dissolve can be used as an explicit signal. Cuts in general signal a smaller change in a theme.

An establishing shot which shows the whole scene should be used to start a new sequence and provide context. To provide detail of newly introduced object or context, the object is shown filling the frame with a small amount of surrounding scene; whereas to imply a relation or compare two objects a tight two-shot with both objects together in the same frame is advisable. If the start and end state of an action sequence are important, then a "slide show" image sequence may be better than animation, as recall of the details of action may be improved if shown in a set of stills or in slow motion. The onset or change in topographic motion, in which an object moves across the ground of an image, is more effective for attracting attention than internal movement of an object's components.

Linguistic Media (Text and Speech). As with moving image, the literature on layout of text is extensive. Two levels of linguistic media design are considered: first, structuring the text itself to make the segmenting of content clear, and second, design of markers within text to guide the user toward certain phrases and sentences.

Text may be structured to indicate subsections by indentation, formatting into paragraphs, columns, or use of background color. Bullet points or numbered sections indicate order more formally, for example, for procedures. If language is being used to set the context for accompanying media, it is important that the correct reference level is set. For instance, a higher-level concept or the whole scene is described at the beginning of a script. When detail or particular objects are important, then the level of detail is set by introducing single facts or individual objects.

Cue phrases and keyword markers can be used to make phrases and sentences more salient. For instance, when an action sequence or time is complex or unfamiliar, a cue phrase "in the following steps" can be used to explain the change. Sequence cues, for example, "at time x, " "next, " or "just after, " locate an important time point or event, such as the start or end of a sequence, whereas "next, " "until, " "while, " or "if... then... otherwise" indicate order in sequences. Causal relations can be suggested by markers such as "because, " "in order to, " "consequently, " or "resulting-in"; whereas comparisons may be signaled by "in contrast, " "as opposed to, " "on the other hand, " or "either... or. " Finally, voice change (active to passive, first person to third) in text or spoken language can be used to segment text and emphasize different sections. The effects, ordered according to their power in attracting attention in text and speech. These effects are used to draw attention to important information within each medium as well as making clear thematic links between media.

This concludes the method stages, which have now produced a detailed and thematically integrated presentation design. The guidelines will have been applied either to the specification bar chart before implementation or iteratively during a cycle of prototype implementation, evaluations, and critiquing.

Case Study Example

To illustrate the guidelines, an example of a commercial CD-ROM, "The etiology of cancer, " is used. This application was designed for undergraduate training of medical students. The content is directed toward causal explanation and conceptual learning, and the following segment explains how an enzyme repairs a mutation in a DNA sequence. The important facts that should be conveyed follow:

- The identity and attributes of the objects—DNA, with the mutation to be repaired, the photolyase enzyme, the dimer (enzyme bound to damaged DNA), and light energy.

- The actions organized in the sequence of repair—DNA is damaged by mutation, enzyme attaches to damaged DNA, forms dimer complex, light energy activates enzyme, DNA is repaired, enzyme detaches from DNA.
- Causal explanation—That DNA is repaired by the photolyase enzyme which forms a dimer complex with the DNA and requires light energy to activate it.

In the original product, no bullet points were used, and there were only a limited number of text captions to augment the image and speech soundtrack. Part of the presentation used a sequence of revealed captions, with limited animation in the light energy sequence; however, the design did not follow the causal explanation media pattern. The goal was not introduced and no summary of key concepts was given, although the causal sequence was portrayed as a series of still images with minianimations. The whole sequence was not repeated with an animation to integrate the causal explanation.

Several contact points should link the speech and between-image and text components. However, few contacts were implemented in the initial version of the product. Furthermore, no attempt was made to highlight key components, such as the enzyme or the dimer complex. These strengthen coordination between the speech track and image components as well as making key objects more salient. Comprehension tests were carried out on this product before and after improvements using the contact point guidelines. Comprehension was significantly improved for novices after redesign; experts showed some improvement. This experimental evidence demonstrated the value of directing the user's attention with image-based media as well as showing the importance of integration in multimedia.

Conclusion

This chapter described a method for designing interactive multimedia, including modeling techniques and guidelines. The method starts with requirements analysis to capture the users' goals. This is followed by analysis of the users' characteristics; domain analysis to create a profile of the users' knowledge, roles, and abilities; and a description of the system domain, environmental variables, available technology, and domain layout. This information influences media selection and choice of metaphors. Analysis proceeds by task analysis to decompose requirements goals, possibly supplemented by use case description of user-system interaction. The next step is information analysis, which establishes the content for education multimedia and the information needed to support users' tasks. Information units and groupings are classified with a set of amodal information types that facilitate mapping to appropriate media. Media resources are selected for the information types using a set of mapping rules and the presentation is organized in a first-cut script. These are used to create storyboards and mock-ups of the system, which are tested with users to get early feedback on the design. Aesthetic effects modify selection rules and focus on choice of media for attractiveness and arousal. Use of human image can project personality and develop persuasive dialogues.

More detailed design focuses on presentation layout and specification of the user-system dialogue. Dialogues are based on the users' tasks, with additional controls for navigation and manipulation of media. Presentations are specified in screen maps and bar charts, which show the order and layout of windows and playing audio media. Navigation is based on the logical model of information with search and access facilities. The second aspect of detailed design is highlighting information to draw the users' attention to key facts and establish contact points between related information in different media. Design effects for making information salient in each media type are used to add contact points to the presentation.

9

Animation: Design and Effects

Animation

Animation is the rapid display of a sequence of images of 2-D artwork or model positions in order to create an illusion of movement. It is an optical illusion of motion due to the phenomenon of persistence of vision. This could be anything from a flip book to a motion picture film.

Early Animation

There is no single person who can be considered the "creator" of the art of animation, as there were several people doing several projects which could be considered various types of animation all around the same time. (Short, hand-drawn animation scenes could be presented with the Phenakistoscope, the Zoetrope, and other optical "toys" already in the early 1800s.)

The following is a brief listing on those who are often acknowledged as significant to the development of animation. Note that this list is by no means a comprehensive list of contributors to early animation.

Georges Méliès was a creator of special effect films, such as A Trip to the Moon. He used many techniques one of which was to stop the camera rolling, change something in the scene, and then continue rolling the film. This is a very similar idea to that of stop-motion animation. Melies accidentally happened upon the technique when his camera broke down while shooting a bus driving by. When the camera was fixed, a horse happened to be passing by just as Méliès continued to film. The result was that the bus appeared to change into a horse.

J. Stuart Blackton was possibly the first filmmaker in America to use the techniques of stop-motion and hand-drawn animation. Introduced to filmmaking by Edison, he pioneered these concepts at the turn of the 20th century, with his first copyrighted work dated 1900.

Emile Cohl began drawing cartoon strips and created a film in 1908 called Fantasmagorie. The film largely consisted of a stick figure moving about and encountering all manner of morphing objects, such as a wine bottle that transforms into a flower. There were also sections of live action where the animator's hands would enter the scene. The film was created by drawing each frame on paper and then shooting each frame onto negative film, which gave the picture a blackboard look.

Winsor McCay created detailed animations that required a team of artists and painstaking attention for detail. Each frame was drawn on paper, requiring backgrounds to be redrawn, as well characters to be animated. His films such as Gertie the Dinosaur (1914) and The Sinking of the Lusitania (1918) were of an impressive scale, although The Sinking of the Lusitania used cels.

Otto Messmer, in 1919, created the character of Felix the cat for Pat Sullivan's animation studios. The importance of Felix lies in the character's strong personality, created largely through gesture and actions.

Animation Techniques

Animation techniques are incredibly varied and difficult to categorize. Techniques are often related or combined. The following is a brief on common types of animation. Again, this list is by no means comprehensive.

Traditional animation

Also called cel animation, the frames of a traditionally animated movie are hand-drawn. The drawings are traced or copied onto transparent acetate sheets called cels, which are then placed over a painted background and photographed one by one on a rostrum camera. Nowadays, the use of cels (and cameras) is mostly obsolete, since the drawings are scanned into computers, and digitally transferred directly to 35 mm film. The "look" of traditional cel animation is still preserved, and the character animator's work has remained essentially the same over the past 70 years. Because of the digital influence over modern cel animation, it is also known as tradigital animation.

Full animation

The most common style in animation, known for its realistic and often very detailed art.
Examples: All Disney feature length animated films, The Secret of NIMH, or The Iron Giant

Limited animation

A cheaper process of making animated cartoons that does not follow a "realistic" approach.
Examples: The Flintstones, Yellow Submarine

Rubber hose

The characters are usually cartoony, and the animators have a lot of artistic freedom as rubber hose animations don't have to follow the laws of physics and anatomy in the same degree as the other main styles in animation.
Examples: Early Mickey Mouse cartoons, Ren and Stimpy, Popeye

Rotoscoping

A technique where animators trace live action movement, frame by frame, either by directly copying an actors outlines into an animated drawing (e.g. Ralph Bakshi), or use rotoscoped material as a basis and inspiration for a more fluid and expressive animation (e.g. Disney).
Examples: Snow White and the Seven Dwarfs, Gulliver's Travels, American Pop

Stop motion

Stop-motion animation is any type of animation which requires the animator to physically alter the scene, shoot a frame, again alter the scene and shoot a frame and so on, to create the animation. There are many different types of stop-motion animation. Some notable examples are listed below.

Clay animation

A clay animation scene from a TV commercial.

Often abbreviated to claymation, this is a type of stop-motion animation using figures made of clay or a similar malleable material. The figures may have an armature or wire frame inside of them, similar to puppet animation (below). Alternatively, the figures may be made entirely of clay, such as in the films of Bruce Bickford where clay creatures morph into a variety of different shapes.

Examples: Wallace and Gromit; Dimensions of Dialogue by Jan Švankmajer; The Amazing Mr. Bickford; The Trap Door

Cutout animation

In this type of stop-motion animation, the animation is formed by moving 2-dimensional pieces of material such as paper or cloth.

Examples: the animated sequences of Monty Python's Flying Circus (often referred to as Dada animation, named after the Dada art movement); Tale of Tales; early episodes of South Park

Silhouette animation

A type of cutout animation where the viewer only sees black silhouettes.

Example: The Adventures of Prince Achmed, the world's oldest surviving animated feature film, from 1926.

Graphic animation

Model animation

In this form of animation, model animated characters interact with, and are a part of, the live-action world.

Examples: The films of Ray Harryhausen (Jason and the Argonauts) and Willis O'Brien (King Kong)

Go motion

Object animation

Pixilation

Examples: Neighbours

Puppet animation

Puppet animation typically involves puppet figures interacting with each other in a constructed environment, in contrast to the real-world interaction in model animation (above). The puppets generally have an armature inside of them to keep them still and steady as well as constraining them to move at particular joints.

Examples: The Nightmare Before Christmas, Robot Chicken, The Tale of the Fox

Brickfilm

Puppetoon

Computer Animation

Like stop motion, computer animation encompasses a variety of techniques, the unifying idea being that the animation is created digitally on a computer.

2D animation

Figures are created and/or edited on the computer using 2D bitmap graphics or created and edited using 2D vector graphics. This includes automated computerized versions of traditional animation techniques such as of tweening, morphing, onion skinning and interpolated rotoscoping.

Examples: A Scanner Darkly, Jib Jab

- Analog computer animation
- Flash animation
- PowerPoint animation

A completely synthetic, computer-generated scene.

3D animation

Figures are created in the computer using polygons. To allow these meshes to move they are given a digital armature (sculpture). This process is called rigging. Various other techniques can be applied, such as mathematical functions (gravity), simulated fur or hair, effects such as fire and water and the use of motion capture to name but a few.

Examples The Incredibles, Shrek

- Cel-shaded animation
- Morph target animation
- Skeletal animation
- Motion capture
- Crowd simulation

Less common techniques

Drawn on film animation

A technique where footage is produced by creating the images directly on film stock.

Paint-on-glass animation

A technique for making animated films by manipulating slow-drying oil paints on sheets of glass.

Pinscreen animation

Makes use of a screen filled with movable pins, which can be moved in or out by pressing an object onto the screen. The screen is lit from the side so that the pins cast shadows. The technique has been used to create animated films with a range of textural effects difficult to achieve with traditional cel animation.

Sand animation

Sand is moved around on a backlighted or frontlighted piece of glass to create each frame for an animated film.

Other techniques and approaches

- Character animation
- Chuckimation
- Multi-sketching
- Special effects animation

Computer Animation

Computer animation is the art of creating moving images via the use of computers. It is a subfield of computer graphics and animation. Increasingly it is created by means of 3D computer graphics, though 2D computer graphics are still widely used for low bandwidth and faster real-time rendering needs. Sometimes the target of the animation is the computer itself, but it sometimes the target is another medium, such as film. It is also referred to as CGI (computer generated imagery or computer generated imaging), especially when used in films.

To create the illusion of movement, an image is displayed on the computer screen then quickly replaced by a new image that is similar to the previous image, but shifted slightly. This technique is identical to how the illusion of movement is achieved with television and motion pictures.

Computer animation is essentially a digital successor to the art of stop motion animation of 3D models and frame-by-frame animation of 2D illustrations. For 3D animations, objects (models) are built on the computer monitor (modeled) and 3D figures are rigged with a virtual skeleton. For 2D figure animations, separate objects (illustrations) and separate transparent layers are used, with or without a virtual skeleton. Then the limbs, eyes, mouth, clothes, etc. of the figure are moved by the animator on key frames. The differences in appearance between key frames are automatically calculated by the computer in a process known as tweening or morphing. Finally, the animation is rendered.

For 3D animations, all frames must be rendered after modeling is complete. For 2D vector animations, the rendering process is the key frame illustration process, while tweened frames are rendered as needed. For pre-recorded presentations, the rendered frames are transferred to a different format or medium such as film or digital video. The frames may also be rendered in real time as they are presented to the end-user audience. Low bandwidth animations transmitted via the internet (e.g. 2D Flash, X3D) often use software on the end-users computer to render in real time as an alternative to streaming or pre-loaded high bandwidth animations.

A Simple Example

The screen is blanked to a background color, such as black. Then a goat is drawn on the right of the screen. Next the screen is blanked, but the goat is re-drawn or duplicated slightly to the left of its original position. This process is repeated, each time moving the goat a bit to the left. If this process is repeated fast enough the goat will appear to move smoothly to the left. This basic procedure is used for all moving pictures in films and television.

The moving goat is an example of shifting the location of an object. More complex transformations of object properties such as size, shape, lighting effects and color often require calculations and computer rendering instead of simple re-drawing or duplication.

Explanation

To trick the eye and brain into thinking they are seeing a smoothly moving object, the pictures should be drawn at around 12 frames per second or faster (a frame is one complete image). With rates above 70 frames/s no improvement in realism or smoothness is perceivable due to the way the eye and brain process images. At rates below 12 frames/s most people can detect jerkiness associated with the drawing of new images which detracts from the illusion of realistic movement. Conventional hand-drawn cartoon animation often uses 15 frames/s in order to save on the number of drawings needed, but this is usually accepted because of the stylized nature of cartoons. Because it produces more realistic imagery computer animation demands higher frame rates to reinforce this realism.

The reason no jerkiness is seen at higher speeds is due to "persistence of vision." From moment to moment, the eye and brain working together actually store whatever you look at for a fraction of a second, and automatically "smooth out" minor jumps. Movie film seen in a theater runs at 24 frames/s which is sufficient to create this illusion of continuous movement. Many people are tricked into seeing the movement without any stopping because the frames are shot at a quick rate.

Creating Characters and Objects on a Computer

Computer animation combines vector graphics with programmed movement. The starting point is often a stick figure in which the position of each feature (limb, mouth etc) is defined by as Avars (animation variable).

The character "Woody" in Toy Story, for example, uses 700 Avars, with 100 Avars in his face alone. Successive sets of Avars control all movement of the character from frame to frame. Once the stick model is moving in the desired way, the avars are incorporated into a full wire frame model or a model built of polygons. Finally surfaces are added, requiring a lengthy process of rendering to produce the final scene.

There are several ways of generating the Avar values to obtain realistic motion. Motion tracking uses lights or markers on a real person acting out the part, tracked by a video camera. Or the Avars may be set manually using a joystick or other form of input control. Toy Story uses no motion tracking, probably because only manual control by a skilled animator can produce effects not easily acted out by a real person.

Computer Animation Development Equipment

Computer animation can be created with a computer and animation software. Some examples of animation software are: Amorphium, Art of Illusion, Poser, Ray Dream Studio, Bryce, Maya, Blender, TrueSpace, Lightwave, 3D Studio Max, SoftImage XSI, Alice, and Adobe Flash (2D). There are many more. Prices will vary greatly depending on target market. Some impressive animation can be achieved even with basic programs; however, the rendering can take a lot of time on an ordinary home computer. Because of this, video game animators tend to use low resolution, low polygon count renders, such that the graphics can be rendered in real time on a home computer. Photorealistic animation would be impractical in this context.

Professional animators of movies, television, and video sequences on computer games make photorealistic animation with high detail. This level of quality for movie animation would take tens to hundreds of years to create on a home computer. Many powerful workstation computers are used instead. Graphics workstation computers use two to four processors, and thus are a lot more powerful than a home computer, and are specialized for rendering. A large number of workstations (known as a render farm) are networked together to effectively act as a giant computer. The result is a computer animated movie that can be completed in about one to five years (this process is not comprised solely of rendering, however). A workstation typically costs $2,000 to $16,000, with the more expensive stations being able to render much faster, due to the more technologically advanced hardware that they contain. Pixar's Renderman is rendering software which is widely used as the movie animation industry standard, in competition with Mental Ray. It can be bought at the official Pixar website for about $5,000 to $8,000. It will work on Linux, Mac OS X, and Microsoft Windows based graphics workstations along with an animation program such as Maya and Softimage XSI. Professionals also use digital movie cameras, motion capture or performance capture, bluescreens, film editing software, props, and other tools for movie animation.

Hardware Animation Display Technology

When an image is rendered to the screen, it is normally rendered to something called a back buffer. There the computer can draw the image, making any necessary changes to it before it is done. While the computer is rendering, the screen is showing the contents of what is called the primary or active buffer.

When the image is completed, the computer tells the screen to draw from the back buffer. This can be done in one of two ways: the contents of the back buffer can be copied to the primary buffer (or active buffer the buffer which is currently being shown) or the computer can switch where it is drawing from and make the back buffer the new primary buffer. In this case, the primary buffer becomes the back buffer. John MacArthur is the one that thought up this process. This process is usually called double buffering or, informally, "flipping," because the computer is flipping its use of primary and back buffers.

This switching should be carried out when it is imperceptible to the user. Therefore it needs to take place during what is called the "v-sync" or vertical retrace. The v-sync, in CRTs, takes place when the electron guns reach the bottom right of the screen and need to reposition the beam to the top left of the screen. This happens very quickly and the image the guns had just projected remain on the screen as they are moving back to their starting position. While the guns are repositioning themselves, the computer has enough time to flip buffers and the new image will be rendered on the screen on the next pass of the guns. The new image will continued to be displayed until the buffers are flipped once more.

When the computer fails to wait for the v-sync, a condition called sprite breakup or image breakup is perceptible. This is highly undesirable and should always be avoided when possible to maintain the illusion of movement.

The Future

One open challenge in computer animation is a photorealistic animation of humans. Currently, most computer-animated movies show animal characters (Finding Nemo), fantasy characters (Shrek, Monsters Inc.), anthropomorphic machines (Cars, Robots) or cartoon-like humans (The Incredibles). The movie Final Fantasy: The Spirits Within is often cited as the first computer-generated movie to attempt to show realistic-looking humans. However, due to the enormous complexity of the human body, human motion, and human biomechanics, realistic simulation of humans remains largely an open problem. It is one of the "holy grails" of computer animation. Eventually, the goal is to create software where the animator can generate a movie sequence showing a photorealistic human character, undergoing physically-plausible motion, together with clothes, photorealistic hair, a complicated natural background, and possibly interacting with other simulated human characters. This should be done in a way that the viewer is no longer able to tell if a particular movie sequence is computer-generated, or created using real actors in front of movie cameras. Achieving such a goal would mean that conventional flesh-and-bone human actors are no longer necessary for this kind of movie creation, and computer animation would become the standard way of making every kind of a movie, not just animated movies. However, living actors will be needed for voice-over acting and motion capture body movements. Complete human realism is not likely to happen very soon, however such concepts obviously bear certain philosophical implications for the future of the film industry.

For the moment it looks like three dimensional computer animation can be divided into two main directions; photorealistic and non-photorealistic rendering. Photorealistic computer animation can itself be divided into two subcategories; real photorealism (where performance capture is used in the creation of the virtual human characters) and stylized photorealism. Real photorealism is what Final Fantasy tried to achieve and will in the future most likely have the ability to give us live action fantasy features as The Dark Crystal without having to use advanced puppetry and animatronics, while Antz is an example on stylistic photorealism (in the future stylized photorealism will be able to replace traditional stop motion animation as in Corpse Bride). None of them are as mentioned perfected yet, but the progress continues.

The non-photorealistic/cartoonish direction is more like an extension and improvement of traditional animation, an attempt to make the animation look like a three dimensional version of a cartoon, still using and perfecting the main principles of animation articulated by the Nine Old Men, such as squash and stretch.

While a single frame from a photorealistic computer animated feature will look like a photo if done right, a single frame vector from a cartoonish computer animated feature will look like a painting (not to be confused with cel shading, which produces an ever simpler look).

Detailed Examples and Pseudocode

In 2D computer animation, moving objects are often referred to as "sprites." A sprite is an image that has a location associated with it. The location of the sprite is changed slightly, between each displayed frame, to make the sprite appear to move. The following pseudocode makes a sprite move from left to right:

```
var int x := 0, y := screenHeight &div; 2;
while x < screenWidth
drawBackground()
drawSpriteAtXY (x, y) // draw on top of the background
x := x + 5 // move to the right
```

Modern computer animation uses different techniques to produce animations. Most frequently, sophisticated mathematics is used to manipulate complex three dimensional polygons, apply "textures", lighting and other effects to the polygons and finally rendering the complete image. A sophisticated graphical user interface may be used to create the animation and arrange its choreography. Another technique called constructive solid geometry defines objects by conducting boolean operations on regular shapes, and has the advantage that animations may be accurately produced at any resolution.

Let's step through the rendering of a simple image of a room with flat wood walls with a grey pyramid in the center of the room.

The pyramid will have a spotlight shining on it. Each wall, the floor and the ceiling is a simple polygon, in this case, a rectangle. Each corner of the rectangles is defined by three values referred to as X, Y and Z. X is how far left and right the point is. Y is how far up and down the point is, and Z is far in and out of the screen the point is. The wall nearest us would be defined by four points: (in the order x, y, z). Below is a representation of how the wall is defined.

(0, 10, 0) (10, 10, 0)
(0,0,0) (10, 0, 0)

The far wall would be:

(0, 10, 20) (10, 10, 20)
(0, 0, 20) (10, 0, 20)

The pyramid is made up of five polygons: the rectangular base, and four triangular sides. To draw this image the computer uses math to calculate how to project this image, defined by three dimensional data, onto a two dimensional computer screen.

First we must also define where our view point is, that is, from what vantage point will the scene be drawn. Our view point is inside the room a bit above the floor, directly in front of the pyramid. First the computer will calculate which polygons are visible. The near wall will not be displayed at all, as it is behind our view point. The far side of the pyramid will also not be drawn as it is hidden by the front of the pyramid.

Next each point is perspective projected onto the screen. The portions of the walls 'farthest' from the view point will appear to be shorter than the nearer areas due to perspective. To make the walls look like wood, a wood pattern, called a texture, will be drawn on them. To accomplish this, a technique called "texture mapping" is often used. A small drawing of wood that can be repeatedly drawn in a matching tiled pattern (like wallpaper) is stretched and drawn onto the walls' final shape. The pyramid is solid grey so sp its surfaces can just be rendered as grey. But we also have a spotlight. Where its light falls we lighten colors, where objects blocks the light we darken colors.

Next we render the complete scene on the computer screen. If the numbers describing the position of the pyramid were changed and this process repeated, the pyramid would appear to move. ((YEH))

Movies

CGI short films have been produced as independent animation since the 1970s, though the popularity of computer animation (especially in the field of special effects) skyrocketed during the modern era of U.S. animation. The first completely computer-generated animated movie was Toy Story.

Amateur Animation

The popularity of sites such as YouTube, which allows members to upload their own movies for others to view, has created a growing number of what is often considered amateur computer animators. With many free utilities available and programs such as Windows Movie Maker, anyone with the tools can have their animation viewed by thousands.

10

Multimedia Products and Copyright Works

Introduction

The existing categories of copyright works that might eventually be capable of accommodating multimedia products, and having identified the difficulties they would present if they were to serve the needs of these products, one might wonder whether it would be a wiser solution to afford copyright protection to a multimedia work irrespectiveof whether or not it comes within one of the existing categories of copyright works. In other words, one should examine whether the classification of a new work is a necessary prerequisite for the work to attract copyright protection. The essential question therefore is whether a multimedia work can qualify for copyright protection by reason of its originality alone if, of course, it is taken for granted that a multimedia work is by nature a 'work' that is adequately fixed to meet the criterion of fixation in those countries where such a criterion is indispensable for the qualification of a work as a copyright work.

The answer to this question necessarily involves two aspects or considerations. One aspect is whether in all national copyright laws, classification of a work is a necessary prerequisite for it to attract copyright protection. The second is, where such a requirement is not present, whether the option of the protection of a multimedia product outside the special regime of a particular class of works, i.e. as a traditional literary work, a film, a computer program, etc., suffices for its protection and satisfies its needs fully.

Guidance in the Berne Convention

A first element of guidance in this area can be found in the Berne Convention which provides for a minimum standard of protection that needs to be met by all Member States. We will analyse how the Member States have implemented and built upon this minimum standard.

The Berne Convention defines as copyrightable material literary and artistic works, meaning every production in the literary, scientific and artistic domain, whatever its form or mode of expression. Article 2(1) of the Convention gives some illustrative examples of what the concept of literary and artistic works includes: books, pamphlets and other writings, lectures, addresses and so on. Thus, any work which meets this description and which is at the same time original and consistent with what is implied by the notion of 'production' in the same article qualifies for copyright protection. It is clear from the above description and wording that the notions of 'literary works' and 'artistic works' represent generic terms rather than special categories of works in the narrow sense of the term (i.e. traditional literary works). Thus, any work which possesses the essential characteristics contained therein, together with the required creativity that is implied by the nature of these works, qualifies for copyright protection without any further requirement or consideration. Prior classification of a work is not required.

Yet, Berne requires only that all works that come within its scope are protected. How this is achieved is left to the Member States. Two approaches have appeared over the years. A first approach sticks rather closely to the text of the Berne Convention and prior classification does not take place. This approach has mainly been adopted by countries of continental Europe and those that follow their lead.

A first approach

Belgian copyright law keeps the broad generic category of literary and artistic works as the first and only test for qualification of a work as a copyright work. The notion of 'literary and artistic works' is not defined. Article 2 of the Belgian Copyright Act simply refers to literary works as 'writings of any kind' and gives a limited number of examples.

Definitions or examples of artistic works or of sub-categories to the broad literary and artistic works genre are not given. In the German Copyright Act, the generic category of works is the category of 'literary, artistic and scientific works'. The list of works in article 2 of the Act which come within its ambit of protection is only illustrative. The French and the Greek Copyright Acts opt for a category of qualifying subject matter which is linguistically even wider. The French Act refers to any 'work of the mind', whilst the Greek Copyright Act refers to 'works' in general. 'The term "work" designate[s] any original intellectual literary, artistic or scientific creation, expressed in any form, notably written or oral texts.' In all these cases any list of examples is not exhaustive. Thus, in these countries virtually everything qualifies as a copyright work. The criterion that is used to ensure that the quality standard that Berne adopts through the introduction of the terms 'literary and artistic works' is respected is the originality criterion. Only original works will be seen as copyright works and the high originality criterion is there to make the selection.

The 'no prior qualification' approach has also been adopted by the United States. It opts for a general term and definition which, in the first instance, does not immediately refer to literary and artistic works, works of the mind or works generally. Section 102(a) of the US Copyright Act provides that 'copyright protection subsists in original works of authorship fixed in any tangible medium of expression, now known or later developed, from which they can be perceived, reproduced or otherwise communicated, either directly or with the aid of a machine or device'. Similarly in Greek law, the concept of a 'work' is the starting point. However, the American version immediately adds further requirements. In practice there are three necessary prerequisites for a work to qualify for copyright protection. First, it has to be a work, second it has to be original and third it has to be fixed in a tangible medium of expression. Although the US Act later enumerates eight categories of works, these categories play an indicative role only. Works that do not belong in one of these categories may also qualify for copyright protection if they possess the features mentioned above.

At first sight the US three-condition test of qualification seems to be more restrictive than the requirement found in most continental law systems that a work should simply come within the notion of a literary or artistic work in order to qualify for copyright protection. Nevertheless, if one takes into account the loose criterion of originality in the USA, one soon realises that the number of works qualifying for copyright protection in the USA is substantially larger than that on the continent. The broad generic category of literary and artistic works, which is provided for in the continental copyright laws, is substantially restricted by the requirement that a work carry its author's personal imprint. Such a restriction goes a good deal further than the US three-condition test for works.

A Second Approach

The countries we have just mentioned adhere to the first approach in implementing the Berne provisions. A second and rather different approach has been taken by the UK. The CDPA 1988 follows a different route of qualification. Here classification is a necessary requirement. In order for a work to qualify for copyright protection, it has first to come within one of the specifically designated categories of copyright works. According to section 1 of the Act, a work should fall within the description of original literary, dramatic, musical or artistic works, sound recordings, films, broadcasts or cable programmes, or the typographical arrangement of published editions. If that is not the case the work at issue does not qualify as a 'copyright work' for the purposes of this Act. Originality is required only in those cases where it is specifically mentioned. In other words, only literary, dramatic, musical and artistic works have to be original. The originality criterion, as we mentioned earlier, is confined to the issue of whether there is enough skill and labour involved in the creation of the work. It is interesting to note that although the numerus clausus of the copyright categories available in the UK Copyright Act seems to restrict the scope of protection of works, the low originality criterion or the absence of any originality requirement at all in certain cases, coupled with the broad definition and description of these limited categories of works, allows for an extensive number of works to qualify. In this sense, copyright in the UK is much broader than copyright in continental law countries.

The fact that in the UK a work has first to be designated as a particular type of work, for example a literary work, a film, a sound recording, etc., in order to attract copyright protection is not necessarily restrictive to the number of works qualifying. The description of each category of works is usually wide enough to encompass many variations of the same expression. If at the same time the originality and the fixation requirement are respected, this is actually how a work comes within the scope of the CDPA 1988. After this classification the work necessarily qualifies for the regime of protection which corresponds to the class of works at issue, e.g. the audiovisual works regime of protection if the work qualifies as film, the phonograms regime of protection if the work qualifies as a musical work, and so on. However, the risk with broadly defined classes of works is that if a work could qualify for copyright protection under more than one category of works, it might not fit well with the regime of protection of one single category of works. Theoretically, one work should qualify for no more than a single category of works otherwise the general copyright system malfunctions. This view was also confirmed in the case-law. Laddie J ruled in Electronic Techniques (Anglia) Ltd v. Critchley Components Ltd that in some cases the borderline between one category of copyright and another may be difficult to define, but that does not justify giving the author protection in both categories. The categories of copyright works are, to some extent, arbitrarily defined. In the case of a borderline work, I think there are compelling arguments to say that the author must be confined to one or another of the possible categories. The proper category is that which most nearly suits the characteristics of the work in issue.

Thus, if a newly qualified work comes under the classification of films but is not a film stricto sensu and presents a different range of particularities, it is very likely that the regime of protection for films will not serve it well, at least in respect of those characteristics which come on top of the traditional characteristics of the film. The same, of course, applies to any regime corresponding to particular classes of works.

Problems arising from these Approaches

Up to now we have discussed the system of qualification of works as copyright works in relation to both approaches found in the area. Yet both approaches present inherent problems when they have to accommodate multimedia products. We will first deal with the problems deriving from the approach which does not involve prior classification of works.

In the copyright laws where the procedure is usually independent of any prior classification of the work, a work has to possess the general characteristics of the genre of literary and artistic works in order for it to qualify for copyright protection. If that is the case and the work at issue is also original enough, it qualifies for copyright protection without any further requirement. Only in a second phase does classification take place and this happens only when the work possesses the particular characteristics of one of the categories of literary and artistic works for which special rules were deemed to be required. In this case the relevant regime of protection applies. In case classification is not possible by reason of the particularities of the work and the absence of a specific category for multimedia products, then the work is afforded the general copyright regime of protection which coincides with that of traditional literary works. In that case, although the work does not remain unprotected, it can be protected only partially since the general regime of protection covers in essence those parts of a work which come close to a traditional literary work. The issue of how far multimedia products resemble traditional literary works has been discussed earlier in this book, and it is apparent that these two works do not necessarily have much in common. Therefore, if multimedia products were to be protected as traditional literary works it is clear that their protection would not be wide enough to cover their entire scope.

Although the UK approach takes another starting point, it still gives rise to a number of problems. In this case multimedia products cannot be afforded copyright protection unless they are first classified in one of the existing categories. Yet classification is not an easy task here either. The different classes of works have been designed to accommodate specific products, although it is obvious that most of them are worded in very broad terms. Three conclusions can therefore be drawn. First, a work might not qualify for copyright protection at all if none of the categories available is found capable of protecting the work at issue because the work does not come within the definition of any of the categories. Second, fitting the new product into one of the given categories of works, e.g. protecting a multimedia product as a computer program, would inevitably result in protecting the whole product as a computer program and thus attributing features as well as rights and obligations to it which are not relevant or functional in its context. Consequently, the accommodation of multimedia products in any category will inevitably offer copyright protection for those parts of the work that coincide with the characteristics of the works meant to be included in that category of works but not for those characteristics which differ or are additional to it.

The third conclusion that can be drawn is that a work (the multimedia product in the case at issue) might be divided into different parts and each part might be protected on its own merits. However, this is not a viable solution from a market, as well as a practical, point of view. This is because most parts of a multimedia product can be seen only in conjunction with each other and evaluated as a whole. If one misses the value of the interaction of the different components of a new work one also misses the added value which is put on the work exactly by reason of the interaction of these elements. That will inevitably lead us to situations where inseparable and indistinguishable parts (in the sense that they cannot be distinguished or, if distinguished, they give another result) will inevitably stay unprotected. In that sense both approaches present equally grave problems in relation to the protection of multimedia products. Replacing one with the other does not seem to solve the problem. Both approaches are incapable of offering full protection by reason of the difficulty which they will face at some stage in the procedure for qualification of new products. Thus, rejection of one for the sake of the other does not take us very far.

Classification is not an undesirable process, and it is not necessarily that which creates the problems in relation to the protection of a new work as a copyright work. It reflects the need for the appropriate protection for each work. Without classification at either a first or a later stage, a work runs the risk of being misplaced or left partly unprotected. This is also demonstrated in the US White Paper where it is argued that 'however absent the addition of a new category, a work that does not fit into one of the enumerated categories is, in a sense, in a copyright no-man's land'. In addition, the categorisation of a work allows creators and third parties to pursue their rights and fulfil their obligations relating to the particular work. In other words, it is not clear whether an act is permitted under the exceptions to economic acts until one knows whether the work at issue is, for example, a literary work. In the same sense, development of works is neither secure nor even possible if an entrepreneur does not know to what he is entitled. Contract law cannot always close the gaps that are there because of the special nature of intellectual property rights and the existence of ius cogens provisions. Classification is necessary in so far as it determines the applicable regime of protection, and this regime offers the framework within which parties participate in the development, marketing and use of an intellectual property product.

Possible Solutions

From a legal point of view there is much discussion relating to the abandonment of the different categories of copyright works in view of the creation and production of more and more hybrid works which cannot easily be classified. Under the current regime of protection the only possible solution for these works to be protected is their submission under the regime of protection for literary works. That, however, is as unsatisfactory as it is for a work to qualify for any other inappropriate regime of protection. Consequently, only three solutions are possible. First, a new classification must be introduced for the group of new technological productions (which will probably in the future take us down the route of a case-by-case study of copyright works and perhaps necessitate the introduction of new categories of works). Alternatively, there must be an annulment of any specific categories of works and a flexible copyright system, which can be adapted according to the will of the parties and the works at issue, must be designed. A third solution would be the restriction of the scope of copyright only to works which are strictly literary and artistic works (restricting the copyright regime to a core of highly original and creative works as was initially intended), and the design of sui generis rights for the accommodation of the rest. In any event, multimedia products, in view of the difficulties they present when compared with any of the existing categories of works, require special treatment along the lines of either the introduction of a new category of copyright works or the design of a sui generis category of works which will combine copyright and other 'non-copyright' provisions. In addition, they may also call for a combined regime of protection, i.e. copyright protection together with sui generis protection along the lines of databases. From a purely economic point of view, one could argue that there might not be a need for any legislative action in the area of multimedia.

If under the current copyright regimes of protection a class of works is found which can even partly accommodate multimedia products, then the remaining elements of these products, which are not protected under this class of works, could arguably still be satisfactorily protected by the operation of the market. There may indeed be circumstances where the normal operation of the market takes care of the problem and offers adequate protection to multimedia products in the sense that they get the protection they deserve and that that protection goes to the persons who deserve it. On the other hand, it could be argued that multimedia products do not always appear in such circumstances. In the same sense that databases needed a sui generis right to correct a market failure because copyright was not capable of protecting the most valuable aspect of the average database, it can be argued that most multimedia products are not adequately protected by any of the existing copyright regimes. If their real value is found in the combination of various and numerous bits of information, interactivity and integration, no single category of copyright works can offer adequate protection. The aspect of integration is particularly valuable but it is unknown in the current copyright regimes. This means that multimedia products will lose out in terms of protection under any of the existing regimes. The additional value they present remains unprotected and, in a climate of digital ease of copying at a fraction of the original investment costs, the market is unable to correct this failure through its own mechanisms. The result of this is an absence of an optimum level of protection and therefore an absence of an incentive for the creation of new high-quality multimedia products since the creators cannot recoup their efforts nor the entrepreneurs their investment.

In addition, there is no function of the market which can compensate for those parts of a work which are not protected under current law apart from the fact that the first competitor on the market benefits from some lead time, i.e. the time necessary for competitors to prepare and release a competing product. However, in many cases this is a minimal form of protection. The market characteristically favours trading parties which are somehow bound by an agreement or contract. It is therefore not possible for the owner of copyright in a work to bind by contract every third party which has access to his work and which can easily copy and reproduce it. In these circumstances one can reach the conclusion that there exists a market failure requiring correction by the introduction of a new class of works or the creation of a new right. In relation to multimedia products two options are open. Either an adequate classification can be found for a particular type of work or a new type of work or a new (sui generis) right needs to be created.

Conclusion

In conclusion, one can say that under some national regimes of protection a multimedia product can attract copyright protection irrespective of any classification. This is not so in the UK though. Yet under both approaches described above multimedia products are protected either under the general regime of protection for literary and artistic works or under the regime of protection for specific categories of works. In both cases certain aspects of multimedia products remain unprotected. The argument that these aspects can be dealt with satisfactorily by the operation of the market is not convincing. The only feasible solution seems to be the introduction of special rules for multimedia products. The method and content of these rules is a matter to which we will return later.

Qualification of Multimedia Works The way in which the various contributors to a work co-operate can arguably be used as a criterion to distinguish between various categories of works. This is done to a fair extent, for example, in French copyright law. But even there the only real issue for discussion is that of authorship and ownership of copyright. It is worth examining whether such an approach makes it easier to fit multimedia products into copyright.

'Collaborative works' are works in the creation of which more than one natural person has participated. These works are the joint property of their authors and any rights in them are exercised by common accord. 'Composite works' are new works in which a pre-existing work is incorporated without the collaboration of the author of that work, and are the property of the author who has produced them. 'Collective works' are works created on the initiative of a natural or legal person who edits them, publishes them and discloses them under his direction and name and in which the personal contributions of the various authors who participated in their production are merged in the overall work for which they were conceived, without it being possible to attribute to each author a separate right in the work as created. There is a legal presumption that these works are the property of the natural or legal person under whose name they have been disclosed.

Multimedia Products and Collaborative Works

The notion of collaborative works presents certain limited attractions in relation to multimedia products. Multimedia products are indeed the outcome of the contributions of many participants who, according to the traditional copyright axiom, have to be compensated for their work. It is therefore fair enough to bestow on them the quality of author, together with the full panoply of exclusive rights. However, in the context of a multimedia product this presents certain inherent difficulties. First, the number of contributors involved in such a work is substantially larger than the number of persons involved in a traditional collaborative work, often becoming so great as to render any co-authorship and co-ownership of rights impractical to operate in the market. Clearing rights and reaching a common accord in these circumstances are highly difficult and risky tasks since the whole project or any future project depending thereon can be put in jeopardy if one of the authors involved does not co-operate in the end or does not agree to the further exploitation of the work. Second, not all the contributors involved in a multimedia product deserve the status of author. That, of course, is true in relation to other collaborative works, such as films, too. The technicians or people having undertaken non-creative tasks are never given authorship. Yet, in a multimedia context this distinction is not always an easy one to make. Some of the contributions involved, though technical, might also involve creative tasks because of the nature of the multimedia work. Examples are the contributions made by phototypesetters, info-designers, ergonomicists, page and screen designers, index drafters, documentalists, sound engineers, designers of hypertext links, etc. In a collaborative works regime such considerations are more problematic and have to be solved and considered at every stage when the work is used or exploited and not only at the stage of the production of the work. Even if successful financial arrangements are made, there is always the risk that one of the authors might exercise his moral rights in bad faith or want to create problems in the further exploitation of the work

In addition, a multimedia product is not in essence a collaborative work. There is no common inspiration of the persons involved in its production. There is also no common work or collaboration in the same way as in a collaborative work. Even if in the beginning different kinds of individual works are meant to be put together, their individuality soon disappears by reason of the commercial function and appearance of the multimedia product. The multimedia product presents an image of merged works and contributions which can no longer be distinguished or separated. These contributions are put together by one natural or legal person. This is the person who conducts the whole project, edits the various contributions and puts them in the format of the multimedia product. It is occasionally the same person who decides the image and the marketing of the work and makes the funds available. The other scenario is where in the main there are companies that undertake all these tasks (producers) and commission other companies for the physical development, technical organisation, form, packaging and marketing of the final product (makers or developers). It is usually under the second company's trade mark that this product reaches the market. In the regime of collaborative works these practices are not taken into account and therefore there is no legal presumption in favour of legal persons. Another interesting point to note is the fact that in France audiovisual works are de iure collaborative works. If multimedia products were to qualify as audiovisual works they would necessarily qualify as collaborative works as well.

Multimedia Products and Composite Works

Composite works are another potential category for multimedia products. Indeed, multimedia products contain a bulk of pre-existing works and materials in the same way as composite works. It would be unrealistic for the producer of a multimedia product to include only newly commissioned works in such a project. It would be costly, time-consuming and, on most occasions, it would also be commercially unattractive. Although this is usually the case, it would be equally unrealistic for one to suppose that only pre-existing works are contained in a multimedia product. New works can also be included, especially in cases where the persons commissioned to produce such works are needed to offer their services until the last minute in the form of putting the finishing touches to their works once they have been incorporated into the multimedia product and merged with other contributions. However, the participation of authors other than the collector in a work prevents the work from being a composite work. It is apparent that the category of composite works was included to accommodate mainly collections of works and anthologies or derivative works such as translations, adaptations, etc. However, this type of work seems to have little in common with multimedia products. Although composite works also have the advantage of conferring the rights of an author on the person who has realised the collection of the works, i.e., on one person, they are still inflexible on the issue of conferring authorship on any legal person.

Multimedia Products and Collective Works

Collective works seem to come closer to multimedia products than any of the previous types of works. The advantage of this classification is that, irrespective of the nature of the works that are brought together and the nature of the work that results, one can establish a single rule which deals with the fact that there are multiple contributors. For the final work, however, there should ideally be one rightholder. To a certain extent what is achieved by this approach is that a work that results from the collaboration of various authors is given copyright protection and the ownership of that protection can be attributed to one person. Furthermore, given the fact that multimedia products are projects that are essentially undertaken by companies, the law provides in such situations that the company under the name of which the work is disclosed can also become the rightholder of the work. This is particularly helpful if one takes into account that it is mainly companies that invest money, know-how and personnel expertise in the creation of a multimedia product. And given the fact that multimedia products are essentially functional information-based works, the fact that companies can automatically hold the exclusive rights in them substantially facilitates the trade of these works on the international market.

In addition, collective works stipulate that their contents are merged in the overall work without it being possible to distinguish between them. This seems to sit well with the nature of multimedia products, the value of which consists not only in the contributions they contain but in the added value of the overall work in which these contributions have been brought together and put in a particular format. Indeed, on most occasions this format does not allow one to distinguish between the various contributions.

Perhaps the only problem in relation to collective works and multimedia products is that the author of a collective work is the person who edits, publishes and discloses the work under his direction and name. Yet the rights in the work are conferred on the person under whose name the work is disclosed, without any reference to his direction. However, this is bound to cause problems in the context of a multimedia product. As was explained earlier, the practice with multimedia products is that the person or company that edits and publishes the work is not always the person under whose name the work is disclosed. Disclosure and marketing of a multimedia work are usually undertaken by the company that develops its technical base and which happens to have a trade mark that is capable of contributing to its market success. These particularities have not been taken into account by the drafters of the notion of collective works. The notion of collective works is alien to most national jurisdictions. In Belgium and in the UK, for example, there are provisions only on collaborative works and works of joint authorship respectively. Works that involve contributions of more than one person confer authorship on all the persons involved, either individually or jointly. Only at a second stage and through the operation of a contract can a natural or legal person become the owner of the work. However, moral rights remain with the author unless they have been waived in jurisdictions, such as the UK, where waivability is an option.

Summary

The above discussion leads us to the conclusion that the most suitable category for multimedia products is collective works. But even here certain transformations have to be made regarding the tasks of the author and the contents of these works, which clearly come closer to the description of composite works in so far as they contain pre-existing materials. In this sense multimedia works are hybrid works (a mixture of composite and collective works) with prevailing features from the category of collective works. In this light, if one stretches the notion of collective works one might well argue that multimedia products can be considered as collective works. In a French copyright system that means that a multimedia work cannot by definition be an audiovisual work, because then the legal presumption would automatically make it a collaborative rather than a collective work. Therefore, in this case one has either to go down the path of collections, databases, etc., or simply to allow multimedia works (in jurisdictions where that is possible) to qualify as collective works and be given the protection of the general category of works (literary and artistic works). In such a case, of course, the inconsistencies of multimedia products with the various aspects of this regime (other than authorship/ownership) have to be considered separately.

Although this is a valuable conclusion in relation to French multimedia products, it can only be of limited value for those countries that do not provide for the category of collective works in their copyright laws. Even in France though, this conclusion is not particularly helpful for identifying the regime of protection of multimedia products. Identifying a copyright work as a collective work solves only the issue of authorship and ownership. It is not capable of offering a complete regime of protection for multimedia products. In this sense, even if the conclusion that multimedia products are collective works is a conclusion which one can arrive at with a substantial degree of certainty, it is still not a solution capable of solving the problems of the protection of multimedia products. In any copyright system one still has to assess multimedia products on the grounds of their nature rather than the type of co-operation between their various contributors. In conclusion, the approach that starts by categorising a work as collective or collaborative provides only a stopgap solution in practice in those countries where a detailed categorisation by the nature of the work is not required. If a work deserves some form of copyright, then the approach provides workable answers in terms of ownership. The fundamental questions of the nature of a multimedia work and its broader regime of protection are not resolved at all though.

Qualification of Multimedia Works

We also discussed the various classifications provided in the national copyright laws which relate in some way to multimedia products, i.e. traditional literary works, compilations, databases, audiovisual works and computer programs. Thus, we have reached a stage at which we have to draw some conclusions as to the nature of multimedia products and how this nature relates to existing copyright categories of works.

Before we enter any discussion relating to the categorisation of multimedia products, one point should be clarified. Not all multimedia products are the same. There are common characteristics found in all advanced multimedia works which render them distinctive. To what extent these characteristics will remain unchanged by future technological developments in the area is an issue upon which we can only speculate.

Amongst the five categories of copyright works that we examined, three categories can immediately be excluded as candidates for accommodating multimedia products. These are the categories of traditional literary works, conventional compilations and computer programs. We demonstrated that works found in the first two categories, mainly comprising text, or text and images in the case of compilations, are found in a standard hard-copy format and cannot be altered. Interactivity is a notion which is alien to them. In relation to computer programs, it has been demonstrated that the only similarity they possess to multimedia products is that they constitute a part of them: their technical base. Classifying a multimedia product as a computer program would therefore disregard all the visual aspects of the work which make it valuable and which appear in addition to its technical base. The nature of all three of the above categories of works is far removed from the nature of any multimedia product.

The remaining categories of works which come closer to a multimedia product are those of audiovisual works and databases. However, although audiovisual works capture some of the visual effects of multimedia products, they fail to accommodate the variety and changing nature of their contents; interactivity precludes any set 'sequences of images'. In addition, audiovisual works mainly comprise images, whereas multimedia products contain images but only as a part of their contents. In reality they contain all kinds of works and data which on most occasions translate into text.

Databases seem to overcome this hurdle. Any kind of work (e.g. text, images, music, etc.) can be contained in a database. On top of that, no 'sequences of images' are required. In fact, the notion of databases is antithetic to any sequences of images altogether. However, the problem here is that it goes even further than that and requires the elements included in databases to be individually accessible. The presence of interactivity in a multimedia product prevents access to elements in the same way as a database. The contents of most multimedia works are merged in such a way that what is accessed and retrieved contains bits and pieces of various elements that have been entered in the work in a first phase. Entries that have been independently inserted in a multimedia work and which are then as such independently retrieved by users of the work are rarely found in a multimedia product.

In the light of the above, the following conclusions can be drawn. There is nothing to exclude the possibility of multimedia products qualifying as either films or databases as long as they possess the necessary characteristics of one of these categories of works. Yet, parallel qualification of a multimedia product as both an audiovisual work and a database is not possible, not only doctrinally, but also according to the EU database Directive which prevents films from qualifying as databases. Splitting a multimedia work into various parts and protecting them on their own merits is also not a viable solution. It causes confusion on the market as to the identity of the authors/rightholders and the rights owned by them, and loses sight of the multimedia work as a whole (meaning the collection and arrangement of its elements in a way that is both comprehensible and interactive) and its added value.

Although advanced multimedia products might in rare cases qualify as audiovisual works or databases, this might often be the case with multimedia products of the first generation. That is explained on the basis that advanced multimedia products are more complex works when compared to multimedia products of the first generation, with a qualitatively higher degree of interactivity allowing users to manipulate and intervene in the contents of the work through sampling, blurring, etc. They are essentially hybrid works that cut across many categories of works and are not capable of being fitted into any of the existing categories of copyright works. Even if the regime of protection of these categories might theoretically serve the needs of multimedia products well (which as we proved can only rarely be the case), it is not possible to afford them the regime of protection of a category of works with whose nature they have little or nothing in common. Expansion alone of the existing categories of copyright works in order to accommodate multimedia products within their regime of protection would still need separate legislative action in the same way the introduction of a sui generis regime within or outside the scope of copyright would.

Hybrid Product of Copyright Classification

We have come to the conclusion that although multimedia products cut across many categories of works, still there is no perfect match with any of them. We are presented with a vide juridique (i.e. a complete absence of directly applicable legal rules). It therefore follows that if we are to protect multimedia products effectively, new legislation is required as a means of either introducing a separate category of protection within copyright or abandoning copyright protection altogether and heading towards an unfair competition law right. The first solution presupposes that multimedia products are creations which are original and therefore still merit copyright protection. The second one acknowledges that in reality it is the contents and the investment in money, time and effort that make the multimedia product valuable and not the presence of any originality. A third solution would envisage a combination of the two along the lines of the EU database Directive.

One should address the problems deriving from an attitude towards new technology products that the role of copyright is not to protect works (products) and is definitely not to facilitate creation. Copyright law protects authors. Any transformation of the law would only adjust it to this emerging new reality which is not necessarily compatible with the primary objectives of intellectual property, at least from a continental law perspective. Since authors are protected according to the existing copyright regimes, the issues of creation/ production can be solved through the operation of the market, unfair competition law, contract and, lastly, technology. The latter are only side issues when compared to the protection of the author or authors of the multimedia work.

The fact is that, no matter how one defines copyright protection (e.g. protection of the author rather than the creation), one still touches on the relationship between the author and his work. We demonstrated that a regime of protection which is not well placed to accommodate multimedia products can only afford protection to the wrong authors. That, however, cannot be remedied by either the operation of the market or that of the contract. We explained that the market and the contract bind people who are parties to the same deal or transaction. They do not bind third parties who have access to the work and to whose financial benefit it is to copy as much as possible in order to avoid additional costs in the creation of identical or similar products. Such a situation jeopardises the rights of authors by putting at risk their efforts and investments. Without securing their intellectual labour and the investment that is needed to put it in the format of a product erga omnes, the system hits a blockage which cannot easily be overcome, if at all. It is true that the author of new technology works does not have much in common with a traditional author and that increasingly the creation has become a production, the value of which does not depend so much on the personal authoring of the work as it does on teamwork and market needs. This, however, is not a good reason to leave authors of the new era unprotected. Protecting the creation is like protecting the author, and facilitating his work is in fact giving him an incentive to continue to produce. The fact that his productions are dictated by the market and the new reality does not signify that the author is a second-class author, it rather signifies that the needs of present societies have changed and it is on this basis that the authors and their works should be assessed. Unfair competition protection in its turn falls short of taking into account principles of creation, intellectual effort and originality since it is based on a market-orientated approach. It therefore presents problems analogous to those we discussed in relation to the market.

There is little doubt that multimedia works can be original creations of the mind. This is also the reason that justifies their protection under copyright law. The fact that they do not currently fit in any of the existing categories of copyright works is clearly not an indication that they do not deserve copyright protection. It is rather an indication that there is a need for the introduction of a separate category for multimedia works in copyright law which will take into account digitisation, the inclusion of several different kinds of works in one product and above all interactivity.

In this category of works there should not be such a thing as prevailing elements. All kinds of works can possibly be included, irrespective of their nature and initial format. Digitisation will indicate the large factual capacity of multimedia works and their form of expression which clearly departs from any conventional form of expression or carrier without, however, affecting the nature of the works included. The works that are included do not lose their original status once they are digitised. They co-exist as parts of a larger entity. The fact that the elements included in a multimedia work are merged should also be mentioned. As such it does not preclude the instance where some works might not be merged (or entirely merged with others), but it facilitates any potential regime of protection with regard to the rights of the authors of the works included as well as to the rights of users. Interactivity is important from two points of view: first, because no standard sequence or format of contents is required, and second, because the lack of standard format (or the intention of lack of standard format) offers users the freedom to elaborate or intervene in the work without infringing potential rights of authors. The combination of various kinds of works irrespective of their conventional earlier format, digitisation and interactivity will undoubtedly be the essential common characteristics of any new technology products. From that point of view, many future developments in the area can well be accommodated by this new category of works.

Dropping copyright protection in relation to multimedia products altogether is not a viable option. First, copyright has an internationally well-established regime of protection which allows a substantial degree of co-operation and reciprocity between the various states. Over and above that it has proved itself all along to be the most effective means of protection, perfectly capable of protecting new technology products. The common currency of intellectual creations has not been overtaken in any respect and therefore there is no reason to abandon the only protection that is going in this direction. However, this argument is not there to exclude the introduction of any sui generis or unfair competition rights in relation to intellectual property products which come close enough to a practice of industrial production and involve also issues of investment which cannot be successfully dealt with by copyright, especially in relation to creations which are not original. This was the case with databases. Here an unfair extraction/re-utilisation right has been introduced in relation to the contents of a database in the obtaining, verification or presentation of which a qualitatively or quantitatively substantial investment was made. If a database is original, the unfair extraction right comes on top of its copyright protection to prevent third parties from extracting almost the same contents for use in a different structure or arrangement. If the database is not original, the maker of the database would still not jeopardise his investment in bringing these elements together should third parties be ready to copy them. That may also be the case for multimedia products. The investment put in in relation to their elements might be so substantial that it has to be afforded separate protection. This is especially true for multimedia products which are not original and therefore do not attract copyright protection. In addition, the way these elements interact with each other can also form the subject of an unfair competition law right (cf. the sui generis right for databases) if it is commonplace in terms of originality but hard enough in terms of, for example, investment to bring it to realisation. Although interactivity derives from the computer program that operates the multimedia work, the way this operation is projected on screen can still form the subject of a separate right. In conclusion, the best possible solution seems to be the introduction of a new category of copyright works, i.e. multimedia works, plus the introduction of a sui generis right relating to the investment put into the contents of the multimedia work and perhaps to the way its interactivity is presented on screen.

11

Applications and Architectures of Multimedia

Introduction

Ubiquitous computing envisages software in devices spread throughout our environment. Interaction may be through explicit UIs, but in many cases we will be interacting with computers via everyday products and furniture, for example, displays in desks, mobile phones, on glasses, ear pieces and so on. Education and training are key markets for multimedia, and increasingly for VR; however, the contribution from advanced technology to successful learning outcomes is not clear. The second area is design and requirements analysis. Simulation and interactive microworlds are an important contribution of both VR and multimedia. VR in particular has become important for virtual prototyping and refining designs by simulation. Current research in progress in the ISRE project is described and guidance given on VE-driven requirements analysis.

Educational Applications

This short section provides some background guidance on the dialogue design issues for Computer-Aided Learning and Computer-

Based Training (CAL and CBT) with multimedia and VR. First, some words of caution. I firmly believe that 90% of the design effort and corresponding reasons for successful learning products does not reside in the UI, multisensory or otherwise. Multimedia, and to a lesser extent VR, has been the subject of a large amount of unjustified hype. The evidence that multisensory interaction on its own actually improves learning is remarkably hard to find although many believe that it does. Indeed, there is evidence that current products have poor learning outcomes. The objectives of this chapter are not to repeat a tutorial on design of educational software; this would require another book, and there are already plenty on the market. Instead, I concentrate on the intersection of interaction and presentation design for effective learning outcomes. It is difficult to talk about learning outcomes without some view on pedagogical design, so I start with a brief review of the design problem before the UI.

Learning Environments

The education world has been debating the merits of instructionist versus constructionist approaches to learning for several decades. Instuctionism is learning by telling and emphasizes delivery of content; in contrast, constructionist approaches emphasize learning by doing. The latter tradition is generally accepted to be the superior approach. Constructivism advocates tuition in which the student learns by trying out problems, constructing things, and interacting with the world. This makes sense in terms of basic psychology because learning and problem solving are closely linked; the more we think about the subject matter, the deeper the encoding of a memory schema. However, not all learning may need a constructionist approach. Training and more in-depth education have differing objectives:

- Training aims to impart knowledge to usually motivated individuals. The knowledge in training is frequently procedural or task-based explanations, and skilled operation is the expected outcome. Instructionist approaches can be appropriate for training.
- Education aims to create a deeper understanding of a domain than does training. The knowledge that the learners should acquire will be multifaceted, for example, concepts, causation,

and more complex knowledge. Education also aims to teach students about the learning process itself: learning how to learn, and the ability to reflect on experience. Constructionist approaches and their relative, guided discovery learning are more appropriate.

Design of software for training is easier because the learning ambition is lower; however, the boundary between the two is not clear-cut. Many training applications need to impart deeper knowledge, considering the growth of knowledge-worker economy and distance learning.

To lay out the dimensions of the problem, three layers need to be considered: technology, where interactive system design and other artifacts may influence the outcome; cognitive; and social. These levels are examined to illustrate the potential and limitations of multisensory technology.

Individual-Level Learning

At this level the focus is primarily on the individual, although in most contexts the social and cognitive levels are integrated. Motivation is a major cognitive factor influencing learning. Better-motivated students learn more effectively, but the process of motivating people for learning is not well understood. Motivation may be influenced by high level societal values, such as one's career aims; more immediate incentives to do well in an exam or test; or interest in the content itself. Finally, entertainment and fun can motivate learning. Multisensory UIs can help the motivation problem by representing personalities, by choice of engaging media, stimulating dialogues and, in the short term, by the novelty of technology. Content and delivery may be linked to the students' cognitive style. Unfortunately, this property is difficult to analyze. Briefly, cognitive style comes in many variants, but they all tend to boil down to difference in people's ability for abstract thought. Some individuals like to reason with the specific facts and construct ideas "bottom-up." These field dependent students find abstraction more difficult. Other field independent people reason top-down and more abstractly. If these differences could be detected reliably, then field dependent individuals should benefit more from being given abstract structures and analogies, whereas field independent individuals should benefit from scenarios and concrete examples, (i.e. microworlds, virtual environments) to encourage testing ideas. As abstract thought is a trained aspect of human cognition, whether cognitive style exists is a contentious matter. Cognitive style in visualize-verbalize individual differences is probably one of the most dependable design indicators for multimedia.

Social-Level Learning

Learning frequently occurs in groups. When we are puzzled or don't understand something, the most natural course of action is to ask another person to help. Conversations help learning at three levels:

- When engaged in the primary learning task, dialogues with others help to share insights, express problems, and build on each other's suggestions. Dialogues between experts and novices support learning by explanations, critiques, mentoring, and challenging understanding.
- Materials that are not the direct subject matter but help the learner, such as exercises, examples, back-up explanations, illustrative scenarios, and so forth, are referred to as secondary material. Conversations while trying out exercises and discussions of examples help to develop insight into primary material.
- Conversations about the process of learning and material generated during the process, such as comments on difficult concepts, new analogies, counter examples, and learning related to one's own experience, are examples of tertiary karning material. In this case, the conversation itself becomes useful for learning not only when it happens but also as a recorded artifact that can be shared with others. These learning conversations often produce new insights that the instructor may miss.

Social learning can be supported by groupware multisensory systems, also referred to as Computer Mediated Communication (CMC). Some systems are in everyday use such as e-mail and chat, but these share experiences by the impoverished medium of text. Adding multimedia in video conferencing-style interaction provides speech and image but there are several problems in designing CMC systems for effective interaction.

First, there is turn-taking in multiparty conversations. Judging when to speak in groups is complex enough in face-to-face interaction. People use small gaps in spoken discourse, overt invitations to take turns, and a variety of nonverbal cues in body language and facial expression. In spite of the sophistication of natural conversation management, interruptions and shutouts occur. In large groups (more than 5 or 6 individuals), turn-taking can become a problem and moderator roles are used to impose order. Turn-taking can be made more complex in distributed applications when delays in speech transmission make detecting conversation gaps very difficult. Turn-taking is related to the second problem of group-wide views. In natural conversations, we can scan most members in a group of up to roughly 10 to 12 people. In video mediated communication, the view limitations of camera technology mean that either a few participants are shown in sufficient detail to see nonverbal communication or the whole group is visible, but detail of facial expressions and gesture is poor. Of course, two images may be shown, one in foreground detail and the other in background, but then the user has to scan both images to extract the necessary information. Showing a mosaic of many individuals in close-up just makes the scanning problem worse. In short, video conferencing has the television producer's problem: what to show in close-up when it is difficult to predict where the focus of debate will go within a group.

One alternative is to converse in VEs. Avatars replace real-life images. The design question in VEs is how to communicate nonverbal discourse. Groupware VEs have simple facial expressions such as smiles, frowns, and surprise. This has led to more realistic presences with the ability to direct gaze, more facial expressions, and other gestures such as head nods and shoulder shrugs.

When artificial agents are implemented, behaviors can be scripted, but for computer-mediated communication, the problem becomes one of user control. We normally perform gestures and facial expressions unconsciously. Giving people controls to make an avatar frown, laugh, (facial expressions), agree (head nod), or show indifference (shoulder shrug) just gives users a cognitive overload.

Trying to plan nonverbal communication concurrently with speaking causes competing processes in the implication level running both visual and morphological subsystems. New high-level controls are needed so users can express emotional reactions (e.g., surprise, disappointment, joy) in CVEs, as well as mechanisms for turn-taking. In spite of these limitations, multiparty VE conversations do work even with very limited (text or chat) multisensory interfaces in the inhabited worlds of the World Wide Web. In these cases, users have adopted conventions to direct conversation by addressing remarks to individuals in speech and turning their avatars to face the personae being addressed. Alternatively, more formal controls for turn-taking can be provided.

An interesting side effect of media choice in CMC is communication of identity. In video, identity is accessible assuming that the other person is known; however, in e-mail and chat, identity can be hidden by aliases. Some reports suggested that antisocial behavior, for example, being offensive or flaming in e-mail, may be more common when identity is masked. More comprehensive research has shown this not to be the case, and group behavior, negotiation, and building consensus is remarkably similar with or without explicit identity. People circumvent absence of identity by dialogue, asking questions and looking for cues. Design of identity is still a concern, especially for privacy and political reasons. Text media can mask the origin of the individual, organization, and location by eliminating header or address information; speech requires voice modulation; and video images are made anonymous by pixel area blurring. Such techniques are common in television reporting.

The aforementioned discussion has assumed that communication is synchronous; however, multisensory systems can also support learning conversations in asynchronous systems.

In asynchronous communication for both same and different places, multisensory interfaces can help to distribute secondary and tertiary learning materials. Text media are useful because of their persistence: comments can be annotated on learning conversations developed over weeks or months. Speech and video clips motivate learners by making the communication more personal. In synchronous, same-place conversations, the main need is to distribute a lecture to large groups that cannot all fit within the constrained space. Video transmission of lectures is a partial solution. More difficult is giving large groups access to shared demonstrations and simulations. This point is taken up in the following section. Finally, in the same time, different place cell, both multimedia video conferencing and VE communication may be used. Sharing tertiary material usually implies use of text and speech, because this is the usual medium of origin. However, comments and annotations may be made on media that represent primary and secondary learning materials, so groupware environments need to support attachment of voice notes, and drawings and doodles on top of primary learning media, as well as text annotations.

Education Software Technology

The previous section reviewed dimensions of the design problem. We now progress to design implications for multisensory UIs. From the constructivist tradition, several general design principles can be drawn. Interaction is desirable as it encourages exploration and user-directed learning. Active engagement helps to promote active learning because the user has to solve problems via an interactive dialogue. Interactive microworlds and simulations have a long heritage going back to Steamer for interactive simulations and the ARK. The ARK environment provides a game-like world for teaching Newtonian physics, in which students could roll balls down a slide and observe how far the ball flew before hitting the ground. Controls allowed the mass of the ball, angle of the slide, and the strength of gravity to be changed so that different trajectories can be interpreted according to Newton's laws. However, interactive microworlds may not be suitable for all learning domains, so for training, instructionist approaches may be appropriate. In order of increasing complexity, the different styles of tutorial dialogue, with their implications for multisensory UIs, are described in the following section.

Scripted Presentations and Hypermedia

The simplest form of dialogue is a hypermedia model of links. Some interaction is possible so that learners have limited control over content delivery. The user views a presentation that may have several options to explore, presented as menus or different hypermedia hotspots. The dialogue may have differing degrees of branching from a major path with side paths where users are encouraged to follow up on more detail; for example, in a tutorial on animal ecology, the major path explains the food chain from primary producers (plants) through to animals up the food chain. Side links give more details of the types of plants and animals at each level.

More complex navigation can be provided as a multipath network where the student is free to follow many different paths through the learning material. However, to counteract the possibility of getting lost, it is advisable to provide a "guided tour" which takes the student through the preferred path; once having traversed it, students are free to explore on their own. Depending on the level of guidance desired in the learning, hypermedia can converge with scripted presentations; for example, see the following:

- No predetermined pathway—This implies hypermedia in which the user is free to follow any links provided by the designer.
- A preferred pathway is specified but the application also supports exploratory browsing of the material. Recommended pathways may be provided as hints on an overview map, or as guided tours.
- The pedagogical design specifies a predetermined pathway as a scripted presentation.

Although hypermedia is an effective means of promoting user exploration, it is still a fairly passive mode of interaction, and the user is not learning by doing. Once the user has viewed the material, an interactive quiz can be provided, with multiple-choice questions for machine-based assessment. The user is given a score and rewarded with congratulations if he or she gets the answer right, or the opportunity to retry the quiz question if he or she gets it wrong. Although quizzes are popular, they are still only assessing the student's learning after viewing the material. Design issues include how to link components in hypermedia models; and within components, how to integrate multimedia. Learning goals frequently require students to compare information from different sources or viewpoints. Concurrent multimedia help comparisons and cross-referencing because the student can view all the relevant information at once, whereas sequential presentation, enforced by hypermedia, can make this task more difficult. The following principles reiterate the design advice but place it within a learning context:

- When several pieces of information are necessary to achieve a learning goal, display the information concurrently as far as possible, and integrate the content with contact points. Concurrent presentation allows the student to scan all the content without having to burden working memory.
- Place key information in static media, augmented by summaries using text, diagrams, and images. Dynamic media have a stimulating effect and are attractive, but effective information transfer is limited to the gist or high-level concepts. Dynamic media, however, have a role to play in integrating information.
- Integrate information by use of contact point sequences. Revealing elements of a story in a sequence attracts attention and builds up the necessary knowledge toward the learning goal. For instance, explaining the causation of the El Nino weather effect starts by showing ocean temperatures followed by a slide show presentation of the heat build-up reversing flow of currents, transfer of warm water from west to east, increased evaporation near South America, and more rain. Contact point captions point out key items in the image sequence.
- Use video showing people with speech to motivate and attract students. Judicious use of video showing an instructor can attract attention by personalizing the presentation.
- Make the presentation as interactive as possible. Interaction is dealt with in more depth in the next section; however, even within a limited ambition, multimedia interaction can be encouraged. Contact point cues can be embedded in material to encourage exploration of supplementary information. Active cursor techniques with pop-up text can reveal contact points. Questions and miniquizzes can be triggered by exploring items within presentations.

Interactive Microworlds and Active Engagement

This approach is motivated by constructivist learning. The system becomes a multisensory simulation of the domain, which makes the development more expensive, but the payback should be more effective learning. Users interact by direct manipulation in a VE or simulated world, or by changing parameters and observing the effects of different simulation runs. For example, in teaching the ecology of food chains, a graphical image of a pond is shown containing plants, herbivores (tadpoles, mayflies, snails), and carnivores (fish, birds, otters, etc.). Realistic images can be combined with diagrams to show the food chain relations among animals. The user can interact with the simulation by running animations that show plants being eaten by animals progressively higher in the food chain, or by setting parameters to change the numbers of animals and plants at each level and then running the simulation to see the effect of different numbers. The system uses graphs to show the effect on herbivore, carnivore, and plant populations and the image is edited to show fewer or more animals and plants. Alternatively, users can drag and drop various pollutants from different sources (bucket icons); then the Simulation runs to show the effect of pollutants being concentrated up the food chain leading to death of animals at the top of the food chain.

This form of interaction allows users more freedom to explore the Simulation as an interactive microworld and engages them in active learning by experimentation. In VE implementations, the student interacts with the world by becoming one of the actors immersed in the environment. Concepts from drama theory, well understood by games designers, can be employed to improve student motivation, for instance, by planning surprise where exploration triggers agents to appear, which challenge the learner. As the environment is explored, the level of difficulty increases so material is gradually assimilated. This follows the minimalist concept of learning, in which the student is only exposed to the bare essentials at the onset of learning, then the content is gradually exposed with increasing levels of complexity. Linking experience to abstraction is the most difficult part of the design. Students may interact with microworlds but only at the level of observing surface effects, so they may fail to abstract the causal explanation. Use of critique agents to question and challenge students is one answer.

Design of microworlds will vary considerably according to the domain and pedagogical objectives. In simulation environments, the user interacts with a designed world by changing the parameters that run the simulation and observing effects. An example is the interactive Pondworld where pollutant and population parameters can be set to explore the effects on animal and plant populations. In virtual worlds inhabited by the user or a surrogate persona, the simulation may be similar but immersion encourages learning by an enhanced sense of engagement. An example is exploring a dangerous environment to plan crime prevention; the user walks through dark and threatening streets to experience the sense of menace. Environments in which the students can design the solution for themselves are true constructive learning environments in which the learners become designers. They are given the basic building blocks for a solution, hints about how to proceed, and then left to solve the problem by construction. The act of problem solving by doing encourages depth of encoding and learning. An example is the augmented reality system for urban planning where the student can move houses, streetlights, and so forth, to design a new street and then run the simulation to observe the effect on crime statistics, and reaction of the inhabitants.

The essence of microworld-based tutorials is an embedded model of the domain that contains laws governing reactions of objects and agents. The user is provided with those objects and agents as building blocks, and an outline environment in which to design. The system interprets the user's design, so that when it is run, the domain laws can be invoked to predict a probable outcome.

The architecture consists of a model editor that provides the users with components and a means of constructing their solution. The model simulationcontroller interprets the solution and runs it against the domain laws. The consequent effects are displayed to the student within the microworlds with additional summaries where necessary. The pedagogical aspect of the dialogue is implemented by system agents that take initiative to actively tutor the student or help when they have made mistakes, as explainers and critics.

Multisensory User Interface Issues. Many of the multisensory design issues for microworld-based systems are shared with their less ambitious scripted cousins. However, microworlds imply agent roles as explainers, critics, or student representations, and this raises issues of multimodal communication. Ideally, speech is the preferred form of communication; however, the limitations of natural language processing and artificial intelligence will keep human tutors in business for a long time to come. Software tutoring systems may be a useful addition to the battery of teaching aids but they are no substitute for a flesh-and-blood tutor.

In spite of these limitations, advances have been made in automated question answering systems. Restricted natural language and use of question type taxonomies help the system interpret formatted questions from the student. Planning techniques based on Rhetorical Structure Theory enable the system to automatically compose the answers from knowledge (and media) fragments in the content database. Speech will play an increasingly important role in the future.

The link between speech generation and projection of personality by artificial agents is an opportunity for future research. Personality can be mimicked by fairly crude visual representations, especially when integrated with speech.

Once agents have been designed, the next issue is the choice between augmented and virtual reality. If the user is exploring the world by navigation, then VR is sufficient. An example is NASA's Mars explorer in which the student can learn about the effects of climate and geology by flying through a virtual Martian landscape. Little haptic interaction is required. In true constructive environments, haptic interaction is often necessary. In these applications, augmented reality is superior because the student can pick and place components more easily. The system still has to detect where components have been placed so the simulation model can be run, and feedback is projected on top of the augmented reality. Tangible domains such as engineering, architecture, and urban planning are good candidates for augmented reality. In contrast, interaction in more abstract domains can be kept in the virtual world, a good example being the agentsheets construction environment, which can be specialized to create many different simulations.

The final issue is how to represent the user's presence and whether to provide virtual tools in the VE. The student's viewpoint can be set as egocentric, in which case the world is experienced with full immersion. The sense of presence and engagement is greater, which may motivate learning, but the disadvantage is the inability to see the overview. Conversely, an exocentric view allows learners to see their own presence within the VE, and hence, get a better feel for the context of their interaction. There is little research to suggest which view will have better learning outcomes, so the best advice is to consider providing both views, to enable the student to be immersed in the experience and then swap to overview mode to see the wider context.

This concludes the brief review of multisensory UI design for educational and tutorial applications. Much research needs to be done both at the level of pedagogical theory and how to translate theoretical motivations into effective interaction. In the next section, the second application area of design and requirements analysis is reviewed.

Virtual Prototyping

Multisensory interfaces have a great potential for supporting design. Indeed, one of the significant markets for VR is in design exploration and requirements validation, often called virtual prototyping. VEs help designers debug products that have not been built. The appeal of VE design support is saving the cost of physical mock-ups and prototypes. However, the usability requirements for virtual prototypes can be quite demanding. In operational testing, fidelity with the real life design is important. In these applications, the user-tester needs to experience as close an approximation to the reality of operating the design as possible. Furthermore, in design applications, close coupling with specifications and Computer Aided Design (CAD) is important. This was the significant advance in Boeing's use of VR for design of the 777 aircraft. Close coupling of the CAD system with VR simulation enabled designers to visualize the layout of wiring controls and a myriad of other physical design components. They could reason spatially using the VR and then transfer their conclusions to the accurate CAD model that formed the basis for manufacture. Although virtual prototyping has become established practice, there is little understanding of the usability issues involved.

Requirements Analysis with Virtual Environments

Requirements engineering with VEs introduces some interesting parallels with usability evaluation. The VE representation of a design is being investigated, so in some sense a design is being evaluated. The important issue for designers of the VE (rather than the product) is to make sure usability issues do not interfere with assessment of the product.

Having gone to the expense of creating a virtual prototype, it is important to capitalize on the investment. The VE can be used in slightly different versions to gain feedback on several different aspects of design.

- Physical and spatial fit—This is achieved by realistic modeling to check that components can fit into the spaces specified, that movement and composition of objects is physically possible, and that people can move in constrained spaces, reach switches, and so forth. Close coupling of spatial specifications in CAD models is necessary.
- Human operations and tasks are feasible and effective. This set of requirements needs a realistic design including operational controls. Scenarios are walked through to check that the user can find and understand the necessary information portrayed in the design. Limitations of VE come into play here if operations involve haptic feedback. When haptic feedback is important, augmented reality should be considered.
- Operation can take place under a variety of environmental conditions. This is where virtual prototyping really starts to pay off. The VR design can run under a variety of simulation conditions, for example, degrees of lighting, visibility, noise, and so forth. The scenario simulation environment that surrounds the basic design can be changed for different test runs.
- Operation will be effective with different user roles. This is the most complex part of prototyping, with immersed actors playing different user roles, or automated agents are scripted to respond with different degrees of skill.

Scenarios that describe the user tasks are acted out in the VE. The prototype is run against a series of operational user task scenarios with variations of environmental conditions to stress-test the design. As requirements are captured in the form of design critiques, these are recorded in the requirements specification or CAD model and subsequently become design improvements. The cycle of scenario-based testing is repeated until an effective and usable solution is produced.

Designing Virtual Prototypes

The virtual design provides the general layout of the environment, the ship's guns, and details of equipment. The extent of the viewable, external environment will depend on the operational scenario and environmental specializations. For example, in the ship gunnery training system, details of the seascape viewable can be changed for fog, clouds, high seas, etc. The operators are immersed or represented as mannequins that they can control for limited movement.

The design components and interactions in the VE should be represented as accurately and completely as possible within resource constraints. Realistic detail always costs more development effort, so it should be concentrated on areas to be investigated in the scenarios, rather than background and contextual detail. Inaccurate representation can bias results and lead to inaccurate analysis and results. For example, a radar screen is depicted in detail so that tracks can be seen, but the sonar equipment is only represented in outline. Multisensory feedback through the use of visual, audio, and haptic channels improves realism and sense of engagement. Haptic is desirable for complex manipulations of objects, although cross-modal substitution may be necessary if it is available. For example, audio is added for background noise of equipment and spoken communication. Sounds or color changes represent contact and pressure to substitute for haptic feedback.

For operational scenarios, all users will need to be represented as virtual actors in the VE. The mannequins should support the range of actions involved in the scenarios; for example, leaning forward or bending down for testing ergonomic requirements and gesticulation for communication. Ideally, users and operators should be able to move their mannequin to mirror their own body movements. When avatars are represented, ideally, full body suit sensors are necessary to map movement of the real operator's limbs and body to the mannequin. This is expensive and difficult to resource so scripted interaction of mannequins or limited single limb movement are more usual. Anthropometrically precise mannequin tools are available for ergonomics testing of human movements. Devices should be chosen according to the type of interactions involved in the scenarios, so a 3D mouse may suffice for simple interactions but a glove (hand presence) will be necessary for complex object manipulations.

Two approaches are possible for running scenarios. First is scripting operational scenarios so mannequins carry out actions that the analyst can observe; basic ergonomic action scenarios can be preprogrammed and run automatically in the VE. Second, immersed actors can carry out operational tasks. Ideally, these should be potential users of the future system; alternatively, operational scenarios are run with trained operators role-playing scenario scripts. Running scenarios with operators controlling their own presence is more complex.

Immersive (Head Mounted Display or HMD) viewing for close examination and manipulation of objects provides extra realism and sense of presence where needed. CAVE or large projection screens facilitate multiuser viewing and peripheral views including the wider context. This option is useful for complex scenarios involving collaboration between people. Desktop viewing may be chosen for solo tasks not requiring direct interaction or close object examination, and for longer scenarios when immersive interaction is not necessary.

The analyst may be immersed in the VE to observe users directly and experience interaction from their viewpoint, or have an external viewpoint to see interaction in a wider context. An analyst immersed with the users or operators will have a better sense of the shared experience, but the ability to gain an overview is lost. Moreover, no two users' viewpoints will be the same. In shared VEs, one user has to be the dominant actor whose movement controls changing the viewpoint. Other users receive the dominant user's viewpoint, which is less than 100% natural. Another consideration is that audio in the VE or the use of immersive displays may obstruct users' verbal reports.

The trade-off for the analyst's viewpoint is how closely the analyst needs to mirror the user's experience so usability problems can be interpreted. One compromise is for the analyst to observe the immersed users first and note problem areas, then follow up with solo immersed walkthroughs to inspect specific problems. Controls for changing the analyst's viewpoint on the VE are desirable, so that user interaction can be observed from different angles. In complex VEs, map-like displays of the environment showing the current position of users may be helpful in tracking their progress and location in the VE. In group scenarios, if one user is controlling the view, then the analyst's view, should to be tied to this. Otherwise, switching between the overall and individual viewpoints to obtain more detail can help. Having covered the design of virtual prototypes, the next step is to review the process for requirements analysis with VE designs.

Scenario-Based Requirements Analysis

Requirements analysis with virtual prototypes shares many techniques with usability evaluation of VEs. Indeed, the two processes are similar and share the same objective of design improvement. In usability evaluation, the focus of attention is on improving the usability of the VE itself, whereas virtual prototyping concerns design refinement prior to building a real product. Virtual prototyping with scenario analysis can be carried out using one of two different approaches:

- Design walkthroughs—This approach involves the analyst walking through the design using himself or herself as a surrogate user, and asking questions at set points in the operational scenario. The walkthrough produces a checklist audit of design faults and recommendations for improvements. Walkthroughs are quick and cheap to do, but may suffer from the analyst's lack of domain knowledge.
- Observation of user problems—In this approach, human operators follow scripts and act out tasks in the VE. The requirements analyst observes the operators and asks them to think out aloud. Problems are detected by observing difficulties in operating equipment, by failure to achieve operational performance targets, or by misunderstanding and difficulties reported by users during interaction or in debriefing interviews. Analysis is diagnostic in nature, that is, when the

user experiences some difficulty, the analyst has to trace the problem back to either a fault in the design or a problem in the operating procedure or possibly a false assumption about what is humanly possible.

In walkthroughs, the participants follow the scenario scripts to the best of their ability, role-playing the actions as closely as possible to real life. The analyst follows their interactions, making notes of any difficulties. The user is encouraged to provide a running commentary of what he or she is doing and his or her perceptions. Unexpected behavior and the user's comments on the system are noted, especially critical incidents or breakpoints indicating difficulty in interaction or understanding. The point in the scenario script when the incident occurs is noted, as well as any design features implicated in the problem.

After the walkthrough, debriefing interviews follow up on observed issues. Comments and positive or negative views are gathered to help understand the design and validate requirements. Observed problems need to be attributed to design features or the testing environment. Problems are categorized into the following sets:

- User training problems – Users do not understand or follow the scenario script; these problems are caused by poor user domain knowledge or training, or misunderstanding of the scenario script.
- Usability problems – Users experience difficulty with VE features that do not directly represent the design solution, such as the navigation method or additional controls. For example, problems in controlling movement, navigation, or conceptual disorientation, limited realism or haptic feedback, mean that manipulations appear to be more difficult than they would be in reality.
- Design problems – These involve users having difficulty with an aspect of the VE that directly represents the prototype design. These problems point to requirements issues and design refinements.

The output of this approach is a set of observed problems cross-referenced to the scenario context in which they occurred and the design feature involved.

Future Trends

In this volume I have concentrated on UIs that are currently grouped under the headings of multimedia and VR. In writing about multisensory UIs I have tried to show that there is really little difference between multimedia and VR: both are just part of a trend toward richer forms of humancomputer interaction. This trend has been with us since the transition from text and command line UIs into direction manipulation and GUIs. No doubt sensory enrichment of human-computer interaction will continue, but it will probably take two quite different paths. In the final part of this chapter, I look at the prospects for multisensory UIs: first, along the path of increased intelligence in communication, the natural language route; and second, convergence with topics so far only mentioned in passing, ubiquitous and mobile computing. In the quest to make computers useful, usable, and universal, we can try to make the computer smarter, enhance its ability to communicate with us in a variety of ways, and integrate it into our everyday environment so that communication is not a conscious act and interaction becomes part of our experience.

Intelligent Multisensory User Interfaces

Adapting to the user, anticipating needs and automating more complex tasks have been quests of intelligent user interface (IUI) research for a number of years. I will not review the user modeling and adaptable UI debate; if the reader is interested in such subjects, there are plenty of papers in the IUI conference series and the journal User Modeling and Adaptable Interfaces, Instead, my focus is on the prospects for developing intelligence for enhanced communication. There are several prospects on this path.

First and most predictable is natural language processing. Speech recognition systems are already approaching reliabilities in the order of 98% accuracy in speaker-dependent word recognition, but correcting two errors in every hundred is still an annoying burden. Ironically, in human-human communication, we put up with similar or higher error rates in speech, and hardly notice the error correction problem. Machine-based systems have yet to achieve a similar vertical integration from speech recognition through semantic analysis and parsing, to pragmatic resolution of ambiguity.

Once this is achieved, speech recognition systems will not need to improve their basic accuracy. Higher order processing will automatically correct errors, just as people do.

Natural language interaction, however, still has to solve the problem of the knowledge acquisition bottleneck. General-purpose natural language understanding with common sense reasoning will probably take some time to solve, but limited-domain language processing is already possible. Whereas we use around 8,000 words in our everyday vocabulary, when we converse about technical subjects, sublanguages restrict the scope of reasoning and communication to a narrow domain. Examples are legal arguments, air traffic control dialogues, and the communication of foreign exchange dealers. Small vocabularies, restricted syntax, and constrained knowledge for pragmatic interpretation characterize sublanguages. This simplifies natural language processing by reducing the complexity of the domain knowledge base required for efficient processing.

Alternatively, software systems can extend their own vocabulary by being taught or asking the user to explain the meaning of words. Systems with extendable vocabularies work well initially, but as the user extends the system lexicon (by adding new words to existing categories then adding new subcategories), the system knowledge becomes inconsistent. Learning systems with better knowledge acquisition dialogues may be able to cure this problem.

Natural language will also become more pervasive as an output or generated form of communication. One limitation to date has been the complexities of planning utterances in the context of what has been said by the human party. Understanding and generation are closely linked; however, natural language planners can now create sophisticated dialogues that integrate gesture, nonverbal communication, speech, and the content being communicated. Intelligent agents with multisensory interfaces will become increasingly capable of holding complex dialogues that integrate communication on different modalities. Where understanding breaks down, improved dialogue repair planning will enable the conversation to continue even when there is misunderstanding, as happens in natural human-human dialogues. The second limitation is the naturalness of synthetic speech where the technical difficulties of generating natural voice intonations are being solved. Soon synthetic speech will no longer sound artificial and intelligent agents will be able to express emotion, surprise, and so forth, in a natural sounding voice.

Intelligent agents will become a common feature of multisensory UIs. Developing rules that govern natural conversations with intelligent agents will require dialogue planners based on discourse theory, and agent representations that behave with appropriate personalities and emotional responses according to the user's dialogue, task, and context, conversational agents are already with us that can talk while communicating with appropriate facial expressions and gaze. Other social agents can be given characters and react with simple models of emotion to show surprise and disappointment. The frontiers are making automated virtual agents more believable and realistic with more sophisticated models of motivation and emotion while increasing the sophistication of facial expressions, gaze control, and expression of emotional response by blushing, and so on. Another challenge is design controls so users can inhabit virtual agents and control them with appropriate facial expressions, movement, and gaze. Robotics will converge with UI design for complex virtual presences. Encapsulating knowledge from social psychology and linguistics within interaction planners for agents will be a considerable challenge.

The vision of intelligent multisensory UIs revisits the debate on system initiative between advocates of passive representation of system facilities and active system support. The role of representation will remain important because people will want to remain in control in many domains. However, the inexorable drive to embed software intelligence in products from cars to homes will mean that intelligent multisensory interfaces are inevitable. Because intelligent agents will always make mistakes, we can only hope their designers make them humble enough to admit it, and have users in control.

Frontiers for Multisensory Interaction

In this volume, there has been a tacit assumption that multisensory interaction is dominated by visual and audio modalities. Haptics got a look in occasionally; olfaction and gustation only appeared in the introduction. In the future, that balance will change.

Olfaction and gustation will use standardized rendering and detecting devices in multisensory workstations (if workstations still exist). We will be able to send complete sensory experiences to each other. The 3D immersive video of our holiday will include the sound of the seaside, the smell of the forest, and the taste of exotic food. This will require considerable advances in generative technologies, but the principles of generation of aerosols for smell and solutions for taste are known. Smell and taste can already be generated at resolutions way beyond human capabilities, so with the development of standardized coding schemes for chemical smells and tastes, full multisensory communication will be a reality.

The future of haptic and proprioceptive interaction is less sure. One view is that there is a law of diminishing returns in building ever more complex haptic feedback devices. Most haptic devices are currently point pressure systems, working on one fingertip at a time. Engineering whole-hand haptic feedback devices is very complex given the variety of potential movements that the human hand can make and the sensitivity of touch. Exoskeletons have tackled proprioceptive feedback for limbs where the freedom of movement is more restricted. No doubt these devices will become more sophisticated, but there is a question about whether users will want to wear these cumbersome, heavy, and intrusive devices. Future advances will probably come from electro-sensitive materials, transforming haptic feedback into a wearable computer. The material deforms to express pressure and resistance for force feedback, and thixotropic properties change to mimic touch. The other alternative is to accept that VRmay not always be the best solution. When touch and physical interaction are important, augmented devices may be superior.

Finally, visual interfaces still have a considerable potential for advances. VR currently uses projected displays. Laser-generated holographic images will be exploited in the future. Virtual environments will develop from the current CAVE technologies so that everyday rooms will become immersive 3D environments with holographic images of agents. Shared 3D environments for teleconferencing and many other tasks will become ordinary. We will share our real augmented reality desks with others in virtual teleworking environments. Immersive 360-degree audio is already impressive, and this too will develop so that long-range soundscapes can be projected. The boundaries between virtual and real reality are already beginning to disappear. The virtual world is projected onto a fine water spray curtain so the user can interact as in an immersive VE; however, the user can then walk through the virtual world projected on the spray curtain into reality, enjoying a seamless virtualreal experience, albeit at the expense of getting wet. This technology has been used in collaborative theater where actors play out scripts partially in the VE world and then reenter reality.

The long-range vision for multisensory environments is to eliminate the interface completely. First, the technology will become invisible as it is engineered into the walls and furniture of our everyday environment. Then, the technology will become wearable and part of us. We owe the vision of ubiquitous computing to Weiser, who conceived a world in which computers become pervasive and embedded in our everyday world. No longer will we interact with a PC; instead, computers in our cars, desks, furniture, and floors will respond to speech, touch, and gaze. Interface technology may go even further and become part of us, as implants. The idea of direct implants into our brains for computer-mediated communication tends to make us squirm. However, surgery for the biotechnology interface is already with us. Electrodes are being implanted to give the blind a crude sense of vision. In the near future, multisensory technology will allow the blind to see and the deaf to hear via biosoftware interfaces. The biotechnology interface in the future may not require any invasive surgery. Use of radio, ultrawaves, and manipulation of electric circuits in the brain from wearable devices may allow multisensory experience to be directly transmissible from one person's perception to another person's memory. This raises interesting questions of how such experiences are sent and perceived. The fact that we see and hear the world via memory will not change, so sending a multisensory experience from artificial devices directly into a person's mind will create different experiences according to the preprocessing provided by the designer. Also, swapping sensory experience from our memories may create weird effects of how we experience the event (a wedding) compared with the receiver's view (the bride's). We may indeed be finally able to see into each other's minds. No doubt younger readers of this volume will be around to experience some of these conundrums. I now turn to how multisensory interfaces may merge into the environment, in the growth of ubiquitous computing.

Ubiquitous Multisensory Experience

Computers and their interfaces are starting to blend into the everyday world. Mobile phones become computers with Internet access; interactive televisions are computers; software and microchips are embedded in our homes, offices, and cars. We can even wear computers as fashion accessories, intelligent garments, and augmented reality devices. The days of the computer as a standalone PC are numbered. In the future, we will use a variety of software-augmented appliances. As computers merge into the world, the classic UI of keyboard, VDU, and mouse will vanish. The interface will become our environment. Augmented reality will come of age in a new sense of software driven interfaces within everyday artifacts from refrigerators to cars and phones. We will still need information, and text will still play a role with diagrams and graphics. However, delivery of information will be where we want it, mobile, and with us, on demand via projected displays on our glasses, useful for the ageing population who wear them, or in displays in our mobile phones, watches, office furniture, walls, and ceilings of our homes. Tasks will still drive interaction, but many cognitive tasks such as decision making, planning, and judgment will be carried out with the support of mobile and unobtrusive interfaces. Ubiquitous computing has been with us since Weiser developed the vision of pervasive, unobstrusive technology. Ubiquitous systems extend the view of the user's context in the following "five-Ws" framework:

1. Who? – The system needs to be aware of the individual user. This is manifest in the growing trend for customization and personalization of the interface; the problem for the machine is knowing who it is interacting with if it hasn't been told (i.e., by the person logged on). Future systems will be enhanced by perceptual mechanisms such as image recognition and identification from eye iris or fingerprint patterns.

2. **What?**—This involves guessing what the user is doing. It is a longstanding ambition of intelligent UIs to acquire a model of the user's
behavior. This is still a difficult research problem of understanding activity from low-level data. Future systems might have improved input from model-based scene recognition; image-understanding systems with a semantic model that enables them to interpret what they see.
3. **Where?**—This is a quintessential ubiquitous mobile property, but even with Global Positioning Systems (GPS), it isn't as easy to detect. GPS is only accurate out of doors and even then accuracy is limited to 10m. Improvements may come with local wireless communications such as BlueTooth networks that may be able to track receivers more accurately. "Where" also raises the interpretation problem. The system not only needs a model of the user (who, what) but also a map.
4. **When?**—Time is an important thread of interaction. Many of our interactions are long-running and intermittent. We start a task then pick it up later and elsewhere. Mobile devices need to keep track of our time line, so we can be advised of meetings wherever we happen to be. Time also has an interpretation problem when linked to activity; for example, just how long does looking at something indicate real interest as opposed to absent-minded gaze?
5. **Why?**—This is the most difficult question because it revisits the user modeling problem. To infer just what a human user intends and why requires intelligence bordering on the human. It also needs some understanding of human emotional responses, currently being studied in affective computing (Picard, 1997).

One consequence of mobile and ubiquitous interfaces is that they will become context and location aware. Multisensory interfaces should adapt to suit the user and his or her task, but mobility adds another layer of complexity. Adaptation to the environment is the first level of customizing multisensory interfaces. For instance, the system turns the sound up in a noisy environment, improves contrast and adjusts color balance in bright sunlight, or chooses the appropriate modality according to the context. Thus, my mobile phone selects text and low frequency sound communication when I take it diving, and speech and graphical GPS sensitive compass and map when I am driving.

All this requires more awareness by the device of where it is and the context. This makes multisensory input a key factor in the next generation of devices. Unless the system can perceive its environment it will not be able to adapt to it. Simple solutions such as embedded transmitters in the environment to tell mobile devices their location are a stopgap solution. Transmitters have to be designed to broadcast information to a heterogeneous population of mobile devices, and their (users') needs will be difficult to prediet. Furthermore, instrumenting the environment is an enormous task, which is likely to be unacceptable on economic and environmental grounds. Nobody will want microtransmitters in every tree and street corner. Consequently, systems themselves are going to have to sense the world. UIs will converge with image recognition and speech understanding systems, to say nothing of chemo-sensing and gravity perception. Image interpretation has been a challenge in computer vision and robotics for many years, and current systems have reasonably reliable abilities to recognize simple worlds. However, machine vision is no different from human vision what you see is what you know so the need to interpret sensory input still has to overcome the domain knowledge acquisition bottleneck. In spite of this problem, the ability to integrate information from different modalities will help machines understand their environment. In mobile applications, the challenge is to synthesize information from motion sensors (accelerometers, gyros for position) with external sources of location (GPS and wireless triangulation techniques), with interpretation of visual and audio input. The system will require a world model to interpret even simple aspects of the world, such as awareness of being indoors or outdoors. These problems, of course, have concerned robot designers for many years. Robots have to make sense of the world because they are mobile. The lessons from robotics are that learning about the world is a difficult task. Humans do it in the early years, as babies crawling around experimenting with everything in their environment. Intelligent multisensory systems will have to do the same. Advances in neural computing promise that development of autonomous learning machines should be possible in the midterm future.

So, will multisensory systems be robots, agents that bring artificial reality to life? Will virtual agents live on in artificial worlds? No doubt both. The interface of the future will become part of our reality. We will interact by manipulating objects in our environment. Feedback and output will come from a variety of devices; some will be recognizable displays, others may be robots embedded in the environment. VR and telesensory experience will become accepted as part of our communication infrastructure, which will be ubiquitous and personalized. Thus, if this vision becomes true, UI design and humancomputer interaction will have achieved the ultimate success of solving the problem of interaction, because we will no longer see the problem. The computer, as Norman predicted, will have become invisible.

Conclusion

In computer-aided learning, it is a mistake to focus on the multisensory interaction alone. Most of the problem lies in pedagogical design; nevertheless, multimedia and VR can enhance the design of learning environments by providing rich interactive microworlds for problem-oriented learning. Multisensory UIs can also facilitate social learning by computer-mediated communication; however, several difficult problems still await solution to improve this technology; for instance, the video conferencing and the viewpoint problems.

In design and virtual prototyping, VR gives us the ability to experience our designs before we have to create tangible artifacts. Furthermore, VR allows us to simulate a variety of different scenarios so the design can be tested in a range of operational conditions. Virtual prototyping needs a systematic approach to select the necessary scenarios for testing, and evaluation by immersion poses new problems of interpretation when the problems arise from usability or are design faults in the virtual application.

In the future of multisensory interaction, natural language and intelligent UIs will increase the expressive power in inhabited spaces where the identity of the human and the artificial will become increasingly blurred. Sensory communication will become enhanced by new ways of 3D visual realism, augmented reality with haptics, natural language, as well as olfactory and gustatory communication. Furthermore, machines will have to sense and interpret the world as much as they provide a rich and natural way of communicating with humans. As computers become universal, ubiquitous and wearable, the convergence of multisensory interaction and intelligent agents will lead to a real world inhabited by ourselves communicating with varieties of software entities. Some will be simple devices embedded within our environment, some will be things we wear, others will be agents with personas that assist us in real or artificial worlds; ultimately, some will be artificial life forms in our world.

This leads me to my epilogue. Most of what I have written, I hope, will be useful as design guidance for multisensory interfaces as well as providing some theoretical background for the design process. Design support tools have received little attention, primarily because there are few such tools, although Kaur and Faraday and Sutcliffe are some exceptions. In the future, designing multisensory UIs may itself be a redundant activity. No doubt we will still design computerized agents, but the environment in which they interact will become part of our infrastructure and the agents will learn to adapt to our need. Asimov's laws of robotics and Kubrick's HAL will have joined our world.

Bibliography

Anderson, J. R. (1990). *Cognitive psychology and its implications.* New York: W.H. Freeman.

Biocca, F. & Levy, M.R. (1995) *Communication in the age of virtual reality.* Hillsdale, NJ: Lawrence Erlbaum.

Card, S.K., Moran, T.P., & Newell, a. (1983). *The psychology of Human-Computer Interaction,* Hillsdale, NJ: Lawrence Erlbaum.

Dannenberg, R. & Blattner, M. (1992) The trend toward multimedia interfaces. In Blattner, M. and Dannenberg, R. (Eds.) *Multimedia Interface Design.* New York: ACM Press.

Davenport, G. (1994). Seeking dynamic, adaptive story environments. *IEEE Multimedia,* (3) , 9-13.

Davenport, G., Evans, R. & Halliday, M. (1993). Orchestratingdigital micromovies. *Leonardo, 26,* 4.

Eberts, R.E. (1994). *User interface design.* Englewood cliffs, NJ: Prentice-Hall.

Falk, D., & Carlson, H. (September, 1992) Learning to Teach with Multimedia. *T.H.E. Journal,* pp. 96-101.

Goodman, D. *The complete Hypercard 2.x handbook.* Bantam Computer Books.

Grabowski, B. & Pearson, R. (1988). The development of a research agenda and generic disc

Hudson, T. & Holland, S. (1992) Interactive Multimedia Instruction in Video Production Classes. *Journalism Educator,* 47 (3) 18-26.

Hudson, Tim (1992) Consonance in Depiction of Violent Material in Television News. *Journal of Broadcasting and Electronic Media, 36* (4) 411-425

Kinzie, M.B. (1990). Requirements and benefits of effective interactive instruction: Learner control, self-regulation, and continuing motivation. Education, Technology, Research and Development, 38(1), 5-21.

Locatis, C., Charulıas, J. & Bonvard, R. (1990). Hypervideo. Educational Technology, Research and Development, 38,(2), 41-49.

Magel, Mark (February, 1992) An Introduction to Authoring Languages: Part One. *A V Video Magazine*, pp 120-129.

Nelson, K. R. & McNeil, B. J. (1991). Meta-analysis of interactive video instruction: A 10 year review of achievement effects. Journal of Computer-Based Instruction, 18, 1-6.

Ohkubo, M., Kobayashi, N., Nakagawa, T. (1993). *Design of an information skimming space. ACM Multimedia* 93, 365-371.

Park, William T. (May, 1994) Future Trends in Authoring. *New Media Magazine* pp. 52-54.

Ramanathan, S. & Rangan, P.V. (1994, Spring). Architectures for personalized multimedia. IEEE Multimedia, 37-46.

Salvaggio, J.L. & Bryant, J. (1989). *Media use in the information age: Emerging patterns of adoption and consumer use*. Hillsdale, NJ: Lawrence Erlbaum.

Thompson, J. & Gottlieb, S. (1995). Macromedia Director Lingo Workshop. Indianapolis: Hayden Books. Jacobson, L. (Ed.). *Cyberarts, exploring art and technology*. Miller Freeman.

Utz, Peter. (March, 1994) *All You Need is LV.*

Van Tassel, Joan. (1996). *Advanced Television Systemsl*. Newton, MA: Focal Press

Waern, Y. (1989). *Cognitive aspects of computer supported tasks.* Chicago, John Wiley

Waring, Becky (May, 1994). Video Scan Converters: Not as Simple as they Seem. *New Media Magazine*, pp. 37-42.

Index

2-D Artwork, 226

A

A Scottish Multimedia Cluster, 102
Advance Publications, 45
Advertising Industry, 84
Aesthetic Motivations, 206
Agglomeration, 103
Amateur Animation, 239
Ambiguity, 2
America Online (AOL), 65
Animation, 226
  Techniques, 227
  Design and Effects, 226
Applications and Architectures of Multimedia, 262
Asia Business News, 173
Audiovisual Works, 19

B

Bayerische Landesanstalt Für Neue Medien (BLM),, 97
Bayerischer Rundfunk (BR), 82
Bayern Online, 98
Belgian Copyright Act, 28
BMG Entertainment International, 81
Book Publishers, 80
Broadness, 2
Business Information Services, 46

C

Cable TV Networks, 67
Catholic University of Eichstätt, 78
CGI Short Films, 239
Clay Animation, 229
Cluster-Representing
  Organizations, 120
  Networking and Sociotechnical Constituen, 102
Cognitive Resources, 139
Collaborative Works, 250
Columbia Broadcasting System (CBS), 45
Communication, 1
Compact Disc – Interactive, 2
  Read Only Memory, 2
Compilation Alternative, 37
Computer Aided Design (CAD), 274
  Animation Development Equipment, 234
  Animation, 230
  Integrated Manufacturing (CIM), 170
  Mediated Communication (CMC), 265

Programs, 27
Aided Learning, 262
Based Product or Service, 20
Based Training (CBT), 84, 262
Concurrent or Sequential Presentation, 211
Constituency-Builders, 110
Content and Software (N2K), 53
Distribution, 40
Packaging and Marketing, 40
Context Switching, 150
Corporate Giants, 45
Creative Destruction, 64
Culture of Real Virtuality, 44
Cutout Animation, 229

D

Data Discman, 2
Department of Trade and Industry's (DTI), 127
Design Approach and Technology, 189
Features, 151
Method, 188
Designing of Multimedia User Interface, 186
the Reading or Viewing Sequence, 218
Virtual Prototypes, 276
Deutsches Sportfernsehen (DSF), 82
Diamond of Alignment, 111
Digital Compact Cassette, 2
Compression Techniques, 6
Environment, 7
Technology, 5
Video Disc, 2
Digitisation, 4
Direct Contact Points, 219
Domain Density, 48
Modeling, 193
Dow Jones and Co., 45

E

Early Animation, 226
Ease of Manipulation and Copying, 22
Economic Development Board, 166
Education Software Technology, 268
Educational Applications, 262
Electronic Commerce, 40
Data Interchange (EDI), 57
Data Processing (EDP), 57
Error Diagnosis and Recovery 152, 159
EU Legislation, 25
Software Directive, 28

F

Fernsehstudio München, 82
Film/Radio/Television, 81
Financial Services, 40
Fixation, 21
Foreign Direct Investment (FDI), 116
Frontiers for Multisensory Interaction, 282
Full Animation, 228
Interactivity, 8

G

German Copyright Act, 242
Gross National Product (GNP), 164
Guidance in the Berne Convention, 241

H

Hardware Animation Display Technology, 235
Producers, 101
Head Mounted Display or HMD, 277

Hollow Corporation, 63
Home Order Television, 83
Hover Text, 216
Human Professional Services, 58
Resource Supply and Development, 166
Hybrid Product of Copyright Classification, 257
Hypermedia Dialogues, 214
Hypertext Design, 215

I

IMAX Screen, 209
Independent' Contents, 26
Indirect Contact Points, 219
Individual-Level Learning, 264
Individually Accessible, 27
Accessible' Contents, 26
Industry Structure, 176
Informatics and Digital Communications, 21
Information Retrieval, 40
Technology (IT), 163
Types, 196
Institutional Shaping of IT, 179
Thickness, 41
Integrated Communication Agencies, 61
Communication Networks, 61
Integrating Resources and Action, 152
Intelligent Multisensory User Interfaces, 280
User Interface (IUI), 280
Interacting Technologies/ Constituencies, 115
Interaction Models, 144
Interactive Guides in Museums, 1
Media Association of Scotland (IMAS), 120
Microworlds and Active Engagement, 270
Telecommunications Program (ITP), 49
Television, 1
Interactivity, 7
Internet Advertising, 53
IT 2000, 169

J

J. Stuart Blackton, 227
Johnson's Task Knowledge Structures, 139

K

Knowledge-Intensive Service Networks, 61

L

Layers of Protection, 9
Learning Environments, 263
Limited Animation, 228
Interactivity, 8
Linguistic Media (Text and Speech), 222
Literary and Artistic Works, 242
Local Enterprise Companies (LECs), 124

M

Magazine Publishers, 79
Manual Interactivity, 8
Mass Media and Broadcasting Hub, 173
Media City Munich, 73
Integration and Design for Attention, 218
Selection and Combination, 200
Medienstadt München III, 73
Model Animation, 229
Modeling Multisensory Interaction, 134
Models of Interaction and Designing, 131
of Multimedia Interaction, 134
Moving Image Media, 221

Multimedia and Industrial
Restructuring, 163
Clusters, 101 ·
Conversations, 136
Databases, 24
Infrastructure, 92
Interaction, 153
Networks, 40
Products and Collaborative Works, 250
Products and Collective Works, 252
Products and Composite Works, 252
Products and Copyright Works, 240
Products As Databases, 32
Products, 18
Profiling and Regional Restructuring, 72
Multinational Corporations (MNCs), 121
Multisensory User Interface Issues, 272
Multiuser Dungeons, 150
Object Oriented Systems, 150
Münchner Gesellschaft Für Kabelkommunikation (MGK), 97
Music Television, 208

N

National Broadcasting Co. (NBC), 45
Science and Technology Board (NSTB), 170
Navigation and Control, 213
Exploration Cycle, 156
Network Operators, 101
Networking, 53
New Management Orientation, 165
Media, 44
School of Social Research, 49
York New Media Association (NYNMA), 50
Newly Industrialized (NIE), 163
Newspaper Publishers, 78
No Interactivity, 8
Nonfunctional Requirements (NFRs), 191
Norman Cycle, 143

O

Online Community, 53
On-Line Databases, 1

P

Paper Prototypes, 190
Parsons School of Design, 49
Perceptual Motor Extension, 132
Pioneering Emerging Technology, 112
Possible Solutions, 247
Presentation Scripting, 210
Print Media, 51
Production and Working Conditions, 90
Pseudocode, 237

Q

Qualification of Multimedia Works, 249

R

Radio and Television Programmes, 43
Research, Development and Design (RD&D), 104
Rotoscoping, 228
Rubber Hose, 228

S

Salience Effects in Single Media, 220
Scenario-Based Requirements Analysis, 278
Scottish Cultural Resources

Access Network (SCRAN), 120
Electronics Forum (SEF), 124
Enterprise (SE), 116
Multimedia Working Group (SMWG), 125
Scripted Presentations and Hypermedia, 268
Second World War, 76
Secondary Copyrights, 15
Sectoral Transformation, 164
Siemens-Nixdorf Informationssysteme, 85
Silhouette Animation, 229
Silicon Alley, 41
Singapore Cable Vision (SCV), 181
International Media (SIM), 181
Single Material Support, 20
Social Consensus and Policy Instruments, 124
Design of Technology, 179
Level Learning, 265
Sociotechnical Constituencies (STC), 102, 105
Soft Location Factors, 73
Software Development and 'Generic' Applications, 40
Still Image Media, 221
Stop Motion, 228
Strategies of Innovation, 40
System Initiative Cycle, 158
Initiative Model, 148
Systematic and Methodical Arrangement of Contents, 29

T

Task and Information Modeling, 194
Action Model, 145
Technologies With Indirect Network Externalities, 112
Telecom Infrastructure, 122
Telecommunication, 88
Information Technologies, Media, 75
Television Corporation of Singapore (TCS), 181
The Etiology of Cancer, 223
Hearst Corporation, 45
Three-Dimensional Objects, 34
TIME Industry, 75
Traditional Animation, 227
Transition Path Diagrams (TPDs), 133
True and Versatile Interactivity, 8
Two-Dimensional Format, 34

U

Ubiquitous Multisensory Experience, 285
UK's Copyright Act, 26
Unimedium Multiwork, 3

V

Viacom, 45
Virtual Environments, 283
Prototyping, 274
Reality Walkthrough, 154

W

Wall Street Journal (WSJ),, 46
Window Management, 211
World Trade Organization, 163
Wide Web, 44
Worldwide Waste Management Information System (WWI), 85